Another Country

SEXUAL CULTURES

General Editors: José Esteban Muñoz and Ann Pellegrini

Another Country

Queer Anti-Urbanism

Scott Herring

NEW YORK UNIVERSITY PRESS
New York and London

NEW YORK UNIVERSITY PRESS
New York and London
www.nyupress.org

Library of Congress Cataloging-in-Publication Data

Herring, Scott, 1976–
Another country : queer anti-urbanism / Scott Herring.
p. cm. — (Sexual cultures)
Includes bibliographical references and index.
ISBN-13: 978–0–8147–3718–7 (cl : alk. paper)
ISBN-10: 0–8147–3718–8 (cl : alk. paper)
ISBN-13: 978–0–8147–3719–4 (pb : alk. paper)
ISBN-10: 0–8147–3719–6 (pb : alk. paper)
1. Rural gay men—United States. 2. Rural lesbians—United States. I. Title.
HQ76.3.U5H468   2010
306.76'620973091734—dc22   2009049618

New York University Press books are printed on acid-free paper,
and their binding materials are chosen for strength and durability.
We strive to use environmentally responsible suppliers and materials
to the greatest extent possible in publishing our books.

Manufactured in the United States of America
c 10 9 8 7 6 5 4 3 2 1
p 10 9 8 7 6 5 4 3 2 1

For Shane Vogel

Whatever our sensibility may be, New York gays are justifiably proud of their status as taste-makers for the rest of the country, at least the young and up-to-date segment of the population. Our clothes and haircuts and records and dance steps and decor—our restlessly evolving style—soon enough become theirs. . . . In return for the costliness and inconvenience, the squalor and discomfort of our lives, we get to participate in whatever is the *latest*. We are never left out of anything; we know what's happening.
      —Edmund White, *States of Desire: Travels in Gay America*

Aesthetic intolerance can be terribly violent.
      —Pierre Bourdieu,
          Distinction: A Social Critique of the Judgement of Taste

And I find I keep asking the same question, because of the history: where do I stand in relation to these writers: in another country or in this valuing city?
      —Raymond Williams, *The Country and the City*

Contents

Illustrations

Acknowledgments

THIS BOOK, BY no means a life's work, was nevertheless a life's lot for several seasons. The main idea hit me as I trudged into the Foxhole Lounge during a personal winter of 2003. I later refined the thesis when I visited Mary's in the spring of 2006, and I enhanced my arguments after an evening spent at Uncle Elizabeth's in the summer of 2008. Across this long half-decade, I composed portions in the Happy Valley, the City of Brotherly Love, and the City Too Busy to Hate. I completed its bulk in what a well-known Minnesotan once termed "the vast obscurity" of the Middle West, and in 2009 I revised it 51 miles south of the Circle City, 760 miles west of the Capital of the World, and 2,278 miles east of the City by the Bay. When granted the weak light of hindsight, I see that initial research was first conducted in the so-called Magic City of the South in the late 1980s. The words that follow pay tribute to the worlds I got out of and, at the same time, I have never left behind. They also commemorate places that have failed to receive the sometimes dubious honorific of a nickname.

It's "the loneliest kind of lonely," sang Mama Cass Elliot, who then added that "to do your thing's the hardest thing to do." I have often found her lyrics to be true enough, but I also do not forget the many who steered me through what could have been "rough going." I want to first thank those who took their time—their time out—to sit down with my prose. These include Alison Bechdel, Barbara Ching, Michael Cobb, Ed Comentale, Denise Cruz (phenomenal), Tim Dean, John Duvall, Jonathan Elmer, Maria Farland, Jen Fleissner, Jonathan Goldberg, John Howard, Julia Kasdorf, Keguro Macharia, Victor Mendoza, Richard Meyer, Michael Moon, Charles Morris, Ben Ogrodnick, Andy Oler, Richard Rodriguez, David Román, Ranu Samantrai, Siobhan Somerville, Rachel Teukolsky, Karen Tongson, Sherrie Tucker, Angela Ward, Sarah Withers, and, especially, Patrick Johnson and Robert McRuer. These last two readers offered cut-to-the-chase commentaries on the manuscript as it reached final submission, and the writing was that much stronger for their attention. As this book slowly came home, with each of you I embrace the principle of debt incurred.

I next want to thank those who took time to sit down with my Capote-on-steroids delivery. Oftentimes a public query—I well remember those made by Susan Belasco, Carrie Tirado Bramen, Jennifer DeVere Brody, Judith Brown, Chris Castiglia, Nick Davis, Alex Doty, Lisa Duggan, Rae Greiner, Matt Guterl, Sharon Holland, George Hutchinson, Jeffrey Mc-Cune, Sam Otter, Lloyd Pratt, Marjorie Pryse, Guy Reynolds, Ramón Rivera-Servera, Francesca Royster, and Jani Scandura—helped pitch me out of my hardheaded rut. Other audience members did likewise at the University of Tennessee–Knoxville, the University of Nebraska–Lincoln, two Modernist Studies Association conferences in Burlington and Long Beach, Northwestern University (a dozen and one white roses to Sarah Blackwood for organizing an American Cultures Colloquium panel), the Deep Localities: The New Critical Regionalism symposium at Indiana University, the Emerging Rural, Nonmetropolitan, and Working-Class Perspectives in LGBTQ Studies symposium orchestrated by Nadine Hubbs at the University of Michigan—Ann Arbor, several American Studies Association conferences in Albuquerque, Oakland, Philadelphia, and Washington DC, the University at Albany–SUNY, the University at Buffalo–SUNY, and the Northwestern Center for Global Culture and Communication Summer Institute.

I found the staff at New York University Press—particularly Eric Zinner, Ciara McLaughlin, and Nicholas Taylor—remarkable in their efficiency. Both editors for the Sexual Cultures series, Ann Pellegrini and José Esteban Muñoz, offered keen feedback at every step of the process. Before the final manuscript was overnighted to this Big Apple crew, my work-study assistant, Alexis Wilson, did a pitch-perfect job of proofing for five months in early 2009. Likewise, Shawn Wilson was always available over at the Kinsey to answer any of my questions and all of my concerns.

A smallish portion of chapter 1 was published in *Modern Fiction Studies* 52, no. 1 (2006): 66–91, as "Catherian Friendship; Or, How Not To Do the History of Homosexuality"; and an earlier version of chapter 2 was published in *American Quarterly* 59, no. 2 (2007): 341–72, as "Out of the Closets, Into the Woods: *RFD*, *Country Women*, and the Post-Stonewall Emergence of Queer Anti-urbanism." Sections of chapter 3 split down the middle to appear first in *GLQ* 12, no. 2 (2006): 217–36, as "Caravaggio's Rednecks"; and later in *American Studies* 48, no. 2 (2007): 37–48, as "Southern Backwardness: Metronormativity and Regional Visual Culture."

I thank the Mid-America American Studies Association for permission to reprint from this last journal.

While I lucked out most of the time with copyright and courtesy, deep appreciation still goes to Michael Meads, Sharon Bridgforth, Sister Soami at the Short Mountain Sanctuary, Sherry Thomas, Carmen Goodyear, the staff at Firebrand Books, and Jeremy Hobbs. Some of this motley crew did not agree with my final conclusions, but I was humbled by each individual's willingness to share—and to release—their materials.

Shane Vogel, needless to say, also gave me world rights for my odds and for my ends, but this sentence stumbles away when it comes to his proper citation. Daily, I'm reminded that we don't always need bright lights to make our own lightning, that life in Bloomington is OK. So thanks, yet again, for taking me on.

I last make mention of the many who did not make mention in these pages, but who nonetheless helped mold the book. These are those whose thoughts and images live on in the folders of the laptop, the snapshots on the memory card, the weekend minutes on the bill cycle, the conversations on the cassette. They include Cornelius Mabin, author and editor of one of the first queer of color newspapers in Little Rock, Arkansas; participants at the lesbian and gay Rodeo on the Rock held at the Arkansas State Fairgrounds in 2006; Curt McKay, director of LGBT Resources at the University of Illinois; the editors of *Prairie Flame*; Joey Carolino, a *Southern Voice* cartoonist; Charles Canada, now ensconced on a ranch in Abiquiu, New Mexico; several who answered my call for papers in a recent issue of *RFD*; and the trans-migrant workers of Plainville, USA. As this book began to take its present shape, my contacts with each of you recalled a quote by Winnicott: "But if I fulfill myself I must remember that I climbed to this over the dead bodies of my friends who died fighting." The difference here is each of you remains in the trenches. The key is you all just keep on keeping on.

Introduction

I Hate New York

country, country bumpkin, rube, hayseed, Hoosier, hillbilly, clay eater, redneck, yokel, yooper, hick, Hicksville, backwater, boondocks, trailer trash, the middle of nowhere, the midwaste, flyover country, the sticks, the backwoods, the hinterlands, the outskirts, Sticksville, Shitsville, shitkicker, jerkwater, Podunk, Bumfuck, East Bumfuck, East Bumble-fuck, East Butt-Fuck, BFE, Butt-Fuck Egypt

Urban Legends

I hate New York. It's not just the oppressive summer heat, or the dearth of affordable housing, or the lack of decent water pressure. It's not simply the city's awesome capacity to imagine itself as the be-all and the end-all of modern queer life (no small feat, mind you). What I really hate is the casualness with which this move is dispatched, the taken-for-granted assumption that you want to be on that tiny island (but not some of those outer boroughs) and be there soon. That you want to get there someday, somehow, and *get out* of this godforsaken town. That the promised land awaits just a hub or two or three away. I hate that no queer in New York has ever had to apologize to other queers for wanting to live there, unlike those of us who did not wash up on its shores. And I hate that the more I hate what New York stands for, the more I feel like the kind of shitkicker its queer denizens have too often defined themselves against.

Here are two small examples of what I am trying to describe, a hazy sense of having missed out on something that turns into an acute feeling of being left out of everything, a feeling I've often experienced as a queer form of social death. One is an old club listing from Chelsea, the other a single-line quotation from a prominent queer theorist. Though separated by nearly two decades, they converse in aspiration and intent. My first example is a full-page ad taken from the inside front cover of a 1982 *HONCHO*, a Sixth Avenue–based glossy whose subtitle once informed

1

Figure 1.1. "*HONCHO* Hangouts: New York." *HONCHO* (1982). HONCHO™ is a registered trademark of and published monthly by Mavety Media Group Ltd. Courtesy of Mavety Media Group Ltd. and the Kinsey Institute for Research in Sex, Gender, and Reproduction.

readers that it was *The Magazine for the Macho Male,* and that, at its height, reached many across the nation (fig. I.1).

I could critique this image for its phallic aggrandizement, and I could critique its unquestioned masculinity, its handy racial normativity, and its conflation of one particular white gay male subculture with an iconic emblem of New York—the Empire State Building—that it packs between a pair of button-fly jeans. But mainly I want to critique the ad's fine print. As the copyright at the bottom of the advertisement implies, the visual culture of this metropolitan dick was disseminated as a print culture across the nation during the early 1980s. The photo, *HONCHO* tells readers, is "available as a card through Nice and Sleazy, NYC." Stripped of its numerous Chelsea addresses on the left side of the ad (many now closed, a few like Rawhide still in operation), the erect skyscraper offers itself as a calling card for a certain urbanized vision of queer (male) readership throughout the post-Stonewall United States. One horizon of possibility among the many—the beacon of an enriching clone aesthetic for some—magnifies into the horizon of fantastic possibility for all. What starts off as an open invitation to select *HONCHO* Hangouts potentially becomes a standardizing guidebook for late modern U.S. queer life.

My second example is from the tail end of a chapter from Michael Warner's *The Trouble with Normal,* a book that translated some trends of queer theory for non-academic audiences in 1999. It follows a powerful discussion of Manhattan's waning queer public spaces in the wake of the city's draconian zoning laws. Raising the stakes of his local critique to global proportions, Warner surmises that "the sexual culture of New York City serves people around the world, even if only as the distant reference point of queer kids growing up in North Carolina or Idaho, who know that *somewhere* things are different."[1] Like the *HONCHO* ad, this conclusion too is a calling card of sorts, one that captures the lure of "New York City" as an ideal of possibility, pleasure, plenitude, and escape. Yet this line still haunts me since I first read it a decade ago. I remind myself that queer kids in North Carolina have, at last count, over thirty-five listed gay bars (the tip of any social iceberg) in cities and towns such as Raleigh, Winston-Salem, Asheville, Greensboro, Charlotte, Wilmington, and Rocky Mount. I google "Idaho gay clubs" and I am relieved to find two bars in Pocatello, one in Coeur d'Alene, a few in Boise, plus (this may be wish fulfillment) enriching sexual cultures in Idaho Falls, Lewiston, and Twin Falls.

When I marvel at how the sweep of a sentence writes over these regional spaces for queers past, present, and future, I start to wonder if "New

York City" has become something of a pyrrhic victory for queer sexual cultures. That this city is framed—naturalized—as the epicenter of contemporary queer life "around the world" smarts as much as the implicit assumption that the metropolis is the final destination point for queer kids of any gender, class, race, or region. As much as his necessary work critiques the normalization of queer life in the 1990s, and despite what "New York City" may signal for those raised, like Warner, in "the bosom of Jesus," his quotation nevertheless contributes to one of the dominant themes of a lesbian and gay normalization that he and many other critics elsewhere resist.[2] Like the *HONCHO* ad, the possibility inherent in any urban trajectory slides into a limited compulsion to urbanism. Alongside countless other queer productions, it codifies the metropolitan as the terminus of queer world making as many have come to know it.

Another Country takes this urbanism as a starting point, not as an endgame. It agrees that the sexual cultures of global metropoles have always served people around the world, but it contends that cities like New York (or San Francisco or Los Angeles or Chicago or London or Berlin or Paris or Mexico City) have too often been the distant reference point for non-urban-identified queers. Such being the case, it insists that queer folks in places such as North Carolina and Idaho do know—have known for some time—that somewhere things are different than the Big Apple, and it charts how these individuals have coped with, navigated, mourned, side-stepped, muddled through, menaced, and rearticulated the onslaught of queer urbanisms throughout the twentieth century, and beyond.

I know it may seem easy to harp on the urban legends of a single quotation or an ad from *HONCHO*, and I also know that the boroughs that make up New York City (Manhattan, the Bronx, Queens, Brooklyn, and Staten Island) brim with queers who work hard to fail an urbanist creed. But as this book progresses it will become clear that these two examples are just symptoms of a much larger dynamic, one that often crosses genders, classes, and races distinct from any white gay male metropolitan public sex culture. While I could have cherry-picked other instances with which to begin this introduction, I emphasize these two because they present an entwined urbanism that bridges the givens of everyday lesbian and gay metropolitan life in the United States and the shared assumptions of U.S.-based queer studies that have been produced since the 1980s. I could just as easily have started with a few lines from a 1990 Queer Nation manifesto, "An Army of Lovers Cannot Lose": "Let's make every space a Lesbian and Gay space. Every street a part of our sexual geography. A city of yearning and then total satisfaction."[3] Close read these words and you find that "every space" and "every street" collapse into "a city" for "our" sexual geographies. I could have begun with a translated line from Didier Eribon, one of France's leading gay public intellectuals: "Cities have always been the refuge of gay people. At the end of the 1960s, a gay activist described San Francisco as a 'refugee camp' that had attracted gay people from all over the country—people who were running from the impossibility of living out gay lives in the hostile, hate-filled atmosphere of small-town America."[4] Historicize this line (as my second chapter does) and you discover that this gay activist, Carl Wittman, edited one of the first anti-urbanist queer journals as a refuge from the hostile, hate-filled gay atmosphere of the Bay Area at the beginning of the 1970s. I also could have introduced a snippet from a lesbian oral history, such as one informant who, after discovering the Buffalo bar scene in the 1930s, tells her interviewers that "I was standing there with my mouth wide open, like a hick, I was so excited."[5] Why, I have to ask, does the regional smear "hick" become a shared marker for signaling queer ignorance regarding pre-Stonewall urban lesbian subcultures? Why does "hick" conjure a shameful rusticity that someone like queer disability activist Eli Clare will interrogate in a chapter on late modern lesbian chic?

It almost goes without saying that these urbanist elisions have become endemic to what Warner has elsewhere termed the "subcultural style," as well as to the "self-understanding of a metropolitan sexual subculture" that informed political organizations such as Queer Nation.[6] It also almost goes without saying that ivory tower theorizations and high-profile essays by authors such as Eribon have only added fuel to this fire. And it is disheartening for me to see that urban-oriented queer politics and metro-based queer academics often agree with populist forms of anti-ruralism such as the oral history I quoted from above. In each of these cases, the rural (take your pick: Idaho, North Carolina, small-town America, hick) is shelved, disavowed, denied, and discarded in favor of metropolitan sexual cultures such as New York City, San Francisco, or Buffalo. In each the rural becomes a slur, one that has proliferated into an admittedly rich idiom. Suffice it to say that if recent strains of queer theory and recent forms of lgbtq politics (latent and manifest) share common ground, it's usually a dismissal of rurality as such, a dismissal not only commonplace but, let's bet the farm on it, chronic. Much of queer studies wants desperately to be urban planning, even as so much of its theoretical architecture is already urban planned.

While anti-rural episodes such as the *HONCHO* ad were this book's inspiration, they are not its main preoccupation. As I soon detail, others have ably demonstrated the gaps and the silences that accompany the perpetual urbanization of lgbtq politics and queer studies. Extending their findings and pressurizing the urban/rural binary that informs these analyses, *Another Country* contends that queer artists—across decades, media, and idioms—have creatively used rural stylistics to fashion critiques against lesbian and gay metropolitan norms. Though dismissals of the rural are routine in urbanized lesbian, gay, and queer studies, rurality can be and has been redeployed to promote a critical form of queer anti-urbanism. To support these two theses, I gathered together an eclectic archive that includes novels, paintings, do-it-yourself journals, newspapers, memoirs, photographs, comic strips, fashion studies, a performance, a graphic memoir, and some ethnographic interviews. I treat these disparate objects like a coalition that reveals how queer life beyond the city is as vibrant, diverse, and plentiful as any urban-based sexual culture. Of course it is, and this should be obvious enough by now (it still isn't). I use these materials to go beyond this preliminary thesis and contend that the "non-metropolitan" or the "rural"—broadly defined—in visual and print culture, in performance, and in fashion studies is a premier site of queer critique against compulsory forms of urbanization.

Hence my title, an echo of a call made by critics as diverse as James Baldwin and Raymond Williams. If queers way out there—broadly conceived—have too often been stamped with scarlet letters that spell out backwater, rube, hillbilly, hayseed, redneck, shitkicker, and bumfuck, then what happens when this terminology turns against itself? What happens when countrified queers challenge the representational systems that underlie the perpetual citification of modern lgbtq life? In some cases these questions are matters of ideological life-and-death, and we'll see how answers to them fail and succeed in whole and in part. I'll also show that they were always ripe for the taking when it came to visualizing non-urbanist sexual geographies, and I'll detail how ruralized queers have negotiated the urbane metropolitan stylistics that govern—and normalize—them with counter-stylistics of their own. Along the way I track some social constructions of U.S. metronormativity from the early twentieth century to the early twenty-first century. Throughout these readings, my archive will be largely rural-identified, yet I want to stress in advance that the concerns, problems, and potential solutions regarding lesbian and gay urbanism that *Another Country* faces are germane to many U.S.-based queers, irrespective of their geographic particulars. But before I punch your ticket to this proverbial Hicksville—and before I refine what I mean by "queer anti-urbanism" or "metronormativity" or "rural stylistics"—I want to cover my basics and discuss what others have meant by "the urban" and its often maligned converse, "the rural."

From Non-Metro to Anti-Urbanism

What do we mean by "rural" or "urban"? How do we best define these terms? More important, who best defines these terms? At first glance, a quick definitional grasp on "rural" and "urban" seems self-evident. *Webster's* defines "urban" as an adjective: "in the U.S. census use, designating or of an incorporated or unincorporated place with at least 50,000 inhabitants."[7] In comparison, the most recent citation in the *Oxford English Dictionary* defines "rural" as "of, pertaining to or characteristic of the country or country life as opposed to the town."[8] We can contrast this definition with the *OED*'s take on "urban": "pertaining to or characteristic of, occurring or taking place in, a city or town."[9]

Here we see that the pat definition of "rural" is analogous to "country" as much as "urban" is analogous to the "city" or "town." But what, exactly, constitutes a "city" or a "country" when it is "opposed to the town"? Who, exactly, puts them in opposition? We could take a cue from *Webster's* and turn to the U.S. Census Bureau's most recent guidelines, where the bureau's definition of "population density" may help clarify our understanding of "rural/country" and "urban/city." While we should rightly be suspicious of such bio-political number games, the census nevertheless serves as a material and epistemological technology for enumerating and spatializing the geography of the U.S. nation-state. In a formulation that complements the one provided by the *OED*, "Census 2000 Rural and Urban Classification" defines an "urbanized area" as a space that consists of "core census block groups or blocks that have a population density of at least 1,000 people per square mile."[10]

But something weird happens when we detail the Census Bureau's examples of these statistical "urbanized areas." The definitional certainties of what constitutes an "urban" or a "rural" population begin to undermine themselves. In an extended online listing of over seven hundred of these "urbanized" areas, the 2000 census cites my current residence of Bloomington, IN, alongside what the Web site curiously hyphenates as "New

York—Newark, NJ—NJ—CT" and "Los Angeles—Long Beach—Santa Ana, CA." These listings together appear on a lengthy window with sites such as Appleton, Wisconsin, Dothan, Alabama, Altoona, Pennsylvania, and Macon, Georgia, four cities that also fall under the bureau's "urbanized area" file.[11] Given these loose examples of the static term "urban," the geographic pratfalls of numerically defining what counts as a "rural" or an "urban" space should become less transparent. This is especially so when we consider the logistics of "core census blocks" that have, say, a population density of 999 people per square mile and are deemed "rural" by technicality. Or when we question who, exactly, decided to hyphenate "areas" like New York, New Jersey, and Connecticut as a singular "urbanized" population chain. Some folks in the Jersey Pinelands might disagree.

As we make our way through the numerical quagmire that is the 2000 census, its categorical data illuminates just how precarious any proper definition of "rural" or "urban"—along with their counterparts "metropolitan" and "non-metropolitan"—can often be. The more examples that the bureau gives, the more it obscures denotative guidelines that might demarcate "pertaining to country" or "pertaining to town." Designating any area, population, locale, or, by proxy, person as ruralized while defining any area, population, locale, or person as urbanized starts to seem less like a descriptive act and much more like a prescriptive project. When their semantic surfaces are scratched, the terms "rural" and "urban" become a definitional roundabout. Rather than evidence an actual geographic location (does anyone know offhand the ZIP code for "New York—Newark, NJ—NJ—CT"?), they appear to function more like language games, a term philosopher Ludwig Wittgenstein uses to connote context-specific word usage that can be validated as well as overruled by an individual or by a collective. You don't always know the rural when you see it, and it often takes a shared recognition to identify a particular space or place as "non-metropolitan." This suggests that something in excess of empirical geographic specificities or the faulty logic of population density governs the urban/rural divide that informs U.S.-based queer studies. Since definitions of "rural" and "urban" must participate in a rigged language game, any "urban/rural" distinction is as much context-specific, phantasmatic, performative, subjective, and—I'll stress—standardizing as it is geographically verifiable.[12]

This axiom will allow us to advance a practical theory of how queer urbanities and their counterpart, queer anti-urbanisms, work in tandem and in opposition.[13] I'll return to this tension directly. For now, I note that while "rural" and "urban" are often difficult to define, scholars in queer studies have detailed how the historical fictions of these two terms nevertheless sustain a variety of ruralized and urbanized populations across U.S. sexual history. In numerous disciplines, a magpie consortium of social historians, cultural critics, anthropologists, and literary critics such as Lisa Duggan, Michael Moon, John Howard, Kath Weston, E. Patrick Johnson, Elizabeth Povinelli, Robert Reid-Pharr, Judith Halberstam, Jasbir K. Puar, Mary Pat Brady, Robert McRuer, and others have tackled what McRuer terms the "regional elision in queer theory," and all these critics have emphasized, with varying italics, what Weston describes as "the part played by urban/rural contrasts in *constituting* lesbian and gay subjects."[14] Thanks to this critical mass, scholars now have a reservoir of theoretical and historical knowledge that addresses queer life in the Deep South; negotiations of sexual separatism and assimilation in non-urban indigenous populations; the regional and international rise of white lesbian identity in the early twentieth-century United States; and the advocacy of queer rural African American literary and religious cultures in the North Carolina backwoods.[15]

This incomplete list will remain a work in progress. It has been joined by anthologies such as *Carryin' On in the Lesbian and Gay South, Reclaiming the Heartland,* and *De-Centring Sexualities;* memoirs and fictions by Baldwin, Randall Kenan, Cherríe Moraga, Dorothy Allison, Toni Morrison, Eli Clare, Alison Bechdel, and Gloria Anzaldúa; and documentary shorts, video installations, and feature films such as *Small Town Gay Bar* (2006), *The Long Road to Mazatlán* (1999), *Southern Comfort* (2001), *Lavender* (1971), and *Boys Don't Cry* (1999).[16] Together these works have raised a string of questions and concerns regarding "non-metropolitan" sexual non-conformity over the last three and a half decades. Rather than reinforce stereotypes of the "rural" as a cultural Podunk, these artists and authors pay heed to the "non-metropolitan" as a dynamic space of inquiry and sexual vitality. Complicating geophobic claims that ruralized spaces are always and only hotbeds of hostility, cultural and socioeconomic poverty, religious fundamentalism, homophobia, racism, urbanoia, and social conservatism, their works question knee-jerk assumptions that the "rural" is a hate-filled space for queers as they archive the complex desires that contribute to any non-metropolitan identification.[17] Howard, for one, has tracked how black and white queer males forged sustainable communities across ruralized areas of Mississippi from the Depression era onward. Duggan has excavated how the working-class female "farmer or laborer" of the nineteenth century contributed to the crystallization of a normalizing U.S. lesbian identity in turn-of-the-twentieth-century Memphis and beyond.[18] Povinelli, a participant-observer in radical faerie communes, has theorized the anarchic sexual politics of central Tennessee gatherings as they connect to (and sometimes disconnect with) the flows of aboriginal expressive cultures in Australia.[19] And Reid-Pharr has poetically charted his own regional desires as they orbited around "ugly, poor, white trash," Kentucky-identified males throughout his sexual history.[20]

These writings defamiliarize the master narratives of lesbian and gay U.S. urbanism. They offer variations on anti-rural twice-told tales such as the compulsory metropolitan migration from wicked little towns; the city as the sole locus for queer community, refuge, and security; and the non-metropolitan as a perpetual site of isolation and exclusion[21]—so much so that one scholar offers that "urban/rural contrasts have structured the very subjectivity that allows people [in the United States] to think of themselves or others as gay."[22] And, as Reid-Pharr mentions in passing, the "image" of the rural-based queers that he documents are oftentimes "infinitely disruptive" to the metro inclinations of lesbian and gay studies across racial, national, and socio-economic divides.[23]

Reid-Pharr makes this comment in reference to one of his lovers, Rick, a working-class white male he finds "so ugly and country" that Rick's rusticity—heightened by his "scandalously thick Kentucky accent"—implicitly disrupts the smooth operations of an idealizing middle-class black and white gay male urbanism.[24] Reid-Pharr's claim for Rick's "white trash" stylistics is suggestive for our developing theory of queer ruralism.[25] It invites us to consider how representations of non-metropolitan-identified queers are not only complementary, supplementary, ancillary, or, on their worst days, fetishized as out-and-out marginal to the historical development of metropolitan-based sexual cultures in the modern United States, but also how their "image" can be antagonistic to such normalizing urbanism. Building on Reid-Pharr's key insight, I join these recent discussions surrounding queer U.S. ruralism by putting pressure on the "non-metropolitan" as an "infinitely disruptive" formula in the social fantasies that produce idealizations such as "New York." Stated otherwise, *Another Country*'s archive relays a queer-based non-metropolitanism into a queer-laden anti-urbanism.

Such a shift brings unforeseen advantages to anti-urbanism's frequently scandalous—as in frequently outrageous—usage. *Anti-urbanism* is, without any doubt, a word with an embarrassing social history. In the eighteenth century it connoted a Jeffersonian ideal of non-urban agrarian-ism, a point of view suspicious of the metropolis and well documented in a letter Jefferson wrote to friend and physician Benjamin Rush in 1800: "I view great cities as pestilential to the morals, the health and the liberties of man. True, they nourish some of the elegant arts, but the useful ones can thrive elsewhere, and less perfection in the others, with more health, virtue & freedom, would be my choice."[26] The term was often used in the later nineteenth century to describe a politically bankrupt regionalism that functioned as nostalgic code speak for Anglo-Saxon supremacy and anti-urbanization, or what Southern Renaissance writer and fervid Ku Klux Klan apologist Thomas Dixon Jr. referred to as the "horrors of city life" in a 1902 article praising "Old Tidewater Virginia" over the new brown-stones of New York City.[27] Further down the historical pipeline, others would merge Jeffersonian pestilence with Dixonian supremacy when they used anti-urbanism to refer to conservative, urbanoid, and heteronorma-tive "white flights" from the "urban blights" and the supposed "disorder" of the U.S. metropolis, ones that continue to mark many post–World War II middle-class white migrations to the suburbs.[28]

But what's just as nefarious is how queers have also promoted another version of American anti-urbanism. Warner's *Trouble with Normal* was quick to diagnose this problem: "Phone sex, the Internet, and sitcoms cannot take the place of this urban space [New York's Christopher Street] and its often unrecognized practices of sexual citizenship. That is what has been urged by columnists in the gay lifestyle magazines, chiefly Michelan-gelo Signorile. In his *Life Outside*, a jeremiad driven by resentment toward the social network he ambiguously refers to both as 'the party circuit' and as 'gay culture,' Signorile fuses that resentment with a common rhetoric of antiurbanism."[29] Warner uses the term "antiurbanism" in response to Signorile's best-selling call for the "the 'deghettoization' and 'deurbaniza-tion' of gay life in America."[30] Accompanying Signorile's two demands is a plea for queers—actually, just gay men—to ex-urbanize themselves into suburbs, small towns, and unnamed rural areas, to proselytize "small-town values," and to bask in the "quieter life."[31] Such recent anti-urbanism, War-ner correctly diagnoses, functions as a synonym for the privatization of modern (middle-class) gay males in particular and as a symptom of the gentrification of U.S. queer life in general. It contributes to what Lisa Dug-gan has termed "homonormativity," a post-Fordist sexual quietism that binds U.S. queers to global consumption, neoliberal ideals of free market capitalism, and political assimilation.[32]

Citing this common rhetoric, I want to differentiate between a reactionary anti-urbanism and a critical anti-urbanism. My frequent use of the term in *Another Country* counters Michelangelo Signorile's urbanoid intentions—and, for that matter, Thomas Jefferson's. I have no desire to take the place of urban space; I have no issue with a circuit party; and I have no faith in Old Tidewater Virginia. I also have no clue what the "quieter life" means (then again, friends in my "small town" call me gabby). This book wrenches anti-urbanism away from the word's conservative inclinations to torque it into a tactic that has been wielded by non-urbanist-identified queers of varying races and ethnicities, queers with disabilities, working-class queers, and queers inside and outside any metropolitan area proper. When I cite the term "anti-urbanism" in the following pages, I thus mean to follow American Studies scholar Leo Marx who, in a discussion of anti-urbanism's ubiquity in modern American literatures, finds that the term is less of an anti-urban stance per se (like the kind we saw in Jefferson's letter) and actually "a far more inclusive if indirect and often equivocal attitude toward the transformation of society and of culture, of which the emerging industrial city is but one manifestation."[33] Like the non-metropolitan/metropolitan binary on which it depends, Marx's definition of anti-urbanism too is a language game. As an "equivocal attitude" toward a symptomatic "transformation" in U.S. sexual cultures, a queer use of Marx's anti-urbanism may trouble lesbian and gay urbanisms and function as an "inclusive" mode of critique.

Given that the pernicious etymologies and the current usages of anti-urbanism aren't going away anytime soon, I know that I'm threading a delicate needle. But as a transformational mode of social and aesthetic critique that questions certain transformations in U.S. sexual cultures, a queer anti-urbanism—grounded in the geographic configurations of the non-metropolitan—gets at what Kath Weston means when she writes that rural-identified bodies and stylistics can potentially, though not inevitably, rupture any standardizing lesbian and gay urbanism. "Significantly," she writes, "the same narratives that use urban/rural contrasts to set up the gay imaginary may also contain elements that disrupt the characterization of rural-urban migration as a move from surveillance into freedom and isolation into community."[34] A queer usage of anti-urbanism also gets at what Reid-Pharr indirectly refers to when he states that Rick's rural stylistics are "infinitely disruptive." Such critically queer anti-urbanism is precisely what I'm aiming for when I highlight that rurality—at once a geographic entity and a performative space that has often been shunned, mocked, and discarded by the metropolitan-minded—can be a supreme site of queer critique given that stereotypical images of the region or the rural can be used for unexpected ends.

I emphasize that *Another Country* is not a book about the anti-urban (I advocate the "de-ghettoization" and de-politicization of no one). It is a book about queer anti-urbanism. The former is a phobic response to fill-in-the-blank "pestilential" elements that fall under the rubric of "the city" (elegant arts for Jefferson, noisy neighbors for Signorile, non-whites for Dixon). The latter is a means to critically negotiate the relentless urbanisms that often characterize any U.S.-based "gay imaginary," an imaginary "in which the city represents a beacon of tolerance and gay community, the country a locus of persecution and gay absence."[35] To better understand how non-metropolitan-identified artists have produced this queer anti-urbanism across the spectrum of U.S. sexual history, we now explore these "urban" and "rural" sites not as geographic spaces but as social spaces beyond the Census Bureau population count.

City Subversions, Rural Stylistics, Paper Cut Politics

Having worked through a definition of queer anti-urbanism, I return to my earlier claim that any urbanism as well as any ruralism is as much phantasmatic as it is factual—perhaps more so, since the urban/rural divide that guides many U.S.-based queer studies and queer cultures is oftentimes not a geographic but a social space. Even if the "rural" or the "urban" cannot be verified by Census Bureau fact checking, these terms nevertheless subsist as structures of intense feeling that help materialize the geo-representations of urban or rural queerness. Space and place are as much act and experience as they are dirt and rock, concrete and steel. This formulation allows for more flexible readings of how ruralism and urbanism—mutually constitutive—can inform our readings of U.S. sexual cultures. Recognizing that the term "rural" is historically co-dependent on its binary opposition, "urban," we should theorize "rural" or "non-metropolitan" locales as performative geographic positions that have often enabled individuals and group subjects to experience themselves as distinct from dominant spatial performatives of the "urban" or the "metropolitan." Even when this binary appears outmoded (in, for example, recent studies of ex-urban sprawl), it still has residual effects. Thus the binarism "rural/urban" should be seen not only as a geographic marker wedded to an arbitrary population count;

it should also be seen as a social fantasy whose cartographies are as much psychic, emotive, stylistic, and relational as they are geographically or spatially realized without and within any identifiable U.S. metropolis.

This may sound like a paradox, since so many of the sites that *Another Country* visits—a daydream about Solomon Valley, Kansas; a quarterly conceived in Grinnell, Iowa; some soft-core photographs from Eastaboga, Alabama; a threnody for the town of Port Orford, Oregon; and a graphic narrative based in Beech Creek, Pennsylvania—seem non-metropolitan. Others that I present—an oil-on-Masonite painting made in Lancaster, Pennsylvania; a gathering of male inverts around a piano in early twentieth-century Berlin; some fashion magazines from Paris; a bittersweet recollection of a pre-Stonewall Greenwich Village lesbian bar; a pair of leather boots worn by an Oakland lesbian—may not. Nevertheless, when queers use these sites to disrupt rural/urban hierarchies and to launch critiques of queer anti-urbanism, they demonstrate that the language games of lesbian and gay urbanism may traverse any designated city, country, or town. They also use these locales to unsettle queer urbanities not only in the Castro in San Francisco or in Andersonville or Boy's Town in Chicago (or in queer U.S. metro satellites like Fire Island, Saugatuck, Palm Beach, Provincetown, Cape May, Cherry Grove, Rehoboth Beach, Northampton, and Key West), but also, at times, in Macon, Georgia, and Appleton, Wisconsin.[36] They grant that a flight to the city has to start from somewhere. They acknowledge that "rural" spots can be urbanized as much as "urban" environments can be ruralized. They recognize, much like Judith Halberstam does, that "'urban/rural' is not a 'real' binary; it is rather a locational rubric that supports and sustains the conventional depiction of queer life as urban."[37]

Halberstam adds this line as a footnote to what she terms "metronormativity," and *Another Country* uses the rubric of queer anti-urbanism to take up her neologism. By stating this term, Halberstam references a dominant "story of migration from 'country' to 'town,'" "a spatial narrative within which the subject moves to a place of tolerance after enduring life in a place of suspicion, persecution, and secrecy," and that imagines the metropolis as the only sustainable space for queers.[38] In this heightened version of hegemonic lesbian and gay urbanism—one that we have seen in manifestoes, gay male porn magazines, and French histories of the Castro—metronormativity imagines "the city" as an urban mecca to which rural-identified queers must assimilate. Halberstam then adds that this normalizing "physical journey from small town to big city" stereotypically engenders a "psychological journey from closet case to out and proud."[39]

Overlaying the physical with the psychological, these flights of U.S. metronormativity again reveal any lesbian and gay urbanism to be cartographic and performative, psychic and social, imaginary and all-too-materialized.

Such being the case, we can amplify metronormativity's "physical" and "psychological" makeup to sketch how its multitasking must balance six analytic axes:

1. *Narratological*: Metronormativity often appears as a travel narrative that demands a predetermined flight to the city; a mythological plot that imagines urbanized queer identity as a one-way trip to sexual freedom, to communal visibility, and to a gay village (or at least a studio apartment) whose streets are paved with rainbow pride. This narrative usually takes the form of a bildungsroman to imagine queers as young adults or adults-in-the-making, thus depriving queer children growing up in an identifiable city of a recognizable identity. It also presents non-urbanized areas as hinterlands best viewed from the window seat of your plane. This is not to imply, however, that migrations great or small, individual or collective, enforced or self-initiated, have not been essential to queers of various races and ethnicities across sexual history, or that any queer migration is inherently circumspect, or that flights aren't often dictated by socioeconomic demands.

2. *Racial*: On the one hand, a complement to narratological norms, given that the racial logistics of metronormativity frequently traffic in what José Esteban Muñoz terms a "normative ideal" of whiteness, "an image of ideality and normativity that structures gay male [and female] desires and communities"[40] and what Marlon Riggs, in his cinematic critique of the Castro, terms "the absence of black images" in "this great gay mecca" that "was no longer my home, my mecca (never was, in fact)."[41] On the other hand, an unfortunate corollary to narratological norms, given the unfounded assumption that urbanized areas are more racially diverse and racially inclusive than ruralized ones.

3. *Socioeconomic*: Not simply the gas tank for that flight or the down payment for the brownstone thereafter. Rather, a cross-gender, cross-racial per diem (an Atlantis vacation package here, a pair of Prada glasses there, a Dinah Shore Weekend for some much-needed R and R, a late summer Tuscany rental, that Paul Smith tie you couldn't say no to, bamboo everything for the Crate and Barrel registry) that enables prosperous queers to announce, to feel, to mold, and to capitalize on their leisure-oriented urbanism as bourgeois privilege and as niche market. Their

padded wallets fashion what anthropologist Eric Michaels, in a 1982 takedown of "Nautilus, EST, and Coors Beer," deemed "a Dewar's Profile image of the gay capitalist" that stifles "critical, political sensibility."[42]

4. *Temporal*: Exemplified by the oral history simile "like a hick;" the hierarchized assumption that a metropolitan-identified queer will always be more dynamic, more cutting-edge, more progressive, and more forward-looking than a rural-identified queer, who will always be more static, more backward, and more culturally backwater.

5. *Epistemological*: Also exemplified by the oral history simile "like a hick"; the hierarchized assumption that the closer proximity you have to a skyscraper, the more in-the-know, in-the-loop, and up-to-the-minute you must be, irrespective of your weekly alternative's actual entertainment listings.

6. *Aesthetic*: Substantiated by epistemological, temporal, and socioeconomic norms, an aesthetic norm occurs when the lesbian and gay urbanism that informs metronormativity consolidates itself as queer urbanity. Such urbanity functions primarily as a psychic, material, and affective mesh of stylistics informed by a *knowingness* that polices and validates what counts for any queer cultural production; a *sophistication* that demarcates worldliness, refinement, and whatever may count as "the latest"; a *fashionability* that establishes what counts as the most up-to-date forms of apparel, accessory, and design; and a *cosmopolitanism* that discriminates anybody or any cultural object that does not take urbanity as its point of origin, its point of departure, or its point of arrival.[43] These four aesthetic components are most often referenced as "trendy fashion," "chic," "style," and sometimes even "lifestyle," and they are best exemplified by what one queer glossy alphabetizes (this list is already démodé) as "Production Promotion Proenza Schouler Project Runway Protest Chic Puma Quotes Raf Simons Ralph Lauren Ray-Ban Rehab Roberto Cavalli Samsonite Black Label Sexiest Designers Shoes Shopping Sports Street Styles Icon Sunglasses."[44] I sometimes refer to such dominant queer worlding as a cosmo-urbanism.

Together these six axes of metronormativity—the narratological, the racial, the socioeconomic, the temporal, the epistemological, and the aesthetic—help support, sustain, and standardize the idealizing geographies of post-Stonewall lesbian and gay urbanism, an urbanism that facilitates the ongoing commodification, corporatization, and de-politicization of U.S.-based queer cultures in many locales. Yet while such metronormativity may be a supreme component of post-Stonewall homonormativity—a movement that crystallized alongside the rise of "lifestyle" ideologies in the 1970s—I will insist that its roots shoot back to the early twentieth century with the historical emergence of urbanized lesbian and gay group identities.[45] Thus when my first chapter details how three queer artists responded to the sophistications of Anglo-sapphism and the urbanities of New York City's bohemian cultures in the 1910s, 1920s, and 1930s, it shows U.S. metronormativity to be much more than a sign of our times. It may be best, then, to see any particular instance of metronormativity as a historically conditioned social field whose components try desperately to exceed and even more desperately to naturalize this historical specificity. Such moments occur when a queer like Susan Sontag states in 1964 that gay men "constitute themselves as aristocrats of taste."[46] And such moments have been questioned by queers such as Alfred Kinsey and his cohorts, who informed readers two decades before the Stonewall riots that "it is this city group which exhibits all the affectations, the mannerisms, the dress, and the other displays which the rest of the population take to be distinctive of all homosexual persons, even though it is only a small fraction of the males with homosexual histories who ever display such characteristics."[47]

In this quote, Kinsey and his fellow researchers gender racially unspecified 1940s metronormativity as male. Borrowing a page from their sexology, I stress that the analytic axes of U.S. metronormativity do not always intersect in harmony. Sometimes one takes the lead and subordinates the others. Sometimes one axis becomes a metonym for another. Sometimes you don't need a flight to the city to fashion-police in the sticks. The devil's in the details. It's precisely how non-metronormative queers across the decades negotiate these interwoven compulsions as they do or do not align that piques my interest. A quick example to which I later return: while metronormativity is often racially normalizing, its aesthetic norms have not always been the sole property of middle-class urban-identified white gay men. Queer of color men have been just as normalizing when it comes to policing urbane stylistics, and, as Audre Lorde laments in my fourth chapter, so too were queer of color women in pre-Stonewall Village bars. Taken as story, as style, or both, the evolving historical complexities of metronormativity's permutations thus buttress the narratives, customs, and presumptions of many urbane-identified lesbians and gays in the modern United States. Simultaneously, such permutations enable these gays and lesbians to govern the aesthetic, erotic, material, and affective imaginaries of many modern queers—irrespective of "country," "town," or somewhere in between—since at least the first third of the twentieth century.

Another case in point: despite their differences both Sontag and Kinsey remind us that the aesthetic variables of metronormativity—the subcultural styles of cosmopolitanism, sophistication, affectation, knowingness, urbanity, fashion, mannerisms and other displays—often function as an aristocratic guidebook both to what counts for and as queer taste and often to queer group identity at any given historical moment.[48] Independent of any actualized flight to the city, these stylistics frequently naturalize the "urban" not only as an identifiable geographic entity but also as a desired typology and as a commodified fetish, a "city group" thought to be "distinctive of all homosexual persons." Such urbanities tend to coalesce around seemingly supra-historicist matters of "style" that inform something like the epigraph by Edmund White—self-described "urbane, knowing, sophisticated" author, novelist, "grand arbiter of taste," and "cultural critic"[49]—that opens *Another Country*:

> Whatever our sensibility may be, New York gays are justifiably proud of their status as taste-makers for the rest of the country, at least the young and up-to-date segment of the population. Our clothes and haircuts and records and dance steps and decor—our restlessly evolving style—soon enough become theirs. . . . All over the country I saw a replication of quite recent if not current New York styles. . . . In return for the costliness and inconvenience, the squalor and discomfort of our lives, we get to participate in whatever is the *latest*. We are never left out of anything; we know what's happening. (259–60)[50]

Really? How come? Published in 1980 at a peak in U.S. lesbian and gay urbanization and included in his travel narrative *States of Desire: Travels in Gay America*, what White describes here is an urbanized and urbane stylistics that intersects temporal ("up-to-date", "the *latest*", "soon enough"), racial, socioeconomic, narratological, and, adamantly, aesthetic norms. It's "style" as invasive species and it's really impressive. In just a few sentences White manages to encapsulate these stylistics not only for "proud New York gays" and their enclaves but—in what we'll come to see as an all-too-familiar elision—for the "rest of the country" as well. Think of it as circum-Manhattan performance where the remainder of the United States becomes Greater New York City. While his snarky words may aim at the sexual assimilation of gay males across the lower forty-eight, they expand this minoritization into a universalizing model that believes itself "distinctive of all homosexual persons." A small fraction replicates itself as a nationalized aristocracy whereby "New York gays" standardize their stylistics into an Americanized city group.

Despite the squalor and the inconvenience when they sweep the country, these boys don't get to have all the fun. White's panorama finds Los Angeles to be "the national center of glamour" (26); San Francisco "the capital of gay life" (32) and "a refugee culture" "from all those damaging years in Podunk" (37); Boston and Washington DC, "intimate and sophisticated" (297); and Kansas City, by contrast, "the Fifties in deep freeze" (156). I could continue to list his taxonomic hierarchies (White does go on even as he eventually acknowledges his own "snobbism" and his neglect of "lesbians as well as small-town or rural life," "gay Asians or gay Jews," and "gay working-class men"), but you no doubt get the point (334, 336). Metronormative task forces like the one *States of Desire* presents are not static. They are instead dynamic forces whose classificatory efforts demand enormous reserves of material and psychic labor, and such labors reproduce an urbanism whose interpellations have always preceded *States of Desire* and which continue to "restlessly" evolve well into the present. As a recent header for the Atlanta-based *Southern Voice* newspaper—a metropolis White deems "the New York of the South" because "both cities are dynamic, both are fashion and convention centers, both are sophisticated" (249)—proclaims: "All the News for Your Life. And Your Style."[51]

White emphasizes that these "styles of life that are unique to a city" have been a subcultural boon for U.S. queers (69). I'll insist that potentially nourishing metronormative projects can sometimes amount to cultural and subcultural damage. There is, a philosopher once said, no document of civilization that is not at the same time a document of barbarism. Besides the "costliness" and the "inconvenience" of classifying these "styles of life" and reifying them across the nation, something else is happening when White tells readers that "we know what's happening." When the memoirist privileges New York gays' "status as taste-makers," he unwittingly confirms a claim made by his contemporary, French sociologist Pierre Bourdieu, which this book takes as an axiom: "Aesthetic intolerance can be terribly violent" (56).[52]

Published in French a year before White's *States of Desire*, Bourdieu's *Distinction: A Social Critique of the Judgement of Taste* takes classificatory practices like White's to task as it investigates the operations of what the sociologist calls "the space of life-styles" (208). To distill *Distinction*'s complex arguments and ethnographies, a social class establishes hegemony when its stylistics—particular affectations, manners, foodways, dress, comportments, and other displays—substantiate themselves as natural, "legitimate," supra-historical, and superior (56). In so doing it renders intolerable other aesthetic possibilities relevant to other social classes (56). For Bourdieu, you either have it or you've had it as your aesthetic choices make you worth more—or worthless—in the symbolic hierarchies of stylization. "At stake in every struggle over art," he writes, "there is also the imposition of an art of living, that is, the transmutation of an arbitrary way of living into the legitimate way of life which casts every other way of living into arbitrariness" (57). In *States of Desire*-speak, "we are never left out of anything" as "the rest of the country" tries in vain to catch up.

The offspring of petit bourgeois parents from a village in the Béarn region of southwestern France, Bourdieu may have meant his critique of status and taste primarily for de Gaulle–era bourgeoisie, but it's clear to me that the urbane stylistics of metronormativity also consolidate cultural capital for queers then and now. When White informs readers that New York gays "know what's happening," he betrays how early-eighties Big Apple urbanity functioned as a specific classificatory scheme in what Bourdieu terms "habitus," one with which queers still grapple (170). Habitus encompasses the productive positions of a "social space" whereby the stylistics of any particular class are confirmed, upheld, discarded, and, with a little luck, manipulated (169). "It is an incorporated principle of classification," he argues, "which governs all forms of incorporation, choosing and modifying everything that the body ingests and digests and assimilates, physiologically and psychologically. It follows that the body is the most indisputable materialization of class taste, which it manifests in several ways" (190). This process of tastemaking—of incorporating or refusing or disputing the dominant stylistics of a social space that establishes the boundaries of a particular social class—is both a conscious and an unconscious effort that plays itself out on anybody's affects and effects, and queer bodies have been no exception to this rule.[53] Hence we can see how a normalizing habitus of "clothes and haircuts and records and dance steps and decor" too often excels at embodying what counts for queer urbanity since "taste, a class culture turned into nature, that is, embodied, helps to shape the class body" (190). Likewise, such habitus (with a big boost from global capitalism) too often succeeds at incorporating queers into an assimilated "stylistic affinity" of urbanism that promises: "All the News for Your Life. And Your Style" (173).

With this social practice of urbanized queer space behind us, we can now complicate my original thesis. We should envision the urban/rural divide that often guides U.S.-based queer studies and U.S.-based queer cultures to be less an identifiable geographic space and more a materialized "social space"—a habitus—governed by dominant metropolitan stylistics (169). Halberstam, Sontag, Kinsey, White, and Bourdieu enable us to see that any lesbian and gay U.S. imagined community is regulated not only by the spatial categorizations of geography, but also by the complementary and frequently damaging classificatory practices of urbanized stylistics. While queer critics have long considered "styles of life that are unique to a city" to be subversive strategies for negotiating the physiological and psychological abuses of heteronormativity—and I don't deny anyone these life rafts—we can also see how dominant versions of metropolitan queer stylistics often work internally to intimidate, to normalize, and to box queers into urbane habitus formations. This may be one reason why lesbian and gay urbanism is so often etymologically and materially linked to lesbian and gay urbanity, and it may also account for why representations of urbane queer "style"—in print culture, in moving image, in fashion, in comportment, in music—can so easily reproduce geographic idealizations of U.S. urbanism. But if you don't want to take my word on this matter, try Esther Newton's: "To talk about homosexual style, it is necessary to bear in mind the broad distinctions among lower-, middle-, and upper-status homosexuals."[54] "Low-status homosexuals," she goes on to note, are "socially avoided and morally despised" by "the sophisticated" members of "the gay world."[55]

Far too many have taken Newton's description as a prescription. Though aimed at queers in New York City, Chicago, and Kansas City, her comments from 1972 justify why some "low-status" ruralized queers might still consider elite urbanized queer stylistics an acquired taste. When framed in this manner, we can better understand how some hold a far more inclusive if indirect and often equivocal attitude toward the dynamic metronormative transformations of U.S. queer cultures. To tweak my thesis again, a habitus of metropolitan stylistics can be and has been manipulated, sidestepped, confounded, and superseded by queers resistant to normalizing lesbian and gay urbanities. Building on Bourdieu, I note that any "space of life-styles" is also a restlessly evolving "field of struggles" (244), "the struggles between agents over the representation of their position in the social world and, consequently, of that world" (253). And thankfully, "the order of words never exactly reproduces the order of things" (481). For our present concerns, this means that metronorma-tive stylistics have long inspired metro-subversions, and there have been countless strategies for countering cosmopolitan lesbian and gay habitus within and without, betwixt and between, any identifiable U.S. metropo-lis. The radical urban-based politics of the Gay Liberation Front (GLF), to take but one example, were integral rejoinders to the racial, gendered, and class-based codes of homonormativity that emerged in the early 1970s, even as the GLF oftentimes promoted one aspect of metronormativity—rural-to-urban migration—in its frequent emphasis on an urban-based politics of "coming out."

I have more to say about this when I turn to the rise of the radical faer-ies and commune-based lesbian separatism in chapter 2. For now, I note that the primary modes of metro-subversion that *Another Country* consid-ers are what I term "rural stylistics." If cosmopolitanism, sophistication, knowingness, refinement, wordliness, and trendy fashion—all under the umbrella term "queer urbanity"—inform idealizations of U.S. metronor-mativity, then I turn the tables to chart how stereotypically ruralizing sty-listics of rusticity, stylelessness, unfashionability, anti-urbanity, backward-ness, anti-sophistication, and crudity try to undercut the metronorma-tive demands made on modern queer life. Taken in part or in sum, these low-rent stylistics put little faith in innocuous images of the "non-urban" as an idyllic pastoral or as a romanticized plain and simple place (though these conservative tableaus, chapters 3 and 4 demonstrate, do have their own resistant potential).[56] Rather, counter-stylistics beholden to queer anti-urbanism negate ideals of queer urbanity in the homogenizing wake of U.S. metronormativity. Such stylistics could—like some working-class aesthetics—be considered what Bourdieu terms a "dominated 'aesthetic' which is constantly obliged to define itself in terms of the dominant aes-thetics," but they will always attempt to make you feel more like (not less than) that proverbial hick, and we should pay close attention to the felt experiences of their non-urbanized embodiments across "the rest of the country" (41).[57] To return to Robert Reid-Pharr's earlier comment, at op-portune moments the rural stylistics of a queer anti-urbanism can be "so ugly" and "country" that they become "infinitely disruptive" or, even bet-ter, aesthetically intolerable. They are the potentially unincorporated (and often positively disavowed) queer spaces in any spatialized story that lesbian and gay urbanity likes to tell itself, and, according to Bourdieu, these stylistics may thus have "the evocative power of an utterance which put things in a new light" (479).[58]

Remember that a "stylistic" or a "style" is not just a "mode of deportment," or a "literary feature," or "a fashionable air," or a "particular method of display," or a "particular manner of life or behavior" that legitimizes itself between the pages of *HONCHO* or in the oral histories of upstate New York lesbian bars or in the rhetoric of Queer Nation or through the header of a *Southern Voice*.[59] Just as the word "queer" can be and has been pried from its homophobic use for new ends, so too does the *OED* remind us that stylistic or a style is also a "weapon of offence"—as in "to pierce with a stylet" or "to execute with a stylus"—and this book argues that non-urbanized queer stylistics can and have been used to disarm the standardizing functions of metronormative habitus.[60] These are scrappy tactics fostered and shared by lesbians, gays, and queers of disparate colors and classes and regions, sometimes across racial lines, sometimes between socioeconomic divides, and sometimes under the national radar—sometimes not. We'll see, in fact, that these queers did not always succeed in their struggles with assimilating social spaces, but their fraught negotiations and their refusals to comply with the iconic geographics of compulsory U.S. metronormativity nevertheless set precedent. They teach us how to grapple with—how to sometimes discredit—the contemporary incorporations of an evolving queer taste, and their stylets always tried to antagonize the phantasmatic urban/rural divide.

We could call this *paper cut politics*. By itself, a paper cut rarely does significant damage since it never punctures the body's deep tissue. It does, however, cause a considerable amount of discomfort, often more annoying than dire. But an aggregate of paper cuts is another country. They may interfere, prod, agitate, and pester from a point of distraction to a point of disruption, and the political aims of the queer anti-urbanisms that I am about to put on display may do likewise. At their most successful, they are constant nuisances to the idealizations of any urbanized lesbian and gay imaginary, "capillary interventions" aggravating a queer body politic that insists, "We know what's happening."[61] At their most engaged, they become cultural remainders that, no matter how costly or inconvenient, thrive in the so-called boondocks of aesthetic intolerance.

Outsider Artifacts

Moving back and forth among VHS and canvas and pixels and the printed page, *Another Country* adopts a battery of these ruralized counter-stylistics and offers up an eclectic archive (inventory sounds more apt) that spans almost one hundred years of metronormativity. Many of the items soon to be featured are not always conversant with one another, but they all share a fierce commitment to queer anti-urbanism. Some, such as the neo-Confederate portraits of working-class white males that the third chapter introduces, would be hard-pressed to find commonality with the "Down Home" African American bulldagga performances by Sharon Bridgforth that I discuss in chapter 4. Others, such as Alison Bechdel's graphic memoir *Fun Home*, stage a cross-generational conversation with urbane, pre-Stonewall stylistics that the radical fairies and the rural-identified lesbian separatists of my second chapter sought to disavow. I recognize that these subjects may sometimes seem strange bedfellows, but one of my main goals is to introduce an assortment of queer counter-stylistics that readers can make later use of, and, if they like, remodel for further ends. I mean this book to be expansive rather than definitive and by no means exhaustive or even comprehensive. The database of anti-urbanisms I have compiled is diverse enough so that you can take what you need and flexible enough so that you can leave what you don't.

In tandem with the multi-mediated nature of these objects of study, *Another Country* also draws on a range of disciplines. I bring together a variety of fields and methodologies—studies in print culture, literary close reading, performance studies, fashion studies, modernist studies, new media studies, and studies in the visual culture of photography and painting—to present an interdisciplinary reading of how the urban/rural divide still haunts U.S.-based queer studies and doesn't seem to be going away anytime soon. These portable modes of critical inquiry are, without doubt, all over the place, but that's precisely the point given that many of my objects have been forgotten or discarded or, in one egregious case, forcibly incorporated into the social fantasy of what now counts for a metronormative habitus. When I began this project I found myself confronted with what anthropologist Gerald W. Creed and cultural critic Barbara Ching once described as "the lack of a conceptual vocabulary for articulating the blend of psychic, cultural, and 'real' geography" regarding any critically queer anti-urbanism, and so this book creates the argot that it needed.[62] Over the course of five chapters, I introduce keywords and phrases—critical rusticity, bicoastality, modernist metronormativity, cosmo-urbanism, regional shame, anti-cosmopolitanism, unfashionability, and queer infrastructure—that I develop alongside previously elaborated terms such as queer anti-urbanism, metrosubversion, and compulsory urbanity to facilitate later forays into the backcountry of critique.

With this terminology in tow, I map the metro-subversions offered by rural stylistics from their quickening in the early twentieth century to the present day. Loose in its chronology, my chapters gravitate toward a few key instances in the as-yet unwritten history of U.S. metronormativity. The first two chapters tackle critical moments in metronormativity's emergence—what one historian terms the making of the "gay world" and what another scholar deems the "Great Gay Migration."[63] Each focuses, respectively, on a cluster of artists (Willa Cather, Charles Demuth, and James Weldon Johnson in chapter 1) and a cluster of journals (*RFD* and *Country Women* in chapter 2) that countered the demands of lesbian and gay metronormativity during the 1910s, 1920s, and 1930s as well as its configurations in the decades immediately preceding and immediately following Stonewall. The following three chapters approach later forms of queer urbanity from the 1980s to the present. These chapters rattle U.S. metronormativity's cultural dissemination by turning to the photography of Michael Meads in the late 1980s and early 1990s; a performance piece by Sharon Bridgforth staged in the mid-nineties; and a graphic memoir by Alison Bechdel published in 2006.

Taken separately, each chapter responds to specific pressures of a dominant queer urbanism: a millennial vogue of "lesbian chic" that winds its way back to the "dyke chic" of the 1950s in chapter 4; the historical emergence of nationalizing newspapers and glossies such as the *Advocate* in chapter 2; the aesthetic peer pressures of queer modernist sophistication in chapter 1; the rise of mid-1990s lgbtq Internet chat rooms in chapter 3; and the mythology of Interstate 80 as the road that propelled post–World War II flights in chapter 5. Taken together, the chapters try to rile the veneration of the U.S. metropolis as the epicenter of any queer community. Writ large, they puncture this fantasy. They ask that we learn to live without metropolitan idealization, and their critical takes on so-called remote locations reveal urbanism to often be a geographic desire full of diminishing returns.

I know that this is much to ask of a few choice sites, and I don't expect the scenes I discuss or the images I reproduced in these pages to halt the onslaught of cosmo-urbanisms once and for all. When I compiled this book's thirty-seven images, they seemed paltry when compared to the visual overloads of any monthly feature in any contemporary queer glossy. To be honest, I really don't mind since we often neglect the small differences that counter-stylistics do manage to accomplish, and these outsider artifacts are no less vital for failing to infiltrate any totalizing metronormative imaginary.[64] Situating themselves beyond this charmed circle, their anti-urbanisms instead dented the idealized imaginaries of something like "New York" when they insisted on stylistic alternatives to "the cultural ascendancy of urbanity."[65]

Indeed, we're going to find that metronormativity is not always easily punctured or displaced, so before we turn to the pages ahead, let's momentarily review a few epistemological traps and intellectual fallacies, lest we inadvertently re-instantiate the very norms we seek to weaken:

First, there is a danger of vulgar ruralism, of reinforcing the fluid urban/rural binary and presenting the rural as more authentic. By no means are ruralized identifications more original or genuine than urbanized ones, as if the country ever came before the city or as if any queer gemeinschaft ever antedates any urban gesellschaft. The ruralized stylistics that this book details are as much historically situated as any singular or collective performance of queer cosmopolitanism or sophistication. Likewise, these chapters have no desire to substitute a dominant lesbian and gay urbanism with a dominant ruralism (suffice it to say that across these pages the rural is not the new urban). But *Another Country* is invested in tracking how non-metronormative subjects negotiated and upset this binary as it continues to inform queer social spaces, even if the binary does not always announce itself as such, and even as rednexuals have been spotted across the land.

Second, there is a danger of conflating the rural with the regional or the intra-regional. Regionalism, like ruralism, has a specific social and aesthetic history.[66] It too is a contested term within modern political, cultural, or social group formations inside or outside the urbanized geographies of the United States. And like ruralism's hierarchized relationship to urbanism, discourses of regionalism have also been used to shore up a nationalizing identity as they too function as spatialized language games. Yet while I try to respect the integrity of these two concepts, I am nevertheless concerned with frequent slippages between the "regional" and the "rural," how, for instance, the queer regionality of an imagined Deep South in chapter 4 intersects with the ruralized bodies that Sharon Bridgforth introduces in her performance piece *no mo blues*. I'm concerned, that is to say, with how the deep localities of queer regionality, queer ruralism, and queer rural stylistics often share a critically anti-urbanist orientation.

Third, there is a danger of homogenizing any city (or, for that matter, any ruralized or regionalized locale). I cannot emphasize enough that the sexual cultures of identifiable metropolitan areas are never uniform, never uncomplicated, and always ripe with non-normativity across and between socioeconomic and racial lines. There's a world of difference between living in a city and living in a world of metronormativity, and the two need not go hand in hand. I also stated at my start that cities are often testaments to possibility, plenitude, miscellaneity, and pleasure (and, it needs to be said, hostility, cultural and socioeconomic poverty, religious fundamentalism, homophobia, racism, urbanoia, and social conservatism). But when a dominant facet of any urban-identified queer population attempts to homogenize itself as legitimate, its arbitrary citified styles can often become compulsory. Thus as much as this book is not about the anti-urban but rather about critical anti-urbanism, it is also not about metropolitan-identified sexual cultures but rather about queer non-metronormativity. Many of the aesthetic and social strategies that this book offers can be—and have been—introduced across any urbanized or ruralized population.

Fourth, there is a danger of allowing the definitional contours of metronormativity to grow static. I earlier suggested that U.S. metronormativity consists of six structural attributes, but we must attend to their historical specificities as well as their historical dynamism as we pluralize this term. Though these norms may want to appear supra-historical, we might envision their labor as akin to the "dominant-residual-emergent" framework introduced by Raymond Williams to characterize the "internal dynamic relations" of many cultural forms.[67] We might then agree with Williams and see, as he does in *The Country and the City*, that these ideas "are changing historical realities, both in themselves and in their interrelations."[68] Concomitantly, we need to attend to the specificities of lesbian and gay ruralities as they align together and as they depart from one another. It was to my surprise that, when I completed this book, most of these chapters managed to pair up across gender: Willa Cather alongside James Weldon Johnson alongside Charles Demuth; *RFD* alongside *Country Women*; Roland Barthes alongside Audre Lorde and Sharon Bridgforth; and Alison Bechdel alongside her father, to name but four examples. In hindsight I see that this move was a calculated wish to trace a continuum of urbane stylistics in the wake of gender-segregated critique, but, to riff on a line from Eve Kosofsky Sedgwick, "there can't be an a priori decision about how far it will make sense to conceptualize lesbian and gay [metronormativities] together. Or separately."[69]

Fifth, there is a danger of neglecting transnational movements as well as the urbanities of other nation-states. Given convincing arguments that "the metropolitan gay model will be found in Johannesburg, Rio de Janeiro and Delhi, as well as New York and London, in interaction with traditional local, non-metropolitan models,"[70] and given recent critiques in queer transnational studies against the "globalization of a 'gay' identity that replicates a colonial narrative of development and progress that judges all 'other' sexual cultures, communities, and practices against a model of Euro-American sexual identity," we should not assume that the critical models introduced in these pages will apply beyond any U.S.-based study, even as an uncritical model of metronormativity likes to think that it applies beyond every U.S.-based study.[71] Hence one of our goals will be to fulfill Halberstam's challenge to "complicate our understanding of sexualities *within* the 'West.'" [72] To do so, we trace the intra- and potentially subnational movements of queer anti-urbanisms as they attempt to undercut the nationalization of a U.S. metronormativity that imagines itself across "the rest of the country" and beyond. This occurs in chapter 1, where we follow New York–based modernist metronormativity to London, Paris, and Berlin; in chapter 3, where we mix the Mediterranean with the Heart of Dixie; in chapter 4, where we revisit the City of Lights; and in our epilogue, which turns to rural-to-rural Mexican migrations in the American heartland.

Sixth, I am open to the charge that I cannot see the splinter in my own eye. Like many forays into U.S.-based queer studies, these analyses were written from a space of professional assimilation, one that I see went hand in hand with an acculturation into certain facets of metronormative habitus. Though I now find myself at the peak of what linguistics terms the Hoosier apex, I no longer have much of a southern accent and I can't turn back that clock. A scholarship boy made good, I cannot recapture the outrageous personal losses that these moves entailed. Many of them I was not—still am not—consciously aware of when I consider my own psycho-geography. Lest I forget my station, please take this sometimes infuriated book as an irrecoverable record of their high cost. Its pages mark geographic and psychological breaks with my own complex identifications as a lower-middle-class queer white male from a town that will never ever get a Zagat rating. This announces itself primarily through the self-reflexive stylistics of a southern-based vernacular that seeps into the cadence of my prose, one I hope against hope might diminish the homogenizing idioms of our scholarly communications. I wish that these brief moments of regionalized discourse—a word here, some sass there—complement the ruralized counter-stylistics I detail. I wish that they succeed as speed bumps in any urbane reader's assimilation of *Another Country*'s case studies. But despite my own privileges of knowingness, I'm nobody's fool.

Nor were any of the artifacts or enactments I'm about to trace in this book. I again stress that the hard-earned protests of queer anti-urbanism I feature may not overhaul the ossifications of any macro-scene. This is more than okay (we ask way too much of our objects). The following studies, you'll find, accomplished a lot by accomplishing little. Each held a mirror up to the smooth operations of a blistering queer habitus. Each recorded the violence of aesthetic intolerance. Each recognized queer urbanity to be an incomplete, uneven project. Each vexed social spaces that are nothing more than small factions of the queer population. And each found (sometimes founded) expressive cultures that realized their supposedly backwater productions. For those of us caught in the undertow, they recorded the difference between what one ex-urbanized queer—himself no stranger to hating New York and imagining another country of critique—once termed "deep water and drowning."[73]

1

Autobiographies of the Ex-Urban Queer

Metropolitan life has never satisfied her, blunted her impatience with its more cheap and intrusive aspects.
—Elizabeth Shepley Sergeant on Willa Cather, 1940

I am so tired. Maybe it is my health, but I suspect it is more from hearing so often, "I must go to Berlin, or Rome, or Vienna, or Florence, or the East, or the South Seas. I know there must be something there for *me*." I so often wished at hearing them that some would, or all would, go to hell.
—Charles Demuth, 1921

New York City is the most fatally fascinating thing in America.
—James Weldon Johnson, 1912

Modernist Metronormativity

If Willa Cather, Charles Demuth, or James Weldon Johnson ever show up on a walking tour of lesbian and gay New York, know you're being led down a blind alley. Recent promotions by lesbian and gay historical tour companies notwithstanding, none of these artists wholeheartedly endorsed the city's pre-Stonewall queer urbanisms. They did, however, share two traits that probably won't receive mention in a contemporary walking guide—geographic proximity to modern urbanized lesbians and gays that fast became geographic misgiving with regard to modern lesbian and gay urbanization.

Each of these New York–based artists orbited bohemian cultures that facilitated the flourishing of lesbian and gay group identities across the early twentieth-century United States. After moving from Virginia to Nebraska to Pittsburgh to New York, Cather occupied a series of Greenwich Village apartments for more than two decades. Moving from his hometown of Lancaster, Pennsylvania, Demuth occupied a studio apartment on

Washington Square South in 1915 and became a habitué of Village clubs until the early 1920s. Moving from Jacksonville, Florida, to New York's Tenderloin in 1899, Johnson settled in this black bohemian district in 1902 and documented its queer nightlife in his anonymously published 1912 novel *The Autobiography of an Ex-Colored Man*.[1] But despite their proximity to (and their on-again, off-again participation in) these formative spaces, all three intuited the exclusions, the foreclosures, and the normalizations that this gradual shift toward queer urbanization entailed. As my epigraphs collectively note, all three grew disenchanted with the promise of what was to become lesbian and gay New York. In the face of myriad differences across race, class, and gender, Cather, Demuth, and Johnson were the first of many U.S.-based artists to dispel early idealizations of what later queer scholars would come to call metronormativity.

I know it may seem strange to consider versions of metronormativity in the first three decades of the twentieth century since the term often seems bound to what Lisa Duggan deems the "new homonormativity" of turn-of-the-twenty-first-century queer politics.[2] For Duggan, the political operations of this "new homonormativity" recast an older model advanced by mainly bourgeois "homophile movement organizations" of the 1950s and 1960s such as the Mattachine Society, ONE Inc, and their publications.[3] Such homonormativities, we'll see, would continue to gestate in the post-Stonewall print cultures of the 1970s that the next chapter details. For now, it makes just as much sense to push close critiques of U.S. metronormativity back even further to lesbian and gay group identity's historical emergence in the 1910s, 1920s, and 1930s, given that the historical constructions of these group identities and the historical constructions of normalizing queer urbanities often went hand in hand. Indeed, many narratives of late modern queer urbanity continue to rely on these earlier formations as they conjure a sense of continuity and historical inevitability that helps glue "metropolitan" to "queer" across the decades. Hence Didier Eribon's whimsical contention that "from at least the beginning of the century, even from the end of the nineteenth century, certain cities such as New York, Paris, or Berlin had reputations that attracted waves of 'refugees' from a wide area, even from abroad, refugees who thereby helped to consolidate the reason for their coming: the existence of a 'gay world' that they joined and to which they brought the enthusiasm that characterizes new arrivals."[4]

We have only to return to Judith Halberstam and a few historians to get a critical sense of this "enthusiasm" for the urban gay world. After

Halberstam outlines her definition of metronormativity—a dominant "story of migration from 'country' to 'town,'" "a spatial narrative within which the subject moves to a place of tolerance after enduring life in a place of suspicion, persecution, and secrecy"—she later notes that this commitment to urbanity was a fairly modernist idea: "Just a quick glance at some of the most influential high-culture texts of queer urban life would reveal guidebooks to Oscar Wilde's London, Jean Genet's [and Proust's] Paris, Christopher Isherwood's Berlin, E. M. Forster's Florence, Thomas Mann's Venice, Edmund White's New York."[5] To this international male-dominated list I might name-drop other pre-Stonewall tour guides such as Richard Bruce Nugent's New York, Ralph Werther's New York, Carl Van Vechten's New York, Charles Henri Ford's New York, Parker Tyler's New York, Gore Vidal's New York, and Frank O'Hara's New York.

This cast of thousands is, admittedly, a massive conflation that spans eight and a half decades of literary history. But that Halberstam singles out early twentieth-century male modernists like Isherwood, Forster, and Mann as her primary exemplars of an emergent metronormativity should come as no surprise, especially for those of us who do American-based literary and cultural studies. John D'Emilio, for one, has charted how shifts in U.S. capitalism at the turn of the twentieth century "made possible the formation of urban communities of lesbians and gay men and, more recently, of a politics based on a sexual identity" that implicitly proselytized flights to major (and minor) U.S. cities before and after the Second World War.[6] And in his overview of New York City's early-century sexual cultures, historian George Chauncey has revealed that many modern-identified urban queer males were metronormative by default. Chauncey insists that the city's "gay world" was an "urban phenomenon" (131) dominated largely by bourgeois gay (white) men who "created a place in middle-class culture by constructing a persona of highly mannered—and ambiguous— sophistication" (106).[7] Promoted across and along racial lines, these stylistic sophistications were matched by aestheticized habitus of knowingness, irony, camp, "Anglophilia" (106), "decorum in their dress and style" (105), and "reverence of the elegance and wit attributed to the English gentry" (106). Advanced by U.S. capitalism, they made possible a certain recognizable version of urbanized male homosexuality, a representation of the "gay male" as both a marginalized sexual identity and as a resistant subculture that was disseminated nationally and internationally through word-of-mouth, silent film, performance, painting, photography, and, especially, medico-legal and literary texts.

To be more specific, I should emphasize a certain dominant version. There is no doubt that such stylistics function as what Chauncey, following political theorist James Scott, terms "tactics of the weak," or collective strategies for negotiating the developing heteronormativities and homophobias of this period (5). But these modern stylistics also incorporated much of the cosmopolitanism, the fashionability, the sophistication, and the knowingness that constitute a main artery of many queer urbanist impulses past and present. In a comment that recalls Esther Newton's contention that "to talk about homosexual style, it is necessary to bear in mind the broad distinctions among lower-, middle-, and upper-status homosexuals,"[8] Chauncey notes that middle-class gay male stylistics came at a steep cultural price, what he terms a "*class* antagonism" toward working-class fairies (106); a "distaste for the fairy's style of self-presentation" (106); and an emphasis on "the prosperous sections of Harlem and Times Square" (106). To this pervasive class bias, I would throw in a geographic bias as well: an aesthetic intolerance for the non-urbane and a commitment to cosmopolitanism that disdained regionalized or ruralized spaces as culturally inferior even as they may have been vaulted into a pastoral. Reproduced and disseminated via modernist visual cultures and "influential high-culture [literary] texts," such privileged subcultural stylistics fostered what could be called a "modernist metronormavity" that complemented other international productions (like *À la recherche du temps perdu* or "The Beast in the Jungle" or *Death in Venice* or *A Room with a View*) to internally police and to socially normalize queers into urbane social geographies throughout the early twentieth century.[9]

Women were certainly not excluded from this mix, and some of the same can be said for urbanized white middle-class lesbians at this time. When she cites her list of male modernists, Halberstam also presents a complementary international catalogue of "Euro-American lesbian writers like Radclyffe Hall, Djuna Barnes, Jeanette Winterson, and Gertrude Stein," noting their emphasis on globalized "urban locations like Paris, London, and New York."[10] If we bracketed Winterson's late modern writings, other critics seem to agree with Halberstam's claim, arguing that many cultural forms of urbanized lesbian and proto-lesbian group identity announced themselves through sophistication, glamour, decorum in dress and style, and transatlantic chic.[11] Hall's image, to cite but one example, was iconic in both the United States and Britain several years prior to the furor over her 1928 novel *The Well of Loneliness*. As cultural critic Laura Doan highlights in her overview of early twentieth-century lesbian subcultures in Britain, Hall and her lover, Lady Una Troubridge—both "of the upper middle and upper classes" and the latter an elegant member of the English gentry—were "so famous for their taste and style" that numerous Anglophilic literary public spheres in the 1920s recorded, admired, mimicked, and lampooned them.[12] Functioning alongside, inside, and, at times, in contrast to gay male urbanizations, lesbian-centered metronormativity too seemed to produce citified compulsions for a variety of disparate women across class, racial, and frequently national borders.

I wish that it was needless to say how much went by the subcultural wayside as these historical constructions gathered force, but I want to follow up on Doan's passing remark that modernist queer female urbanity "undoubtedly foreclosed some promising directions in modern fashion and artistic production."[13] For my present concerns, it is the verb "foreclosed" that interests me most. If now-recovered and often-celebrated lesbian and gay urban phenomena weren't "so small, nor so isolated, nor, often, so hidden" as previously assumed (Chauncey, 7), then could we also suppose that these sexually non-normative populations produced certain subcultural norms—certain foreclosures of the non-urbane—that were, perhaps, advanced by the aesthetic dictates of something like a modernist text? I'm well aware that urban-identified figures like the working-class fairy might have undercut this aestheticized metronormativity with their self-stylizations from without; but if critics such as Halberstam, Chauncey, and Doan concur that artistic icons of modern lesbian and gay urbanity were beholden to sophisticated stylistics marked by racial normativity and class antagonism from within, then can we also imagine possibilities for intra-class or intra-racial critique? What would this lesbian and gay worlding begin to look like if we concentrated on in-house productions that failed to adhere to metronormative stylistics, that voiced dissatisfactions from inside the confines of queer urbanized modernism? What other promising counterexamples might then be reintroduced?

For Cather, Demuth, and Johnson, these questions were not rhetorical. This chapter explores how these three artists negotiated and countered the historical emergence of a predominantly, though by no means exclusively, U.S.-based modernist metronormativity with anti-urbanist stylistics based in "high-culture" literature and painting. To do so, it focuses on internal critiques of queer modernism as these three artists declined the developing international traditions that informed and fomented an emergent U.S. metronormativity that would intensify over the decades. All three reveal what it felt like to be shortchanged by the urbane stylistics of a prevailing sexual modernity. All three produced artworks that perceived the aesthetic intolerance of subcultural subversions. And all three—in various mediums—returned to left-behind geographies to highlight the "peripheral modernity" that contradicted the macro-codes of sexual urbanities guiding so much of the early twentieth century's artistic productions within Western modernism.[14]

I visit three concentrated sites—a few paragraphs in Cather's 1925 novel *The Professor's House* set in Solomon Valley, Kansas; Demuth's 1927 Lancaster-based oil painting *My Egypt*; and an internationalized Berlin gathering of Wilhelmine Era inverts in Johnson's *The Autobiography of an Ex-Colored Man* (published anonymously in 1912, reprinted under Johnson's name in 1927)—to substantiate these claims. When seen in juxtaposition, these sites show dispirited individuals failing and foiling the compulsions of a galvanized metronormativity. One offers a critical indictment not just for men but for women as well. Another does the same for queers of color. In so doing each site responds to dominant and developing urbanizations with an aestheticized strategy of critically queer anti-urbanism. Forming a loose web of critique whereby anti-urbane stylistics surface amid queer U.S. modernism, they present us with a guidebook to a few social and geographic spaces that urbanized high-culture texts tried and failed to remainder.

Gone-to-Kansas

Just as she proved herself to be all too familiar with the sensational 1895 trials of Oscar Wilde (she denounced the playwright/novelist in the Lincoln, Nebraska, *Courier* that same year), it is safe to hypothesize that Cather was likely aware of urbanized (homo)sexual developments in New York City across the first three decades of the twentieth century. These may have included but were not limited to the obscenity trial of *The Well of Loneliness* in 1928–29, heated controversies over Edouard Bourdet's sapphic play *The Captive* (1926), the phenomenal success of Edna St. Vincent Millay's *Renascence, and Other Poems* (1917) and *A Few Figs from Thistles* (1920), and the public visibility of bohemian lesbians in the Village. As earlier noted, from 1906 until her death in 1947 Cather, with her longtime companion, Edith Lewis, lived on and off in a series of New York apartments around the Village. With much of her daily life centered on Washington Square, "all of New York—its high arts and sidewalk low life, and all the sights a habitual walker in the city glimpsed in between—enriched her mind and imagination," Merrill Maguire Skaggs has suggested, and "the bohemian ferment of Greenwich Village in which she lived . . . challenged and provoked her."[15]

There's no denying that Cather was certainly invested in if not necessarily enthralled by the fermentations of Manhattan in general and Village bohemia in particular. She wrote from Pittsburgh as early as 1897 that "we spend our time down here trying to fancy that we live in Gotham."[16] Yet despite these imaginative bouts of urbanity in the Steel City, strains of her queer anti-urbanism repeatedly crop up when one examines her fictional writings, and even more so when one follows her deep investment in the non-urbanized same-sex male bonds that persist from her earliest short stories to her more modernist novels of the 1920s. We have only to think of her 1905 tale "The Sculptor's Funeral," where Cather traces how a small-town Kansas lawyer, Jim Laird, buries "the thing in him that [his Boston friend] Harvey Merrick had loved" and shuttles this passion "under ground with Harvey Merrick's coffin."[17] Or the Archbishop Jean Marie Latour and his traveling companion, Father Joseph Vaillant, surveying the deserts of the nineteenth-century Southwest in *Death Comes for the Archbishop* (1927). Or the "warm affection" forged between the Compte de Frontenac and his "young friend," Robert Cavelier de La Salle, in *Shadows on the Rock*, a 1931 novel set in the French colony of seventeenth-century Québec.[18] Or Claude Wheeler's adoration for David Gerhardt in *One of Ours* (1922), a novel set against the historical backdrop of a war-torn French countryside. Or, for my main argument here, the "strange," "fantastic" midwestern coupling undertaken by Professor Godfrey St. Peter and his pupil Tom Outland in her experimental 1925 novel *The Professor's House* (257).[19]

The recurrence of these same-sex relations in Cather's corpus suggests a cross-identification with men as well as a counter-identification with the lesbian-based literary metronormativity sponsored by writers such as Hall. I emphasize cross-identification because, as many of her best critics have long noted, Cather repeatedly ventriloquized her queer desires by voicing them between men. I emphasize counter-identification because, as her friend Elizabeth Shepley Sergeant observed in the first of this chapter's epigraphs, "Metropolitan life has never satisfied her, blunted her impatience with its more cheap and intrusive aspects."[20] To spin Sergeant a bit, despite the city's bohemian ferment, Cather was never really satisfied with the inchoate metronormativity of an urbanized lesbian identity, and her writings bear this out. Placing the author in contrast to "other literary lesbians of the period, such as Hall or Barnes or Edna St. Vincent Millay" (63), literary critic Christopher Nealon stresses that the New Yorker declined the "glamorously mobile" (63) styles of these "wandering cosmopolites" (9) and was far more interested in "rural people of little means" (63).[21]

Unimpressed by the transatlantic urbanities of sapphism, Cather's writing had little psychic investment in the urbanized lesbian or gay subcultures of New York even while the city may have "enriched her mind and imagination." Nor did she have much interest in an international metropolitan lesbian identity that might now fall under the rubric of sapphic modernism. Such being the case, her regionalized modernism provokes us to think about something more than the literary championing of an urbanized lesbian or gay modernist metronormativity as it also challenges readers to imagine geographic and social spaces that surpass the aestheticized artifices of urbanized queer subcultures. If so, we might then begin to see her passionate same-sex male relations as more devoted to possibilities of the non-urbane in lieu of an easily recognizable metropolitan queer subculture complete with its own dominant stylistics.

Set in the pseudonymous upper midwestern town of Hamilton, *The Professor's House* tracks Cather's dissatisfaction with this modernist queer metronormativity by featuring a relationship between a married elder male (St. Peter) and his young pupil (Tom Outland) that one critic describes as "sensuously Whitmanesque."[22] Their bond begins as cliché: a brilliant and uncultivated student—a diamond from the southwestern rough—looks to an accomplished scholar for intellectual guidance and a chance to study at a university. The working-class boy's talents with the Latin language impress St. Peter, and the professor commits his energies to Outland and ensures him a place at Hamilton's university. What starts off as a rather staid teacher-student relationship, however, becomes something more. Over the course of several years, the two embark on an unlikely companionship. Under one roof, they study, eat, and banter together. They swim together daily, and eventually become traveling companions, much like Cather and Lewis did on their trips to the Southwest in 1912 and 1915. "Two years after Tom's graduation," we are told, "they took the copy of Fray Garces' manuscript that the Professor had made from the original in Spain, and went down into the South-west together. . . . The next summer Tom went with the Professor to Old Mexico. They had planned a third summer together, in Paris, but it never came off" (259).

Critics have often read this relationship as a cosmopolitan middle-class gay married man's long-standing affair with his student, and many depictions do seem to support this claim.[23] St. Peter is a world traveler; he's fond of "luxurious" hotels and a "big city" like Chicago (91); he repeatedly aestheticizes the homoerotics of his relation with Tom; and his wife "withdrew her favour" when St. Peter "began to make a companion" of Outland (173). At the end of the novel's first section, we find a bourgeois St. Peter and Outland fine-dining under the "night fall" of a summer evening while his wife and two daughters vacation in Colorado: "When he cooked a fine leg of lamb, *saignant*, well rubbed with garlic before it went into the pan, then he asked Outland to dinner. Over a dish of steaming asparagus, swathed in a napkin to keep it hot, and a bottle of sparkling Asti, they talked and watched night fall in the garden" (176). With the narrator informing readers that this "was just the sort of summer St. Peter liked, if he had to be in Hamilton at all" (176), the trappings of this urbane pastoral appear to exemplify the "the highly mannered—and ambiguous—sophistication" that Chauncey identifies as a central component of modern urbanized gay male habitus. Culinary ways here become aestheticized markers for St. Peter's class-based cosmopolitanism, signifiers of a Francophile urbanity that connects the small-town professor to an internationally queer community.

But the queer anti-urbanism of another summer evening that closes down *The Professor's House* overturns this scene as well as the novel's prior commitments to such makeshift sophistication. With his family in absentia and Tom a casualty of the First World War, a solitary Godfrey begins to take up another improbable dalliance between another boy and an elder male—himself. I quote the following passage at length because it encapsulates much of my larger argument:

> St. Peter had always laughed at people who talked about "day-dreams," just as he laughed at people who naïvely confessed that they had "an imagination." All his life his mind had behaved in a positive fashion. When he was not at work, or being actively amused, he went to sleep. He had no twilight stage. But now he enjoyed this half-awake loafing with his brain as if it were a new sense, arriving late, like wisdom teeth. He found he could lie on his sand-spit by the lake for hours and watch the seven motionless pines drink up the sun. In the evening, after dinner, he could sit idle and watch the stars, with the same immobility. He was cultivating a novel mental dissipation—and enjoying a new

friendship. Tom Outland had not come back again through the garden door (as he had so often done in dreams!), but another boy had: the boy the Professor had long ago left behind him in Kansas, in the Solomon Valley—the original, unmodified Godfrey St. Peter.

This boy and he had meant, back in those faraway days, to live some sort of life together and to share good and bad fortune. . . . After he met Lillian Ornsley, St. Peter forgot that boy had ever lived.

But now that the vivid consciousness of an earlier state had come back to him, the Professor felt that life with this Kansas boy, little as there had been of it, was the realest of his lives, and that all the years between had been accidental and ordered from the outside. His career, his wife, his family, were not his life at all, but a chain of events which had happened to him. All these things had nothing to do with the person he was in the beginning. (263–64)

St. Peter had previously characterized the Solomon Valley—a couple of hours drive south from Cather's second childhood home of Red Cloud, Nebraska—as a space of sensory deprivation: "When he was eight years old, his parents sold the lakeside farm and dragged him and his brothers and sisters out to the wheat lands of central Kansas. St. Peter nearly died of it" (30).[24] In retrospect Godfrey's response to this internal migration is typically metronormative. He views this ruralized space of Kansas as a dead end, a badland culturally bereft, socially frozen, and unassimilated into his urbane/urbanized inclinations. Far from embracing the developing ideal of the U.S. Midwest as a pastoralized heartland, and far from acknowledging that the valley once supported revolutionary immigrant and African American pioneer settlements in towns such as Nicodemus,[25] St. Peter instead invokes what Emily Dickinson once called "a gone-to-Kansas feeling" when the poet moved from her Pleasant Street house back to her Old Main Street house in Amherst, Massachusetts, in 1855.[26]

Yet in these three paragraphs St. Peter's sunbathed return to Solomon Valley helps to enrich his mind and to resuscitate his imagination. A striking contrast to his previously ingrained tastes, St. Peter's description undercuts his queer urbanity and reconnects him to the ruralized Middle West that he had previously shirked. What he finds on his sand-spit is what Eve Kosofsky Sedgwick, in her preface to the second edition of *Between Men*, terms "that second and belated life," "those tardy, wondering chances at transformed and transforming self- and other-recognition" that function as "the more than Balzacian founding narrative of a certain modern identity for Euro-American gay men"—yet he finds this new narrative with a twist.[27] Sedgwick deems this alternative life "the metropolis," but Cather via St. Peter stakes out a complementary obscure destiny.[28] Pining for Kansas, his belated life concludes in a flight to the country, and his return to Solomon Valley is a "productive immobility" that signifies on the "glamorously mobile" lesbian metronormativity that Cather turns inside out. His dream (and hers) is not one of connecting to a larger transnational or transatlantic community of urbanized queers but of dissociating from it.

When he connects this "novel mental dissipation" of his Solomon Valley-self back to his earlier friendship with Tom, we could also say that Outland's rusticity helps St. Peter realize this ruralized queer cross-identification. A midsummer's eve of fine wine, steamed veggies, and lamb chops aside, *The Professor's House* repeatedly presents Tom as a yokel. Unsophisticated, uncouth, and unrefined, he enters through backdoors; he falls down stairs; he stuffs his face with mashed potatoes; he chomps cigars; and he "never learned to eat salad with ease" (78). Figured as working class, such habitus opposes Godfrey's queer urbanity, and the novel explicitly factors Outland's social and socioeconomic ineptitude as a ruralized stylistics. Tom isn't urbanized by upbringing (his parents died "when they were crossing southern Kansas in a prairie schooner") nor is he metronormalized by inclination (115). When he recalls a journey to the big city of Washington DC, he finds several urbanized lives there "so petty, so slavish" and "all wrong for me" (232, 175). Such lives, he informs Godfrey, "gave me a kind of low-spiritedness I had never known before" (233). Having lived a "rough life" in the non-metropolitan Southwest (124), Tom renounces the compulsory urbanity of this East Coast environment and wants instead to romantically remain one of the roughs, to inhabit "a free life [where he can] breathe free air" (236). In another instance of their queer pedagogy, Outland teaches St. Peter how to ex-urbanize himself. Always a quick study, Godfrey returns the favor with "the boy the Professor had long ago left behind him," one who is "not nearly so cultivated" as previously assumed (263, 265).

Curiously, St. Peter's miseducation into these ruralized stylistics of Kansas and the U.S. Southwest also invokes the "sensuously Whitmanesque" codes of modernist metronormativity. When Cather emphasizes Outland's "rough" life, she references Whitman's self-identification as "one of the roughs" from his 1855 edition of *Leaves of Grass*.[29] Cather was deeply influenced by Whitman,[30] and the narrator's description of

Godfrey's "half-awake loafing" also recalls the poet's "Sun-Bath" in *Specimen Days* (1882), as well as the lines "I loafe and invite my soul / I lean and loafe at my ease observing a spear of summer grass" from "Song of Myself."[31] But here the novelist does not solely invoke the working-class homoerotics so often associated with the New York–based poet. Her thick citations also call to mind the evolving Whitmanian metronormativity rampant in her era (and ours). With poems such as "Song of Prudence" (1856), "Mannahatta" (1860), and "City of Orgies" (1867), Whitman proved to be a decisive influence on modern(ist) American and British queer authors such as Edward Carpenter, Alain Locke, Hart Crane, Langston Hughes, and numerous others. His poetics helped many of them make sense of themselves as queer urbanites, and they do so well into the present. Notes poet Mark Doty in a recent ur-narrative: "[Whitman is] someone who moves from a farm into New York, finds a world of possibility there and then connects to an alternative sexual community. . . . That is the beginning of modern urban gay life and he stands right at that moment when gay men are finding freedom and possibility."[32] Complementing Doty, a historical overview that Chauncey wrote for the *Out Traveler* in 2008 likewise informs readers that New York City's "cultural sophistication" nurtured an "international gay circuit that connected London; Berlin; Paris; Havana; San Juan, Puerto Rico; and Mexico City," where queer modernist artists (he cites Federico García Lorca) were "drawn by Walt Whitman's mesmerizing descriptions of this great 'City of Orgies.'"[33]

Cather's Solomon Valley does not comply with these idealizing stories: it undoes the Whitmania that continues to champion certain facets of New York to this day. Her citations of Whitman in these paragraphs fail to attach Godfrey to an "international gay circuit" through high-culture literary allusion or through membership in an imagined literary community. Redeploying Whitmanian metronormativity, Cather pines for a modern lesbian and gay unworlding whereby St. Peter uses his sunbathing to travel back to a ruralized Kansas, a space that removes the Spanish historian from a social historicization of queer urbanity that Cather daily witnessed on Village streets. Like his ruralized friendship with the working-class Outland, this "vivid" relation to a Kansas boy never convincingly translates "new friendship" into a dominant urban homosexual identity. Godfrey, a self-identified "primitive" "only interested in earth and woods and water," unlearns the prevailing tendency to see lesbian and gay urbanization as a beneficial historical development (265).

Reintroducing the "earlier state" of an unincorporated non-urbanity into modernist metronormativity, Cather's novel thus inaugurates what Mary Louise Pratt, in a critique of metropolitan-based Western modernisms as they relate to Latin American modernist writings, calls sexual "experiments in nonurban aesthetics, of artistic projects anchored not in the city but in the countryside," or what I introduced as rural stylistics.[34] This ideal of non-metropolitan aesthetic experimentation is precisely where the novel closes (or, depending on your perspective, commences): the narrator tells us in the last paragraph of the book that an unprogressive Godfrey "had let something go—and it was gone" (282). This unspecified "letting go," I propose, signals a freedom from metronormative constraints that then enables the professor to begin to think outside the frameworks of a modernized U.S. gay male group identity. At once novel and outdated, his regionalized male-male bonding with a Solomon Valley child pushes him past the historical designations of urbane subculture and back into a phantasmatic elsewhere. We might term this psychic and aesthetic project a re-racination, an imaginary re-rooting into the places that one, willingly or not, leaves behind.

Then and now, *The Professor's House* asks that our critical energies take up this "glittering idea" of making "something new," even as it acknowledges the leisure time needed for this working through (111, 261). Too often, the novelty of this "something new" has been presented as the quickening of subculturally sophisticated queers in New York, or Paris, or London—rarely, if ever, in the wheat fields of Kansas. Yet the novel recognizes the daydreaming necessary for these fanciful flights from dominant modes of lesbian and gay urbanization. At the beginning of modern urban queer life in the United States, Cather stands right at that moment when some gay men and women were finding freedom from the possibility of urbanity.

Still Life with Charles Demuth

So too, on a different register, does the productive immobility of Charles Demuth. In the winter of 1927, Demuth completed *My Egypt*, which I suggest is the first—perhaps the only—modernist self-portrait of type 2 diabetes (fig. 1.1). It's also the scene of one modernist queer invalid signifying on the most famous modernist queer invalid of the twentieth century, but you'd never guess this if you've ever been lucky enough to view it at the

Whitney Museum of American Art. Three feet in height and two and half in width, oil on Masonite made from local linoleum factories, *My Egypt* seems to depict the John W. Eshelman and Sons grain elevators from Demuth's native town of Lancaster, Pennsylvania, or, more accurately, their abstraction. One portrayal of his hometown among many, the painting is a stunning example of Precisionism, a modernist movement embraced by the Stieglitz Circle (among them Georgia O'Keeffe) headquartered at a 291 Fifth Avenue art gallery in New York City.[35] Together some of these artists built on Cubist tenets to transform the architectures of American modernity into non-figurative aesthetics. Hence Demuth splices Pennsylvania silos into shafts of light that radiate across and beyond *My Egypt*'s canvas.

Interpretations of this painting generally fall into three camps, each turning on Demuth's title. Some take the Precisionist painting as a snicker at the Egyptomania sparked by Howard Carter's excavation of Tutankhamen's tomb in 1922, a discovery that helped inspire a craze for Egyptian art deco.[36] For others it's a wink and a nod at the modernist irony that also informed the poetics of his close friend William Carlos Williams.[37] For still others, writes art critic Robert Hughes, "his title connects to the story of Exodus. Egypt was the symbol of the Jews' oppression; it was also the starting point for their collective journey toward the land of Canaan, the forging of themselves as a collective and distinct people. As an invalid in later life, Demuth was 'exiled' in Lancaster, bedridden in his parents' house, cut off from the intellectual ferment of Paris and the sexual-esthetic comradeship of New York. All these were Canaan; home was Egypt."[38]

Let's decode this last reading. Demuth's "invalidism" refers to his diabetes diagnosis in the early 1920s; "sexual-esthetic comradeship" refers to his participation in Manhattan's queer male subcultures; and the "intellectual ferment of Paris" partially refers to the queer international excitement over Proust's *À la recherche du temps perdu*. The logic of this reading suggests that Demuth's modernist Egyptology extends Proust's fraught analogies between minoritized urban gay men ("descendents of those inhabitants of Sodom") and Jews ("a persecution similar to that of Israel") that the author repeatedly promotes in *Sodome et Gomorrhe*, where he imagines the collective fashioning and dispersal of metropolitan-based homosexuals in "London, Berlin, Rome, Petrograd, or Paris" as a Jewish diaspora.[39] We can then read *My Egypt* as a cross-identification with Proust's Parisian invalidism, a hymn to high modernist metronormativity, and a bittersweet takedown of Lancaster as a Podunk town far removed from the queer

Figure 1.1. Charles Demuth (1883–1935), *My Egypt* (1927).
Oil and graphite on Masonite fiberboard, 35 1/4 x 30 in. (90.81 x 76.2 cm).
Courtesy of the Whitney Museum of American Art, New York; purchase,
with funds from Gertrude Vanderbilt Whitney.

metropolis of Sodom. As one critic remarks, *My Egypt* reveals "Demuth raging against the prison of Lancaster's provincialism."[40]

I want to add here that Demuth read Proust's novel in 1927 but never finished it. Literally and figuratively, he put the book down. The English translation of *Sodome et Gomorrhe* by C. K. Scott Moncrieff was published as *Cities of the Plain* by Albert and Charles Boni the year Demuth worked on *My Egypt*, and the painter quickly grew disenchanted with Proust's opus. On October 30, 1927, he wrote to Alfred Stieglitz: "Haven't seen the Stein book [*The Making of Americans*]. But over the summer have read Proust,— so I've joined the others,— not without reservations, however. It's too much like myself for me to be able to get a great thrill out of it all. Marvelous, but eight volumes about one personal head-ache is almost unreadable, especially when you have your own head-ache most of the time."[41]

Such a claim is suggestive. It begs that we reconsider the critical reception of regional "invalidism" thought to inspire *My Egypt*. It begs that we reconsider how studies of the painting—like, we'll see, social histories of urban gay male identity formation—neglect the complexities of Demuth's critically queer disability. And it begs that we reconsider Lancaster as a provincial prison, an invalid's exile, or, at the very least, a personal head-ache. To do so, this section argues that the Lancaster-based artist, reconsidering his earlier advocacy of metronormative modernism in Greenwich Village and Paris, painted himself as a proponent of queer modern disability following his diabetes diagnosis in 1921. Immobilized by the disease and increasingly invalid during the historical crystallization of U.S. lesbian and gay metro-subcultures, Demuth's oil painting stages a bittersweet critique against the sexual normalization of these urbanized able bodies by championing the disavowed spaces of south-central Pennsylvania. To date Demuth remains one of our best recorders of a burgeoning U.S.-based urbanity. With *My Egypt* he complements Cather's championing of Solomon Valley to also emerge as one of its more stringent critics.

But to get to this point, Demuth had to first reconsider the relationship between disability and urbanity since the metropolitan environments that scholars of lesbian and gay U.S. history have archived are also, consciously or not, often aided by able-bodiedness. Given that queer theorists such as Robert McRuer have recently linked compulsory able-bodiedness to heteronormativity as well as to the historical emergence of U.S.-based heterosexuality at the turn of the twentieth century,[42] we might also find that standardizing sexual codes of queer metronormativity intersect with able-bodiedness, or what David Serlin has called the "codes of urban modernity—what really counts as urban and/or modern—[that] are organized around narratives of normative able-bodiedness."[43] Serlin refers to the modern queer icon of Helen Keller in this quote, but in theory and in praxis gay male metronormativity can be dependent on able-bodiedness, particularly ambulation. This is not just a matter of accessibility for that proverbial flight to the city, but the recognition that much of a city's queered spaces are, more often than not, co-dependent on ambulatory erotic comportments and pathways that facilitate same-sex *flâneurie*. One has only to recall the importance of *Gay New York*'s parks, beaches, back alleys, strolling sidewalks, and walking tours, or its built environments of basement cabarets and speakeasy entrances and exits that contributed to the story of urban gay male subculture formation across the early twentieth century.[44] What would it mean to start thinking about these historically nourishing spaces as possible "mobility impairments"?[45]

For over a decade Demuth had to face this question head on, since he was no stranger to either side of the modernist metronormative coin.[46] A self-styled dandy, he was a privileged participant-observer in New York's queer world scenes as early as 1914, when he regularly roomed at one of two Greenwich Village hotels, the Brevoort and the Lafayette, and later rented a studio apartment at Washington Square South.[47] Likewise, his watercolors during this time record the social, aesthetic, intellectual, and sexual vibrancy of Village queer cultures with titles such as *At the "Golden Swan" Sometimes Called "Hell Hole"* (1919), *The Purple Pup* (1918), *Turkish Bath with Self-Portrait* (1918), and *Cabaret Interior with Carl Van Vechten* (1917). Chauncey uses one of Demuth's watercolors—*Turkish Bath* (1916)—to exemplify the sexual ferment of New York in the early twentieth century,[48] and Demuth confirmed his commitment to this "homosexual milieu" with a snippy 1920 hometown portrait of Lancaster entitled *In the Province #7*.[49]

Some of this changed following Demuth's diabetes diagnosis in the winter of 1921.[50] Though he was affluent enough to count among the lucky few to receive regular insulin injections—batches first produced in 1922—they often failed to work on the artist. Frequently starving (a typical treatment of blood glucose regulation) and facing hypoglycemia, he found himself cast out from spaces of aesthetic and sexual ferment, occupying a second floor Lancaster apartment on 118 East King Street under the care of his mother.[51] This "illness," one of his best critics notes, "forced him to seclude himself from New York society"[52] and "physical survival precluded the resumption of his former life-style."[53] "In 1922," he "seized the occasion to make [Lancaster] his sole residence."[54] Over one hundred and fifty miles from New York and almost eighty miles from Philadelphia, Demuth found himself in a town—a rather large, racially diverse town with a population of twenty-two thousand—that was nevertheless ruralized by the metronormative aesthetics of many East Coast urbanites.[55] In this so-called hinterlands, Demuth was geographically dislocated from the sexual and social circles he once helped watercolor in.

With the painter queered by a historically developing urbanism, his diabetes complications forced him to complicate a metronormativity he previously advocated, to cultivate a novel mental dissipation much like Cather's St. Peter. Like many privileged queers, the scales fell from his eyes when he encountered an invalidism that socially invalidated him, one where he could no longer participate in whatever is the latest. And while the artist continued to make visits to New York, Philadelphia, and other major metropoles, and metro satellites like Provincetown, by train until his death in 1935, Demuth, at times, felt frustrated at his incapacity to engage with cosmo-urbanism in the late twenties and lashed out against the mobility of his middle-class Anglophilic peers. "The party sounds grand," he informed one of his close Philadelphia friends when invited to a soirée in 1929, "—but I am afraid it is no place for me! Now, that I know I can't be there."[56]

Such remarks may better explain why *My Egypt* often seems so unintelligible to urbanist critics. It doesn't make sense to see Demuth as mocking a non-urbanized life. It's more complex than this since he's also railing against a developing gay male urbanism—a railing, I have to stress, that occurred only after the painter found himself incapacitated by diabetes. Hence if Egypt did signify a "mania" for Euro-American audiences in the twenties, and if a Lancaster-based Demuth "exploited the Egyptomania that followed Howard Carter's discovery" in his 1927 Precisionism, then he is also exploiting the mania for another concurrent fad, modernist metronormativity.[57] To the best of my limited knowledge, there's never been a widespread queer mania for Lancaster, though curious urbanites did—still do—figure the town and its surrounding agri-landscapes as the ground zero of Amish rurality starting in the early 1930s. Playing with and on this craze, *My Egypt* stages an ironic mania for those spaces expelled from the urbane gay *internationale* at the same moment Demuth professes his own "mania" for Lancaster.

This means that the painter rethinks the Proustian queer diaspora—another aesthetic mania alongside Egyptology—that became a collective trope for elite urbanized gay male self-understanding. *My Egypt* does so when it makes good on Proust's logistically twisted claim in *Cities of the Plain* that urbanized queers may want to "create a Sodomist movement and to rebuild Sodom" even though they never fully realize this dream: "For, no sooner had they arrived there than the Sodomites would leave the town so as to not have the appearance of belonging to it" and "would repair to Sodom only on days of supreme necessity."[58] *My Egypt* literalizes this muddled allegory as it uses modernist form to cancel out the metronormative modernism advocated by queers such as Proust. In an ironic commentary that exceeds irony (remember that Demuth found Proust "a head-ache" "too much like myself"), the painter turns high literary style against itself, a camping that fails to confirm inchoate international metronorms since it paints neither Sodom nor London, Paris, Berlin, Petrograd, Rome, nor, for that matter, New York City. Demuth thus replaces the exclusionary geographies of high-culture gay male aesthetics with two grain silos that capture the industrial crudity of an anti-cosmopolitan style. He turns the knowingness, sophistication, and urbanity of queer modern aesthetics into a mocking ruralized stylistic by doing the improbable: stylizing Lancaster. In so doing he counter-identifies with the international intellectual ferment of Parisian Sodom by turning grain silos into a re-racinated queer diaspora, a canvassed town that no urbane queer wants the appearance of having to belong to.

Demuth, however, owns this geography with his titular possessive. It's *his* Egypt. Non-urbanized queers may do the same, since the defiant painting may well embrace what Dana Luciano, reading queer invalidism into Henry James's 1881 novel *The Portrait of a Lady*, terms "the pleasures of imagination itself."[59] Note the obvious about *My Egypt*: it's an empty, depopulated scene. There are no men in this static scenario. There's no same-sex cruising. There's no mobility. And there's really no there there (as Stein once scoffed about her not-so beloved hometown of Oakland, a city we'll return to in chapter 4). The painting is a still life. We have two phallic silos and a chimney stack, architectures far removed from the urbanized gay male worlds that Demuth tracked in his earlier Village-based watercolors. Such a scene signifies on pervasive stereotypes of ruralized spaces as devoid of queer potential as well as the absence of queer bodies thought to hightail it elsewhere. But this supposed emptiness and seeming immobilization, like the pun on Egyptology mania, like the swipe at the Proustian anti-diaspora, may also be a metro-subversion. As much as *My Egypt* turns grain silos into abstracted rays of light, it uses Precisionism to turn grain

elevators into abstracted spaces of imaginative potential, the photo negative of À la recherche in terms of its author's "cloistered invalidism."[60]

No stranger to James, having painted watercolors of "The Beast in the
Jungle," "The Real Thing," and "The Turn of the Screw," Demuth may have
borrowed a page from the Master when he turns from sociological realism
to Precisionist abstraction. His watercolors typically record the socio-real-
ist architectures of the everyday urban gay male world. But his oils, often
painted on local Lancaster materials, turn the town's everyday architectures into a fantastic space, an impossible rurality advanced by industrial
modernization and marked by medium shift. In the Demuth corpus, such
a break announces an unincorporated sexual geography that replaces his
previous urban gay mimesis with a critically ruralized one; it realizes Lancaster as a fantastic space discounted from the epicenters of U.S. sexual
modernity; and its abstracted revolt from and to the "province" offers a
critical indictment of an inchoate and able-bodied U.S. metronormativity.
Cut off from Parisian intellectual ferment and New York's sexual-aesthetic
comradeship, Demuth launches a non-mimetic queer disability critique,
a takedown of metronormativity as a form of confinement and as an aesthetic impairment. "I'm really all right here," he wrote a friend the summer
he painted *My Egypt*, "— but at times I *almost* wish I could 'go in for' hys-
terics; but all I can go in for is another picture."[61]

"Go in for" may be modern suburban leisure-class slang for going into
the city for a weekend excursion. With Lancaster so often figured as an in-
hospitable geographic disability, Demuth becomes a disability theorist for
those incapacitated by metronormativity. Along the way he, like Cather,
highlights the "peripheral modernity" opposing the urbanized sexual modernities that dominated much of the first quarter of the twentieth century.[62] In *My Egypt*, at least, he did not help forge a collective gay male
world but instead imagined other spaces of queerness that this world liked
to think it was surpassing (and, at times, incorporating). In museums and
on Web sites and through Lancaster tourism, *My Egypt*'s quiet silos may
continue to do more of the same.

That said, I have to qualify my critique. There's no attention paid to the
working bodies of *My Egypt*'s industrialism, and Demuth would continue
to repair to Sodom on days of supreme necessity when he composed watercolors in the early thirties such as *Two Sailors Urinating* (1930), *Two
Figures in Bedroom* (1930), *Distinguished Air* (1930), and *On "That" Street*
(1932) (fig. 1.2). As aesthetically expansive as it is geographically land-
locked, *My Egypt* nevertheless inaugurates one of the first queer crip

Figure 1.2. Charles Demuth (1883–1935), *Distinguished Air* (1930).
Watercolor on paper, irregular 16 3/16 x 12 1/8 in. (41.12 x 30.8 cm).
Courtesy of the Whitney Museum of American Art, New York; purchase,
with funds from the Friends of the Whitney Museum of American Art and
Charles Simon.

styles—which was also one of the first queer regionalist critiques—of an emergent U.S. metronormativity. If Demuth is now well-known for his portraits of bath houses, beaches, Village clubs, and Manhattan back alleys as the key brushstrokes of New York's gay male cityscape, and if his later "invalid" work in Lancaster is thought to long for these spaces from which the painter was geographically "isolated," we must reconsider Demuth's "province" as sensory deprivation as much as *The Professor's House* reconsiders rural Kansas as a midwestern wasteland. Like Godfrey, he lets something go.

And as Demuth found himself increasingly shortchanged by what sometimes counted for sexual modernity, his love-hate affair with queer anti-urbanism thus realized Raymond Williams's neglected closing remarks included in an essay in *The Politics of Modernism*: "This means, above all, seeing the imperial and capitalist metropolis as a specific historical form, at different stages: Paris, London, Berlin, New York. It involves looking, from time to time, from outside the metropolis: from the deprived hinterlands, where different forces are moving, and from the poor world which has always been peripheral to the metropolitan systems. This need involve no reduction of the importance of the major artistic and literary works which were shaped within metropolitan perceptions. But one level has certainly to be challenged: the metropolitan interpretation of its own processes as universals."[63]

It also gets to the heart of Demuth's exhausted letter to Stieglitz written just a few months after his diabetes diagnosis at the Psychiatric Clinic in Morristown, New Jersey: "I am so tired. Maybe it is my health, but I suspect it is more from hearing so often, 'I must go to Berlin, or Rome, or Vienna, or Florence, or the East, or the South Seas. I know there must be something there for *me*.' I so often wished at hearing them that some would, or all would, go to hell."[64] It is precisely this "international gay circuit" that Demuth shirked when he chose—at first, unwittingly—to make Lancaster his Egypt.

Berlin Story

We will return to Demuth in chapter 3, where later twentieth-century Alabama-based artist Michael Meads makes some interesting revisionary claims to the Precisionist's watercolors. I want to now concentrate more on Demuth's "I must go to Berlin" imperative and its accompanying compulsory urbanity, since this is also what one of the painter's contemporaries—James Weldon Johnson—set out to critique when the unnamed male protagonist of his 1912 novel *The Autobiography of an Ex-Colored Man* tells his travelling partner to go to hell in the German capital.

This exact phrase is never spoken, but the scene that I'm thinking of occurs when Johnson's narrator, a tragic American mulatto passing as a white male in Berlin, informs readers that his "mind was made up" and he decides not to accompany his wealthy partner on any future international travels to "Cairo and Tokio" (144). He instead chooses to return to the U.S. Deep South, "to voice all the joys and sorrows, the hopes and ambitions, of the American Negro," and to aid ruralized black folk (147–48). The impetus behind this weighty decision occurs "one night [when] my millionaire entertained a party of men composed of artists, musicians, writers, and, for aught I know, a count or two. They drank and smoked a great deal, talked art and music, and discussed, it seemed to me, everything that ever entered a man's mind" (140–41). Playing ragtime for this queer gathering, the narrator suddenly realizes that he had "now lost interest in our trip" and tells us that he had "made up my mind to go back into the very heart of the South, to live among the people, and drink in my inspiration firsthand" (142).

I'm going to show that this determination to break with his millionaire in Berlin, like so many heated exchanges in *Autobiography*, is, as Siobhan Somerville has claimed, "at once racial and sexual" and geographic.[65] I aim to tease out *Autobiography*'s rich intersectional critique, one that allows Johnson to promote a takedown of modernist metronormativity that balances out some oversights of our previous two case studies. Somerville notes that most interactions between the narrator and his "millionaire friend" (120) often take on "a more directly sexual relationship,"[66] and prior scenes in *Autobiography* support her claim. When the Ex-Colored Man first lays eyes on the white millionaire in a New York–based club, he cruises "a clean-cut, slender, but athletic-looking man, who would have been taken for a youth had it not been for the tinge of grey about his temples. He was clean-shaven and had regular features, and all of his movements bore the indefinable but unmistakable stamp of culture" (116). Here the Ex-Colored Man sets his sights not just on a fit white male body, but on an urbane one as well. The millionaire's stylistics confirms the "unmistakable" cosmopolitanism, the "ambiguous" ("indefinable") sophistication, and the "decorum in dress and style" that marks elite gay male urbanism during the first decades of the twentieth century in New York. A few paragraphs later the Ex-Colored Man notices that the millionaire's apartment also carries this "stamp of culture" since it too is full of "elegance and luxury" (117). Such findings substantiate Somerville's observation that the millionaire realizes "a somewhat sinister version of fin de siècle decadence, a figure of wealth and forbidden sexuality" that the novel dismisses one action-packed night in Imperial Germany.[67]

I'll get back to this Berlin scene in a few paragraphs. Before I do so, I want to address any lingering suspicions that Johnson may seem to be this chapter's odd man out in terms of both sexual identification and literary technique. To attend to the former: Johnson was married to his wife, Grace Nail, from 1910 until his untimely death in 1938, and by everyone's account the two were a well-matched couple. There's no smoking gun to suggest that the author was gay-identified, though Johnson's wide social circles included just about every queer participant in what would come to be known as the Harlem (New Negro) Renaissance. To attend to the latter: unlike *The Professor's House*'s broken narrative frame or *My Egypt*'s Precisionism, *Autobiography* appears quite realist in its narrative technique, merging conventions of bildungsroman, personal memoir, sociological tour guide, city mystery, and slave narrative. Yet critics have long noted that matters of gender and sexual nonconformity ripple through *Autobiography*, as do typically modernist tropes such as unreliable narration, cosmopolitanism, commitment to irony and parody, and stress on the new.[68] Given these intricacies, *Autobiography* is not just an unexpected but a necessary endpoint to our critiques of modernist metronormativity. As we'll see, the author complements Cather and Demuth to present a damning portrait of an internationalized gay male subculture that re-evaluates modern "rural-to-urban" gay migration narratives only to move this critique beyond its typical Euro-American identifications. While Cather's St. Peter overlooks the racial components of his Solomon Valley excursion into non-urbanity, and while Demuth showed little interest in racial critique even as his watercolors illuminated New York's racialized cabarets, Johnson's queer modernism repeatedly underscores the racial norms that buttress the emergent tale of modern gay urbanity.

This critique occurs from *Autobiography*'s start as the novel courses through various geographies that foreshadow the compulsory and exclusionary identifications the Ex-Colored Man severs in Berlin. The Ex-Colored Man's sexual and racial cross-identifications first appear in a small Connecticut community (the narrator was originally raised in an unidentified "little town of Georgia" [3]) where Somerville points out that

Johnson's young Ex-Colored Man sees himself as something of an invert. Drawing on links between scientific racism and the rise of sexology at the turn of the century, Somerville suggests that Johnson "characterizes him through a model of gender inversion."[69] For her, such characterizations emerge following the Ex-Colored Man's segregation among the African American students in his classroom, and his later self-observation in a mirror where he interprets his blackness through the narrative of a young girl trapped in a young boy's body.

Given this invert identification in a small New England town, it makes sense that when the Ex-Colored Boy becomes an Ex-Colored Man he heads for the Tenderloin after wanderings in Atlanta and Jacksonville, Florida. Arriving in New York, he exclaims: "My blood ran quicker and I felt that I was just beginning to live. To some natures this stimulant of life in a great city becomes a thing as binding and necessary as opium is to one addicted to the habit. It becomes their breath of life; they cannot exist outside of it; rather than be deprived of it they are content to suffer hunger, want, pain, and misery; they would not exchange even a ragged and wretched condition among the great crowd for any degree of comfort away from it" (90).[70] Here we see the convergence of several metronormative axes. Following this major metropolitan migration, the Ex-Colored Man begins to socialize with other sexually non-normative black and white bohemians in the "'tenderloin' life in New York" (140). Later, he becomes a nightly fixture in a bohemian New York club where he first encounters the clean-cut millionaire. All told, readers are privy to a standardizing narrative (one that also signifies on the advent of the Great Migration) as *Autobiography* makes its way to this most stimulating City of Orgies.

Yet the above quote also hints at how quickly *Autobiography*'s initial excitement over New York City's queerness can tip over into disenchantment with the "great" metropolis. This frustration is apparent not just in the reference to opium addiction, but also in a long jeremiad on the perils of Manhattan that precedes these idealizing exclamations:

New York City is the most fatally fascinating thing in America. She sits like a great witch at the gate of the country, showing her alluring white face and hiding her crooked hands and feet under the folds of her wide garments—constantly enticing thousands from far within, and tempting those who come from across the seas to go no farther. And all these become the victims of her caprice. Some she at once

crushes beneath her cruel feet; others she condemns to a fate like that
of galley-slaves; a few she favours and fondles, riding them high on the
bubbles of fortune; then with a sudden breath she blows the bubbles
out and laughs mockingly as she watches them fall. (89)

Pejorative allusions to gender infuse this description. New York City
is a seductress. She is a "witch." She is Fortuna who assigns migrants to a
"cruel" "fate." She is a tempting Statue of Liberty who thwarts them "from
across the seas." But what also stands out in this anti-urbanist (and misogynistic) paragraph is the narrator's racialization of the city's "alluring" urbanity. Looking out into the Black Atlantic, New York possesses a "white
face" that the narrator likens to the captain of a slave ship. At such uneasily
gendered moments, *Autobiography* connects a growing distrust of urbanism to a racial critique of whiteness at the precise moment that it narrates
a rural-to-urban queer/black migration.

Such anti-urbanist inclinations snowball after the Ex-Colored Man
moves from a "fatally fascinating" New York City to pre-Weimar Germany.
After an all-inclusive world tour with the millionaire across Paris, London,
Venice, Spain, Brussels, the Mediterranean, and Amsterdam, the two wind
up in Berlin where the narrator tells his friend that he has decided to leave
the metropolis and head back to the hinterlands of the U.S. South. Given
what we've now established with regard to the Ex-Colored Man and the
millionaire, it's not difficult to read this gender-exclusive Berlin scene with
which I began this section as a queer form of modern gay male internation-
alism.[71] Chauncey tells us that "by the time of World War I, there existed
in Paris and Berlin a highly developed gay commercial subculture that easily surpassed the scale of the gay world in New York" (144),[72] and sexology reports from the early twentieth century agree with the historian. In
his 1908 *Les homosexuels de Berlin: Le troisième sexe*—published one year
before Johnson began to draft *Autobiography*—German sexologist Magnus Hirschfeld reports that the "establishments" of Berlin nightlife "are
very popular and filled with people on Sunday and Saturday nights. The
patrons, the waiters, the pianists, the singers, all there are homosexuals."[73]
Later Hirschfeld cites modern German novelist and dramatist Rodolphe
Presber's *Les types de la capital*, a book that similarly identifies "Uranian
taverns" where one just happens to find "an elegant piano with all of the
stock pieces."[74] Likewise, sexologist Richard von Krafft-Ebing's *Psychopathia Sexualis* includes a "notice from a Berlin newspaper, of February,
1884 [which] seems suited to show something of the life and customs of

pederasts and homosexuals: *The Woman-haters' Ball.*—Almost every so-cial element of Berlin has its social reunions—the fat, the bald-headed, the bachelors, the widowers—and why not the woman-haters?"[75] "From the statements of a high police official of Berlin," Krafft-Ebing reveals a few pages later, "I learn that the police are conversant with the male *demi-monde* of the German capital."[76]

The existence of these (often misogynistic) Berlin hot spots alone is worth our interest, and I don't want to homogenize the complexity of the city's developing queer subcultures. Yet what intrigues me is not *Autobi-ography*'s literary representation of male inversion, but that readers may be witness to a fictional gathering of worldly white men of culture, a high society from which the Ex-Colored Man disaffiliates once he realizes that he's been "wasting my time and abusing my talent" (142). What intrigues me, I mean to say, is why Johnson represents this Berlin scene as both an internationalized demimonde and as a metronormative one. It's worth noting that the New York–based millionaire's "stamp of culture" gels well with Berlin's men of culture: the Ex-Colored Man sizes up the "artists, musicians, writers, and, for aught I know, a count or two" who "talked art and music" (140–41). This connection to a cosmo-urbanism marked by decorum, style, sophistication, elegance, and luxury becomes even more apparent when the narrator recollects that during his international travels "my millionaire took apartments, hired a piano, and lived almost the same life he lived in New York" (130).

But it is the narrator's faintly dismissive "for aught I know" that turns this Wilhelmine Era Berlin scene into a critique of an internationalizing gay circuit rather than an innocuous depiction of cultured Euro-Amer-ican gay men. This line figures the Ex-Colored Man as an ambivalent participant-observer in this scene rather than a full-fledged insider, and its embedded commentary is amplified when we learn that the narrator "could only follow the general drift of what they were saying" (141). Thus when the Ex-Colored Man renounces this tie to his millionaire "man of the world" and to these men of the world around him (131)—ties that bind him to the sophisticated stylistics of modern urban gay male world-liness—he also renounces an elite Euro-American habitus that he has not yet fully incorporated nor yet fully identified with. At the same time that Johnson presents a cross-cultural exchange between Americans and Germans packed with shared recognition and taste, *Autobiography*'s queer diaspora may also be one of the first texts in literary history to critique a certain modern identity for Euro-American gay men as an international identification, one that enables us to further historicize Halberstam's associative link between metronormativity and the "most influential high-culture texts of queer urban life."[77]

The novel does so because it factors sexual assimilation into these urbane scenes—of the degree if not of the kind we earlier saw Tom Outland reject in *The Professor's House*—as a questionable form of racial cultivation. When Johnson has the narrator renounce urbanized gay male cosmopolitanism around a piano, he continues the novel's earlier racial critiques of Mannahatta. The Ex-Colored Man comments: "He had taken me from a terrible life in New York and, by giving me the opportunity of travelling and of coming in contact with the people with whom he associated, had made me a polished man of the world" (143). When the narrator notes that the millionaire "made me a polished man of the world," he emphasizes this queer act of cultivation as a discourse of modern metronormativity, a kind of elite acculturation or transmission that links metropoles like London, Berlin, Rome, Petrograd, Paris, and New York, and that we have seen from Halberstam to Proust to Demuth to the *Out Traveler*.[78]

Yet the text also links these polished stylistics to an internationalized scene of whiteness. Desperately trying to convince his partner not to leave him, the millionaire gives this game away when he tells the Ex-Colored Man that "my boy, you are by blood, by appearance, by education, and by tastes a white man" (144). In Imperial Germany (and in a raft of other major European metropoles), the narrator lets us know that the millionaire has been cultivating him into a dominant and racially normalizing subculture all along. But the narrator's desire to return to the Deep South (specifically, the predominantly black rural Georgia counties outside the city of Macon) reveals his desire for a geographic habitus uncultivated by metronormativity, a space worlds away from "the man who exerted the greatest influence ever brought into my life" (148). At such moments the novel launches a critique of how an international and a U.S-based metronormativity coaches subjects into a gay worlding that is at once racial, sexual, and geographic. When the Ex-Colored Man decides against this queer assimilation into globe-trotting urbanity, he simultaneously refuses racialization into modernist gay male cosmopolitanism.

Like Demuth and Cather, Johnson's critique too has its blind spots. When the narrator tells us that "I made up my mind to go back into the very heart of the South, to live among the people, and drink in my inspiration firsthand" (142), he leaves Berlin behind and eventually makes his way to rural Georgia. Heading into what he calls the "interior" (167), this should have been a lived experiment in non-urbanized aesthetics. But upon arrival he informs readers that "much, too, that I saw while on this trip, in spite of my enthusiasm, was disheartening. Often I thought of what my millionaire had said to me, and wished myself back in Europe" (169). While sympathetic to rural black poverty, he nevertheless scoffs at "these dull, simple people" (169–70) and complains about their "rank tur- nip-tops, and the heavy damp mixture of meal, salt, and water which was called cornbread" (169). Such comments betray an archaic commitment to cosmopolitanism that disdains regionalized foodways and ruralized spaces as culturally inferior—and that we've seen vestiges of in Cather's gone-to-Kansas feeling and Demuth's province #7. While he later notes that the rural U.S. South is a place of internal terrorism and extreme pov- erty after witnessing a horrific lynching, the Ex-Colored Man still abjures some of these ruralized and racialized stylistics even as he sees how they differ from the urbane ones that he previously imbibed.

Likewise, near the close of *Autobiography* the narrator confesses that "I reached a grade of society of no small degree of culture" once he makes a killing in real estate and marries one of the loves of his life, who soon dies after birthing two children (197). Yet the last lines of the novel lin- ger on the Ex-Colored Man's disappointment at transforming into this widowed "man of culture," and his disenchantment here recalls both his earlier disappointment at being a gay man of culture as well as the urban identifications that "keeps me from desiring to be otherwise" (211). To its bittersweet end, then, the novel charts a growing disappointment with an internationalized though U.S.-based metronormativity, and this may be the core of *Autobiography*'s critique: as early as 1912 the city can be a let- down. Almost six decades before these ideals saturated U.S. lesbian and gay cultures following Stonewall, *Autobiography* presents the wanderings of a queer male that do not conform to queer cosmopolitanism (which he rejects) or urbanized migration (which he rejects) or bohemian sub- culture (which he rejects) or queer sophistication (which he rejects) or queer metropolitan belonging (which he rejects). Preceding and pre-dat- ing both Cather and Demuth in its transatlantic observations, the novel is relentless in its critique of modernist metronormativity's emplotment as it churns fatally fascinated queers into urbane white men of culture. In a book so concerned with the possibilities of music (it's when he plays rag- time that the Ex-Colored Man decides to literally head south), *Autobiogra- phy* scores another leitmotif that crescendos around a Berlin piano—the counter-idealization of any well-cultivated modernist metropolis.

Raw Deals

Like Cather and Demuth, Johnson thus traces what anthropologist Kath Weston terms "anti-identification" in his modernist novel's gradual and incomplete turn to ex-urbanization.[79] Weston uses this term to describe the dissatisfaction her interviewees expressed when they arrived on urbanized queer U.S. scenes in the mid to late 1970s, the subject of our next chapter. At the moment of metronormativity's historical quickening in the United States, Cather, Demuth, and Johnson do more of the same. Each introduces distinct forms of regionalized modernism to question the international norms of elite (white) gay male and lesbian subcultures in New York City, Paris, and Berlin. Each presents sophisticates who reject sophistication, middle-class gays queered by their anti-urbanities and socially extracted via their anti-cosmopolitan cosmopolitanism. Taken together, these artists launch a triple-pronged counter-attack: Godfrey learns to live without the pleasures of queer urbanity; Demuth turns his back on metronorms; and the Ex-Colored Man renounces a collective gay cosmopolitanism amid its fascinating promise.

And as self-reflexive ex-urbanites—a term that today implies a settlement beyond the identifiable metropolis often associated with affluent residents—all three were somewhat ambivalent about these moves as they formally experimented with moving toward queer anti-urbanism. Godfrey, a wealthy professor, "learned to live without delight" as he dips his imagination into the rural stylistics of Solomon Valley (282). Economically comfortable thanks to his family's Demuth Tobacco Shop, Demuth still complained in watercolor about life in his supposedly one-horse town. Ending his story as a prosperous capitalist, the Ex-Colored Man scoffs at the southern "backwardness" of rural Georgia folk. Demuth never completely denounced metronormative life, nor Cather, nor, for that matter, Johnson. Despite her dissociation from elite lesbian subcultures and her ruralized childhood, the author of *The Professor's House*—if not Godfrey St. Peter—was often committed to middle-class creature comforts, as was Demuth, and Johnson was certainly no stranger to an urban-based cosmopolitanism.

But even as I qualify these projects, I'm still fascinated by how three respective autobiographies (fictive or not) help literalize and historicize a queer ex-urbanization. At a critical juncture in U.S. social history, when the nation's population was almost evenly divided between what counted for ruralized and urbanized areas, Cather, Demuth, and Johnson gesture toward other possibilities that were artistically foreclosed as cities such as New York, Berlin, Paris, and London became the core of an "international gay circuit" among modern and modernist subjects then and, more so, now. Tracing one thread of late metronormativity's backstory, this chapter attempted to show that it is not so wide a leap from Whitman worship to the *Out Traveler* or from Proustian hagiography to a visit to the Whitney or from *Autobiography*'s grand European tour to a racially normative gay male globalization. Many of these texts inform contemporary metronormativities, and the trickle of urbanities this chapter traced hints at the deluge to come.

In their urgent attempts at queer urban unworlding, these sites are thus some of the first to anticipate later U.S. metronormativities; to invert urbane stylistics via what we would come to know as disability, gender, and queer of color critique; and to scrutinize novel urbanizations—Cassandra-like—as a raw deal. Across developing and uneven forms of sexual inversion, middle-class black and white gay male group identity, white middle-class lesbianism, and working-class eroticism, their unlikely affinities show U.S. metronormativity to be an unfortunate inheritance with which we must wrestle. The resistant strains of these anti-urbanist aesthetics ask that we redo the done deals of modern U.S. lesbian and gay urban history, and they are just three deleted scenes that renounced what began to count for the urbanization of the modern lesbian and gay world. We have too often sidelined aesthetic arguments that refused to cultivate the polished meccas, and to continue to do so leaves modernist studies, let alone modern urban studies, deeply impoverished. We might, like the Ex-Colored Man, like Godfrey St. Peter, and like Demuth in his Egypt, start desiring to be otherwise.

2

Critical Rusticity

I've been trying to get it together for a move to the country—I'm so tired of the city, of the gay treadmill, recyclable people and city trips, but wondering how to made [*sic*] contact with other country-oriented faggots. Then—voila—*RFD*.

—Anonymous, 1974

An Aesthetic of Anti-Urbanity

At first glance, a rural farmhouse in Grinnell, Iowa (current pop., 9,205) seems an unlikely spot for a sustained campaign against the standardization of white urban gay male identity in the post-Stonewall United States. But consider this recollection of one holiday season in the winter of 1973:

> For Christmas that year I had bought Julia, one of my housemates, a subscription to *Country Women*, a rural feminist journal out of Mendocino [a small coastal community in northern California]. Reading and loving *Country Women*, I wondered why there wasn't a similar magazine for gay men. I just *knew* that I couldn't be the only gay man who liked rural life, though it sure seemed that way. The six other inhabitants of our it's-not-a-commune-we-just-live-together farmhouse were straight but lovable. The available gay publications were all urban-oriented full of the latest news of cha cha palaces in San Francisco, shows off-off Broadway, trendy fashions from West Hollywood, Gloria Gaynor's latest album, and how to make a killing in the real estate market. As for rural magazines like *Mother Earth News*, well, let's just call these adamantly heterosexual.[1]

Julia's subscription to *Country Women*'s rural lesbian separatism, it turns out, became the inspiration for the *RFD* (once referred to as "Rural Fairy Digest") quarterly. *RFD* was one of the first anti-heteronormative, anti-urbanist, and anti-middle-class journals for queers to appear as a challenge to and a critique of newly nationalized "cha cha" gay publications like the Los Angeles–based *Advocate*. It was thus one of the first queer journals to extend the non-normative intersectional politics of the Gay Liberation Front to non-metropolitan U.S. audiences.

Nearly two decades later, however, the midwesterners who founded *RFD* would have been hard-pressed to find critiques of normalizing urban gay culture in the pages of the journal they established. Take a spring 2000 issue, when a different set of *RFD* editors published "From Hippie to Fairy at Short Mountain Sanctuary," a historical retrospective that made no mention of the Grinnell farmhouse or of *Country Women*'s influence. Located near the small town of Liberty, Tennessee, the Short Mountain Sanctuary (current pop., 17) had been a central gathering place for radical—not necessarily rural—faeries since 1979, the year that former Mattachine Society founder Harry Hay published "A Call to Gay Brothers" for a "Spiritual Conference" in *RFD*. The 2000 *RFD* essay traced a genealogy of this neo-primitivist gay male collective, a counterculture known to throw weeklong festivals in rural Appalachian mountains, Minnesota north woods, Arizona deserts, and elsewhere across the globe.[2] The article glossed Short Mountain Sanctuary and presented a truncated history of its origins: "Hippies knew how to wear flowing clothes, embrace dirt, and worship the goddess. Gay men knew how to have lots of sex, when to wear black, and why to be attractive. They were all familiar with mind-altering substances. Community values and spiritual inspiration married marijuana and sex: the earth mother and pan. The offspring was the radical faeries, a term coined in the 1970s to reflect the need for a counter-cultural queer presence."[3]

There is much to question in this succinct history—its glib sketch of a historically complex countercultural movement assumed to "embrace dirt"; its unspoken assumption that all "hippies" are male; its turn toward "earth mother" worship; and its spurious cross-identifications with spiritually inspired cultures that many radical faeries stereotypically located in the Native figure of the two-spirit.[4] What is also curious about 2000 *RFD*'s unreflective equation among "hippy," "gay," and "radical faerie" is its unacknowledged reliance on the "values" of a communal "presence" that the journal was originally founded to push against—a sexual group identity that appears exclusively gay, exclusively male, and, ironically enough, exclusively urbanized. With allusions to leisure culture ("marijuana and sex"), style and sophistication ("when to wear black," "why to be attractive"), and knowingness ("Gay men knew," "they were all familiar"), the

Figure 2.1. *RFD* logo, *RFD* issue 122 (vol. 31, no. 4; Spring 2005): 44. Courtesy of Sr. Soami for the *RFD* Collective and the News and Microforms Library at Pennsylvania State University.

history that late-nineties *RFD* offers here seems to be more the offspring of a metro-oriented gay male cosmopolitanism than the issue of a radical, regionalized, and intersectional queer counterculture.

"From Hippy to Fairy at Short Mountain Sanctuary" thus corroborates ethnographer Scott Morgensen's recent claim that many present-day U.S. radical faerie gatherings have erased their political history, "outpaced" "rural men's participation," and now consist primarily of middle-class "urban gay men, who [frequent] gatherings as temporary rural retreats for the cultivation of new cultural identity and spiritual insight for transport back to urban life."[5] When seen in this light, the amnesiac histories that the late-1990s faeries tell themselves about their mid-to-late-1970s origins promotes the mainstream "community values" that they like to think they dance, sing, worship, and write against. And though recent *RFD* articles have imagined male readers who are "not interested in being 'bar clones,' but who . . . explore their uniqueness and spirituality (among other things)," the current publication might be closer to an urbanized—and now globalized—version of normative U.S. gay male "bar clone" identity than it likes to presume (fig. 2.1).[6] In a telling moment, one disgruntled *RFD* reader lamented in 2000 that the journal is "quite a contrast from the early issues of *RFD* that came out in the mid-70s." He demanded: "Please cancel my subscription immediately! I thought your magazine was 'a country journal for gay men everywhere' but it's not! The 'RFD' connotation used to stand for those living a rural lifestyle, country affairs, small town life, etc. but not any more! Apparently your mag is now completely (90%+) a Radical Faery Digest."[7]

The following pages revisit *RFD*'s early-to-mid-1970s "rural lifestyle" to argue that the quarterly did not initially stand in or stand for a radical faerie digest that some leisurely cosmopolites might enjoy as an armchair rural retreat (fig. 2.2). Rather, several working-class white males who politically affiliated with the Gay Liberation Front founded the journal in 1974, and they imagined themselves as the antithesis of what many metro-based radical faeries now consider themselves to be. Quoting a sexological glossary titled "The Language of Homosexuality," historian Jonathan Ned Katz notes in his *Gay/Lesbian Almanac: A New Documentary* that RFD initially connoted the transcontinental sweep of the U.S. Postal Service, or "Rural Free Delivery," an abbreviation that "immediately suggests the rustic scene to the urban mind."[8] In the late 1940s and 1950s, pre-Stonewall white middle-class urban gay males appropriated this postal term to disparage what Katz describes as the "R.F.D. queen—a homosexual who lives in the country or in a small town, and who has homosexual impulses and desires, but who does not understand the argot and ways, or know the habits and places of congregation of the homosexual fraternity in cities and metropolitan centers."[9] Following the popularization of the term in television shows such as *Mayberry R.F.D.* (a spin-off of *The Andy Griffith Show* that ran from 1968–71), in the 1970s these so-called RFD queens re-appropriated this regional slur to express dissatisfaction with the "argot and ways" of an emergent white gay male "ghetto" culture felt to be inherently normative rather than inherently oppositional. Far removed from the queer urbanity that marks the late-nineties *RFD* (and many late-nineties post-Stonewall urbane U.S. sexual cultures), early-seventies *RFD* begins as a riposte to these "habits and places of congregation"—one that critiques via the unsophisticated, the anti-urbane, and the anti-cosmopolitan, and one keen to distance itself geographically, materially, and aesthetically from big-city "homosexual fraternity" through unexpected print alignments with small-town rural lesbians. Through such critiques, *RFD* enabled the queer subjects in its pages and elsewhere to imagine and to inaugurate critical horizons that engaged with those bodies and consciousnesses that were often excluded from the matrix of urbane schemas, even as the journal's non-normative engagements were sometimes incompletely realized.[10]

RFD, that is to say, was one of the first post-Stonewall prints to offer a ruralized counter to a U.S.-based metronormativity that complements and extends the critiques introduced in our previous chapter. As much as artists such as Cather, Demuth, and Johnson engaged with a modernist metronormativity based in high-culture literary texts of the 1910s, 1920s, and 1930s, so too did *RFD* engage with post-Stonewall standardizations that emerged in nationalizing newspapers like the *Advocate* as well as a plethora of urban-

Figure 2.2. *RFD* logo, *RFD* issue 1 (Autumnal Equinox 1974): 1. Courtesy of Sr. Soami for the *RFD* Collective and the News and Microforms Library at Pennsylvania State University.

oriented guidebooks that tracked what began to count for queer publics in the 1960s and 1970s. Notes historian Martin Meeker in an overview of the racial and gender normativity of these interlocking print cultures:

> These brief descriptors [Meeker discusses codes such as *B* for black clientele found in publications like the Damron guidebook] became a nearly uniform feature of the scores of guidebooks produced by small presses and do-it-yourselfers and thus reveals a trend toward standardization and specialization in the gay world. . . . It might be argued that those publications simultaneously allowed homosexuals to see how and where they fit in the gay world—and how and where they did not; it provided them with the opportunity to identify with a portion of the gay subculture but also with the possibility of failing to identify with any of the particularities in the gay world as it was being parceled and its parcels were named.[11]

Following Meeker's lead, this chapter focuses on the "possibility of failing to identify" by extending recent historical scholarship on 1970s lesbian and gay print cultures to analyze the queer anti-urbanism of *RFD*'s early stylistics. It offers an aesthetic archeology of what one initial contributor, Donald Engstrom, later termed *RFD*'s "separatist fag community,"[12] and what one historian of regional U.S. cultures, James T. Sears, sees as the quarterly's "anarcho-effeminism."[13] Building on their findings, this chapter explores how a particular version of gay male urbanity began to reprint itself as a normalizing print style in 1970s glossy magazines and newspapers, and how *RFD*, alongside *Country Women*, responded to this historical packaging with oppositional stylistics of its own. Hence the chapter examines the visual culture and the stylistic productions of rural-based queer print culture—logos, subscription notices, fonts, typesets, front covers, back covers, matrices, drawings, boilerplates, and advertisements— that speak volumes about the calcifications of U.S. metronormativity. Interrogating these paratextual layouts will enable critics to further witness how stylistics functions as a point of political and cultural contestation for gay urbanites and their detractors. The layouts will also show how a rustic 1974 *RFD* logo tried to slow the historical march of what would gradually become the urban sprawl of *RFD*'s 2005 logoscape.

To accomplish these tasks, I return to a pivotal moment in U.S. sexual history that saw the fraught convergence of nationalizing newspapers like the "cha cha" *Advocate*, regionalizing radical-lesbian mimeographs such as *Country Women*, and anti-urbane counterparts like the Iowa-based *RFD*. I start in Los Angeles with an explosion of lifestyle publications that enabled aesthetic standards of gay urbanity in the post-Stonewall United States. I next explore rural-based California critiques launched against these stylistic ideals by lesbian separatists disenchanted with male "ghetto" publications. I finally return to where this chapter began—a Grinnell, Iowa, farmhouse—to chart how *RFD* bounces on the *Advocate* and builds on *Country Women*'s stylistics to advance what I theorize as *critical rusticity*. By critical rusticity, I mean an intersectional opportunity to geographically, corporeally, and aesthetically inhabit non-normative sexuality that offers new possibilities for the sexually marginalized outside the metropolis as well as inside it. Both of these journals, we will find, exhibited complicated, sometimes flawed gender and racial politics as they critiqued the *Advocate*'s metronormativity. Acknowledging their respective complexities, I show how a working-class "country journal for gay men everywhere" tried to present aesthetic opportunities to dominant U.S. gay lifestyles via rural U.S. women's alternative lifestyles. These aesthetics were resistant to the "trendy fashions of West Hollywood" males, but they were also indebted to the anti-fashion cultural politics of *Country Women*.

Bicoastality

RFD emerged at a pivotal moment in post–World War II U.S. lesbian and gay print cultures, one marked by a rising tide of consumer-oriented prints such as the *Advocate*; an increasing emphasis on world cities such as New York, Los Angeles, and San Francisco as the final destinations of internal U.S. lesbian and gay migrations;[14] and an increasing bifurcation of queer print culture into distinct lesbian and gay literary public spheres.[15] I overview some aspects of U.S. lesbian-separatist print culture in the next section of this chapter. First I explore the inchoate literary fields that *RFD* and its counterpart, *Country Women*, worked through and against.

Recounting the publishing climate that led to *RFD*'s first issue in 1974, Stuart Scofield, a member of the initial *RFD* editorial collective alongside Donald Engstrom, recalled that:

> at the same time that *RFD* was being born, the third generation of gay magazines began to appear: the heavily-capitalized "slicks" such as *Blueboy* [begun in 1975], *HONCHO* [begun in 1978], and the new Goodstein version of the *Advocate*. Giving Gay Lib at best lip service, they have grown and prospered since 1974 by avoiding political controversy, selling sex and catering to the so-called affluent "gay lifestyle." Unlike all the preceding publications, these new ones are money-making ventures—from Gay Liberation to a Gay Lifestyle, from attempts to define and establish a separate gay culture and identity to the selling of advertisers' products in just five years.[16]

In his mention of "preceding publications" and other "generations," Scofield references major 1950s and 1960s homophile publications such as the Los Angeles–based *ONE: The Homosexual Magazine* and the San Francisco–based *Mattachine Review* and *The Ladder: A Lesbian Review*. Each tried to politicize a "national gay and lesbian community," although none fully achieved this goal; and the first two, the previous chapter noted, were linked to a burgeoning homonormativity.[17]

Scofield then stresses that "earlier prints" like *ONE* and *The Ladder* were supplanted by local-based newspapers and journals such as *"Gay Sunshine* (San Francisco), *Gay* (NYC), *Gay Alternative* (Philadelphia), the pre-Goodstein *Advocate* (Los Angeles), and *Gay Community News* and *Fag Rag* (Boston)."[18] As I mentioned earlier, many of these coastal-based prints were committed to intersectional Gay Liberation Front politics that engaged with concurrent critiques of racial, imperial, and capitalist norms, or what one GLF member and subsequent founder of *RFD* praised in the San Francisco *Free Press* as the interconnection of "women's liberation," "black [or third world] liberation," Chicano liberation, and "white radicals and ideologues" working against global capital and "Amerikan" imperialism.[19] Likewise, part of the multi-front political aims of these queer prints was to critique the homonormative white gay male ghettos that were developing in global cities such as Los Angeles and San Francisco. As one GLF manifesto noted, "ghetto institutions are still part of our lives. . . . The prices are notoriously high, and the practices are often racist, sexist, and anti-working class. This materially oppresses female, black, and poor homosexuals and also reinforces the false consciousness (racism, sexism, class-chauvinism) which divides us as a group and, in the end, oppresses us all."[20]

The *Advocate*, however, dismissed the ideals of these Gay Liberation prints and affirmed what Scofield sees as a de-politicized "Gay Lifestyle." By the early 1970s, journals such as the *Mattachine Review* were either financially destitute or out of print, and prints such as Boston's *Fag Rag* were nationally if not locally eclipsed by the Los Angeles–based *Advocate*.[21] Emerging at the historical upswing of gay "ghetto"-ization, the publication paradoxically began as an offshoot of U.S. homophile monthlies like *Mattachine* and a complement to urban-oriented gay liberation prints such as *Gay Community News* and *Gay Sunshine*. By the mid-1970s, it surpassed both of these constituencies and "made a killing" as a "gay lifestyles magazine" that promoted "trendy fashions."[22] Historians have often charted the *Advocate*'s devolution into an "affluent" lifestyle weekly as a refusal to maintain previous allegiances to post-Stonewall intersectional politics.[23] Yet even before Wall Street investment banker David Goodstein purchased the publication in 1974, overhauled it into a slick glossy, and added the subtitle *"Touching Your Lifestyle"* to its inside cover, the *Advocate*—despite its *"Newspaper of America's Homophile Community"* header—confirmed a white middle-class cosmopolitanism that marked norms of cultural and socioeconomic capital for many gay men and lesbians, metropolitan or not, and that *RFD* and *Country Women* would later try to counteract.

To do so the *Advocate* imagined gay readers as "heavily capitalized" consumers and interpellated them into a normalized racial and class identity via an aesthetic of chic and fashionability. Scanning the layout of the early 1970s *Advocate*, one is struck by the relentless promotion of this cosmo-urbanism. Alongside second-page coverage of local catastrophes such as the 1973 arson of L.A.'s Metropolitan Community Church (the folded front cover being reserved for a top-to-bottom beefcake photograph), or pedagogical milestones like the inauguration of the first U.S. gay and lesbian studies courses in public universities, you find advertisements for a men's boutique that names itself the Town Squire, and puns that theirs is "the town squire for fashion advocates." You also encounter an endless sea of glittery ads for Persian rugs in Melrose, or skimpy swimwear, or *Art World*, or swank nightclubs, or Eye Mystic jewelry, or David's Divine Dining, or Glendon's fine crystal, or Dresden kennels for your beagles, or advice for buying your perfect boat, or hat stores, or New Look loungewear, or glass tabletops. There are weekly columns with titles like "BODY Buddy," "Fashionation," "The Fine Art of Dining Out," and "Aunti Lou Cooks" (a fancy French stew, more often than not). To be more theoretical, there are ample opportunities for what Pierre Bourdieu, in his sociologies of French taste, terms the "body schema";[24] what José Esteban Muñoz, in his overview of mainstream New York City gay nightlife, terms "the dominant imprint," "a blueprint of gay male desire and desirability that is unmarked and thus universally white";[25] and what I see as the ongoing cultivation of U.S. metronormativity grounded in an *Advocate* Los Angeles "ghetto" yet extending beyond this print metropolis to encompass a globalizing United States. As one March 1970 "Exclusive to the Homophile Society from Coast to Coast" advertisement for "specially designed" Eye Mystic 10K white gold blue sapphire rings promises, "We predict that the Eye Mystic will become the symbol of the Homosexual Society the world over."[26]

If not yet "the world over" (that would come soon enough), then certainly the transcontinental United States as the stylish imprint that fast became the *Advocate: Touching Your Lifestyle* matched the stylish commodified bodies offered between its pages. Witness the following 1970 gray-balance graphic, a subscription advertisement that records a shift from Gay Liberation to "Gay Lifestyle" within an eight and a half by eleven format (fig. 2.3). First, what is most obvious about this ad is its erasure of women. Second, there are no queers of color. Third, it is obsessed with the duplication of leisure-oriented white gay male "ghetto" bodies. Six clustered scenes reproduce approximately thirty-eight persons, all white and none recognizable as female. Potential subscribers instead view exact replications of stylish men who dress the same, share similar chiseled features, and read the same copy of *Advocate* newsprint whose front page reads, "Groovy Guy Gala Goes Ga-Ga," and whose back page reads, "What do 70,000 gay people have in common? The *Advocate*, that's what!"

In this advertising subscription, a developing clone culture operates as an alliterated print culture, and unlike earlier publications such as *Mattachine* or *ONE* or later prints like *RFD* or *Country Women*, lesbians are nowhere in sight. Thus the taut body of a slim white male, hair coiffed, jean cuffs hemmed, calf muscles bulging, and cruising eyes demanding your attention, occupies a good third of the ad's frame. The epitome of

Figure 2.3. Artist unknown. *Advocate* subscription advertisement, February 1970. Courtesy of the History, Philosophy, and Newspaper Library at the University of Illinois at Urbana-Champaign.

"trendy fashion," this clean-cut reader presents himself as a sophisticated cosmopolite for interested subscribers, and if his tight-fitting T-shirt and deliberately placed locks don't alert you to this, a quick historical semiotics of his sidekick poodle—another eager *Advocate* reader—certainly will.

This poodle is, in fact, key to decoding how the *Advocate*'s visual culture stylizes U.S. gay metro-norms and records a shift in the male-centered U.S. metronormativity that first emerged in the early twentieth century. While most of the ad appears sleek, modern, and bulging—from the skyscrapers to the *Advocate* reader's crotch—the poodle appears somewhat

Figure 2.4. Artist unknown. Detail from *Advocate* subscription advertisement, February 1970. Courtesy of the History, Philosophy, and Newspaper Library at the University of Illinois at Urbana-Champaign.

removed from this beefiness. With a bow on its head, it appears dainty, diminutive, and effeminized (fig. 2.4). Yet the fact that the subscription aligns the marginalized poodle with the *Advocate* reader is noteworthy, since the dog functions as a representative carryover from pre-Stonewall metropolitan stylistics, one in which a certain version of white gay male identity was registered through "fancy frills, froufrou, bric-a-brac, and au courant kitsch"—another stamp of the high culture that we first encountered in chapter 1.[27] That the poodle is also an avid *Advocate* reader (look at that cotton-ball tail wagging like a metronome) is just as significant, given that this pre-Stonewall dog reads a post-Stonewall lifestyle magazine rather than politicized prints such as contemporary Gay Liberation Front journals like *Fag Rag*. A recent historical shift in lesbian and gay U.S. print cultures becomes aestheticized as a recent historical re-alignment, and one effeminized mode of gay metro-style is incorporated into—and made subservient to—a more masculinized other.

What the *Advocate* subscription accomplishes here and throughout its pages is, to my mind, significant. Its images translate the gendered, racial,

and class biases of one pre-Stonewall generation of middle-class white urban gay U.S. men—what a male GLF proponent criticized as a "bygone era
of their fantasy world of poodle dogs and Wedgwood tea cups and chandeliers and all the fancy clothes and home furnishings that any queen could
ever desire"—into a hyper-masculinist semiotics of "ghetto" visibility.[28]
This historical move from the 1940s and 1950s to the 1960s and 1970s
is then condensed into the spectacle of an apolitical *Advocate* reader and
his dog. Together these two come to epitomize a certain legend of homosexuality in the post-Stonewall U.S. city, a guidebook of sophistication too
often presumed to be intrinsic to Western gay men regardless of historical
specificities. Notes queer critic Joseph Litvak: "We have learned from gay,
lesbian, and queer theorists that gay people—especially gay men—have
traditionally functioned as objects of such distinguished epistemological
and rhetorical aggressions as urbanity and knowingness. But, in the Western *imaginaire*, gay people also function as subjects of sophistication."[29] To
extend Litvak, Western gay men, along with Western lesbians and queers
of color, within and without the city are "traditionally" subjected to sophistication as an aggressive communal standard not only from outside queer
group identity, but also from inside it. The 1970 *Advocate* ad bears this out
as it turns the "rhetorical aggressions" of an earlier U.S. cosmo-stylishness
into an aesthetic norm that thinks itself *America's Homophile Community*.

To confirm its representative claim, the *Advocate* nationalizes this metronormativity by condensing an imaginary Homosexual Society into four
U.S. cities. The *Advocate* ad is thus one of the first of its historical kind
to push toward another normalizing impulse that early *RFD* and *Country
Women* work against: bicoastality.[30] By "bicoastality," I refer to an idealizing
metropolitan scenario akin to "the flight to the city" that constructs intra-
national, national, and often transcontinental queer identities by imagining the evacuation of the rural into phantasmatic geographies such as New
York, Los Angeles, and San Francisco. In lieu of the international Berlin
and Paris negotiations that marked Demuth and Johnson, the *Advocate* ad
translates localized imaginaries of urban cosmopolitanism into a national
readership that it assumes applies universally to all queers, irrespective of
their geographic particulars. To do so, it subjects readers to a bicoastal *Homophile Community* bookended by geographic stereotypes of New York
City, San Francisco, and Los Angeles with one token midwestern city—
Chicago, a Second (or Fourth) City—tacked on for good measure. Left of
the anonymous reader and his canine are six scenes. One depicts *Advocate*
subscription space. Another depicts leisurely *Advocate* readers outside an

unnamed bookstore. The remaining scenes figure specific geographic lo-
cales. The Golden Gate Bridge, hillside Victorians, and a trolley overflow-
ing with clones signify "San Francisco" and its growing Castro district.
The Washington Square Arch, several raised water towers, and the Empire
State Building register "New York City" or, perhaps, "Greenwich Village."
"Los Angeles" figures as a day at the beach accompanied by seagulls. And
"Chicago" is condensed into a building from the Marina City complex as
well as the Pablo Picasso statue in front of the Richard J. Daley Center
(formally the Chicago Civic Center).

These "extra-regional" metropolitan centers are geographically distinct,
but the *Advocate* ad pools them together through a gray-scale graphic layout of cosmopolitan nationalism.[31] Near the center of the ad, the Empire
State Building's lightning rod penetrates the Golden Gate Bridge, and
one standing *Advocate* reader at the LA beach blurs into another standing *Advocate* reader in Washington Square Park. All told, we view leisurely
San Francisco readers joined with leisurely New York City readers joined
with leisurely Los Angeles readers joined with leisurely Chicago readers
through the *Advocate* subscription as a collective "America." In anticipa-
tion of later urban-oriented U.S. lifestyle slicks such as *Instinct, Curve,
Genre, Out, Details, Clik,* and *MetroSource,* these metropolitan localities
confirm a male-driven *Advocate* imaginary that constructs the urban as the
locus of a nationalizing and nationalized queer U.S. identity. The localities
thus situate "trendy" male bodies into a "ghetto"-ized gay nation, one that
RFD's "rustic" aesthetics will combat by over-writing.[32]

This being the case, we could say that the ad calls for subscriptions to
not only compulsory homonormativity through the body of the *Advocate*
reader to the right (his cloning is obvious enough), but also to compulsory
metronormativity through the bodies of the *Advocate* readers to the left.
Once it demands what "you" know about the *Advocate*—and what commonalities an all-male citizenry of "70,000 gay people" might share from
the West Coast to the East Coast with only Chicago in between—urbanism blends with urbanity blends with knowingness blends with worldliness
to circulate a national and, in due time, global commodification of metro-
based Gay Lifestyle that stands in for "homophile community." Stitched
together through the aesthetic *imaginaire* of a poodle and its owner, the local turns national turns bicoastal through an exclusionary grapho-politics
of open membership. This strategy of stylization will occur throughout the
Advocate in the 1970s, and will continue well into the twenty-first century
(see fig. 2.5 with its shag carpeting and red wineglass).

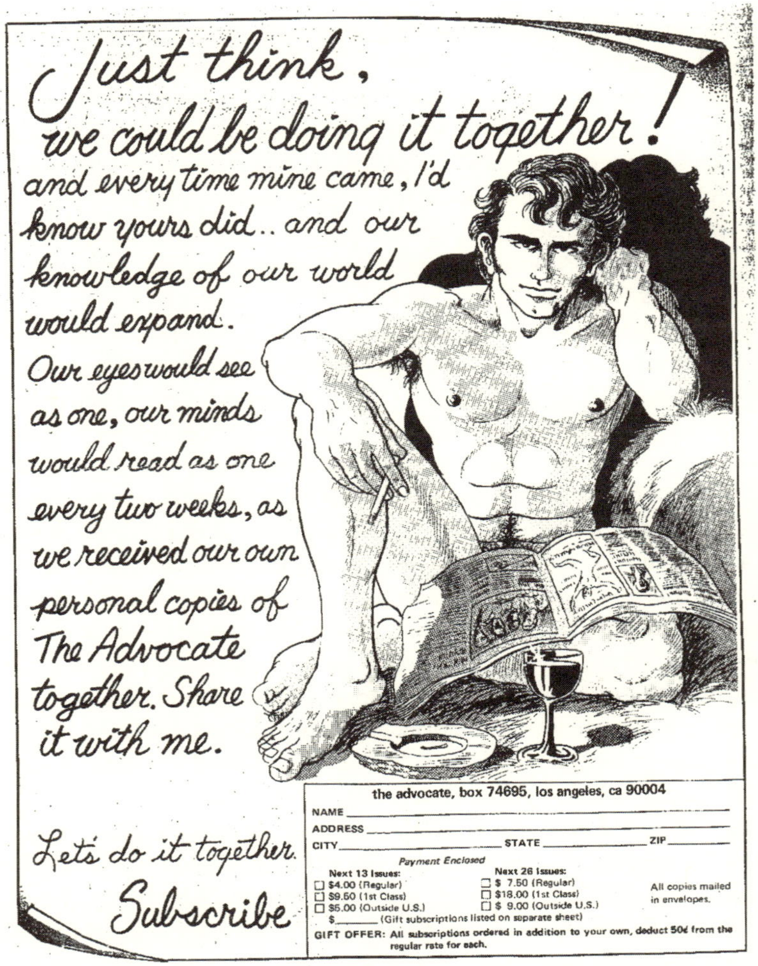

Figure 2.5. Artist unknown. *Advocate* subscription advertisement, January 31, 1973. Courtesy of the Kinsey Institute for Research in Sex, Gender, and Reproduction.

True to my last claim, dozens of weekly *Advocate* issues published at the historical peak of white gay male "ghetto"-ization in the United States (roughly 1970 to 1979) present multiple instances of compulsory metro-identification with its East Coast–West Coast "ghetto" lifestyle norms—so much so that explicit reference to bicoastal "habits and places of congregation" are often no longer needed in many of these ads and subscription notices, becoming instead common knowledge. The following September

1970 subscription advertisement, for instance, shows the reader nothing more than an abstracted typescript of solid black letter AAAs (fig. 2.6). These AAAs are then reproduced ad infinitum as the *Advocate* clones itself into a cohesive and recognizable group identity. In print speak, the advertisement attempts to "boilerplate" a national and cosmopolitan gay male identity for literary public spheres across a post-Stonewall U.S. nation. A term originating from the nineteenth-century press, etymologist Michael Quinion notes that "boilerplate" refers to how:

> in the latter part of the nineteenth century, news agencies and syndicates in the United States would regularly send out material to the many small-town papers across the country. To make it as simple to use as possible, the text was supplied ready to typeset on matrices (commonly abbreviated to *mats*), squeezed paper moulds created by stereotyping, from which type could be cast locally. All the printer had to do was slot it into the right place on the page, often first cutting the mould with scissors in a brutally crude form of editing to fit the text to the space.[33]

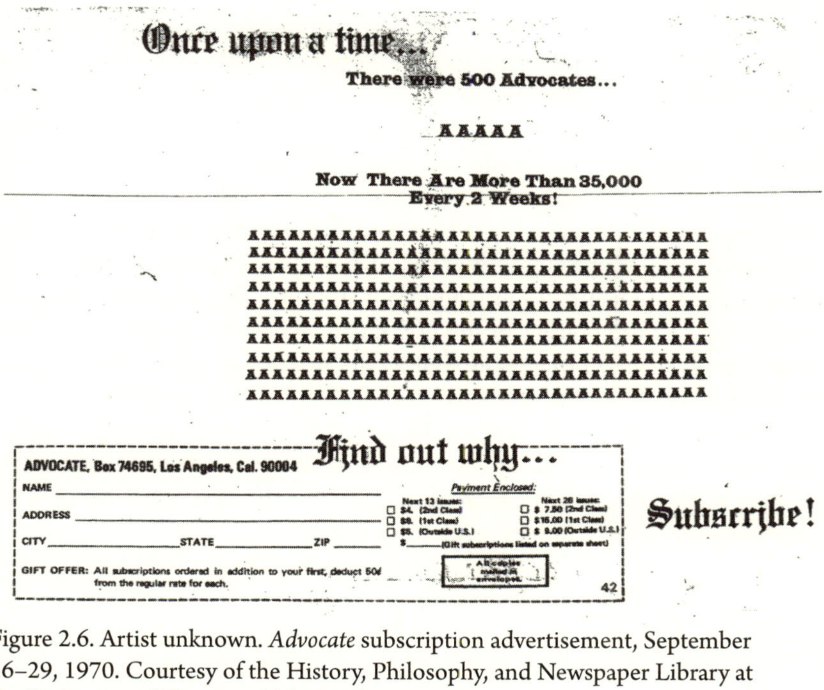

Figure 2.6. Artist unknown. *Advocate* subscription advertisement, September 16–29, 1970. Courtesy of the History, Philosophy, and Newspaper Library at the University of Illinois at Urbana-Champaign.

Hence, according to Quinion, to "boilerplate" a standardized image or text becomes synonymous with the capacity to "stereotype" said image or text when a press reproduced inexpensive prints for urban audiences as well as for small-town readerships.

With its potentially endless string of AAAs, it is clear that this *Advocate* subscription boilerplates a certain bicoastal stereotype of queer urbanity, one that naturalizes mid-1970s metro-norms even as it presents itself as a novel historical entity. Thus the ad hails readers when it begins with a standard narrative cliché—a fairytale "Once Upon a Time"—and ends with an ongoing reproduction of *Advocate* subscribers. Like the "70,000"-plus readers in the previous *Advocate* ad, uniform readers here no longer have particularized bodies as they take on the *Advocate*'s mass public story line. They are instead clones of the same letter, and they constitute a literalized A-list that would come to dominate stereotypes of "Western gay people" in the mid-to-late-1970s lesbian and gay U.S. *imaginaire*.

In so doing, the *Advocate* presents a predominantly if not exclusively bicoastal stylization as a telos of enormous historical potential that will encompass the U.S. nation-state: "Now There Are More Than 35,000." It erases its own print history as it again naturalizes a certain version of metro lifestyle. Presented through the implicit frame of males-only textual reproduction ("There Were. . . ," "Now There Are. . . "), an *Advocate* ad once more reprints an urbanized norm whose font sells compulsory metro-identification to the masses. This could also be called the historical entrenchment of U.S. metronormativity (and flyover country) as an imaginary of the "bicoastal" grafts onto the imaginary of the "urban." This is an ideological representation of the "urban" as a geographic and homogenized space of leisure, wealth, and consumption, and it works to replace the notion and the politics of the U.S. city as a place of racially and socioeconomically diverse queers as well as the urban as a performative space of political contestation, uprising, and revolution that marked numerous metropoles in the late 1960s and early 1970s.[34] This exemplary image is also one among the hundreds published in metropolitan gay lifestyle glossies in the decade after Stonewall, an ideal whose metronormative associations we'll also examine in chapter 5.

Country Women

If the *Advocate*'s "70,000 gay people" subscription notice and its "More Than 35,000" call to cosmopolitanism erased women in general and lesbians in particular, there were numerous rejoinders to this oversight from white lesbian organizations, and they were blistering. Notably, Del (Dorothy) Martin, a former editor of *The Ladder* and now an icon of the pro–gay marriage movement in the state of California, revoked her membership in the early-1970s homophile community and wrote a scathing denunciation of urban gay male lifestyle publications titled "If That's All There Is." In this manifesto, first published by the *Advocate* under the misogynistic title "Female Gay Blasts Men, Leaves Movement" in 1970 and later reprinted in the 1971 collection *Lesbians Speak Out* by the Oakland-based Women's Press Collective, Martin bids "goodbye to all the 'representative' homophile publications that look more like magazines for male nudist colonies" and "goodbye to the gay bars that discriminate against women."[35] In their place, she contends, "it is a revelation to find acceptance, equality, love, and friendship—everything we sought in the homophile community—not there, but in the women's movement."[36]

With this farewell to the *Advocate*, Martin joined a rising number of women's movement coalitions (such as the National Organization of Women) to launch critiques against misogyny, male-oriented capitalism, male-oriented aesthetics, and gay male-oriented "ghetto" print cultures.[37] In fact, Martin became a member of NOW's board after breaking with nationalized homophile publications like the *Advocate* and, soon after, emerged as a key spokeswoman for radical lesbian separatism, a "lodestar of [largely white] Lesbian America in the 1970s" that encouraged political and cultural breaks from straight-male-identified (and gay-male-identified) cultures to promote woman-centric lifestyles.[38]

While there were numerous critiques launched against the racial norms of this lesbian-separatism by queer of color/third world feminists such as the Boston-based Combahee River Collective, Cherríe Moraga, Rosario Moralas, and Gloria Anzaldúa, I want to explore some examples of visual and paratextual print culture of white lesbian separatism to see how it stylized its racial norms as it also critiqued homonormative ideals. Though the *Advocate* editorials were quick to dismiss such lesbian-separatist critique with snippy commentaries on how "Gays, Gals Don't Mix," manifestos such as "Leaving the Gay Men Behind" by New York City's Radicalesbians launched intersectional attacks on economic inequality, gender bias, and sophistication stylistics—in brief, U.S. homonormativity—"as a form of oppression" that they sensed many white urban gay male middle-class publics typified.[39] As self-identified lesbian separatist Karla Jay writes in her influential 1978 essay "No Man's Land":

> I talk of women/lesbian culture and not gay male culture. I believe that culture is one area in which lesbians have greatly diverged from gay men, perhaps because, as I have pointed out, gay men had some-what different roots, and, after all, they *are* men. . . . This is true, as I've said, in part because gay men, being men, with greater stake in the ruling culture, have relied heavily on already established institutions and forms for their "new" culture. Lesbians, twice removed and thor-oughly alienated, have started from scratch.[40]

As many white lesbian-separatists produced this "women/lesbian cul-ture and not gay male culture," some (not all) lesbian-separatists such as Jay launched negative critiques via a politicized anti-aesthetic, a calculated stylization of the "not gay male" that "greatly diverged" from the gay male metronormativity symbolized by the sleek *Advocate* subscription ads fea-tured above. In fact, there was a significant strain of metropolitan-based 1970s lesbian-separatism that promoted "anti-fashion" aesthetics for those "who were striking out against the *Hollywood-Madison Avenue-Playboy* norm and the objectification of women that it promoted," as well as for those, like Martin, who were striking out against dominant homophile publications felt to be more like "magazines for male nudist colonies."[41] Or, as historian Robert Streitmatter explains, "lesbians did not write so colorfully about their culture" as white gay "ghetto" males did, primarily, he assumes, because urbanized U.S. gay men were thought to place more "value on physical beauty."[42]

I have no desire to access the truth-value of this last claim. Nor am I invested in defining radical lesbians of any color, class, or decade solely as anti-sophisticates. Nor am I eager to reproduce stereotypes of 1970s lesbian separatism as "unsophisticated."[43] A quick glimpse into the histori-cal complexities of pre- or post-Stonewall U.S. lesbian cultures immedi-ately proves otherwise, and a materialist critique that attends to white gay men's access to capital and publishing centers would also inform our un-derstanding of these anti-aesthetic discourses. Yet when a prominent les-bian separatist such as Jay cautions that "we do not become the women of gay men," I am nevertheless intrigued by how a particular strain of white lesbian separatism, implicitly or explicitly, challenges the norms of *America's Homophile Community* with its own aesthetic critiques, and how such critiques functioned as both anti–Madison Avenue and anti-*Advocate*.[44]

Likewise, I am interested in how representations of the non-urban often informed these politics, and how these cultivations facilitated *RFD's* critically queer anti-urbanism. One anti-middle-class journal of white-based lesbian separatism—*Country Women*—did just this as it aestheticized Jay's "No Man's Land" into a unique form of cultural criticism that signified on the *Advocate's* bicoastal ideals. In her negative vision, Jay makes mention of "the proliferation of lesbian media after the Stonewall uprising."[45] Amid the numerous journals that she catalogs (*Lesbian Tide, Big Mama Rag, Lesbian Connection,* and *her-self,* among many others), she highlights *Country Women's* dedication to "rural living" and its critique of gay male "ruling culture."[46] Within this growing schism of radical lesbian separatism and gay male "ghetto"-ization—a schism that AIDS activism of the 1980s and 1990s would later help to somewhat bridge—*Country Women* introduced geographic separatism as a possible strategy against middle-class "male culture" as well as the gendered bias of bicoastal aesthetic norms.[47] It "develop[ed] a critical view of urbanity," argues Meeker, as it "struggl[ed] to build . . . outside of and/or independent of America's largest cities where gay ghettos were located."[48]

Originating from the rural community of Albion, California, *Country Women* situated itself 147 miles north of San Francisco's gay "ghetto" and four miles west of Highway 1 in Mendocino County. Printing the journal from 1973 to 1979 with an Anchor Press/Doubleday compilation released in 1976, *Country Women's* collective was composed of working-class and lower-middle-class women who sometimes addressed the sexual politics of opposite-sex communal living as they invoked a back-to-the-land ideology emphasizing local farming and eco-activism.[49] More often than not, members of the collective concerned themselves with publishing the principles of radical white lesbian separatism, "which whilst not exclusively anti-urban, could perhaps best be enacted away from man-made cities."[50] *Country Women* readers and writers thus imagined themselves as an anti-national antidote to male-oriented urban print cultures in general and gay-male-oriented urban print cultures like the *Advocate* in particular. Much of the journal was separatist or "woman-identified" in its back-to-the-land politics.[51]

While this rural lesbian-separatism was often dependent on strategic essentialism, utopian impulses critiqued by queer of color/third world feminists, and an unquestioned reliance on racial normativity, it is clear that the *Country Women* journal tried to advance "alternative (non-urban, non-industrial, non-consumerist) lifestyles" at levels of both content and form.[52] The journal was founded by white blue-collar and lower-middle-class feminists in low-wage occupations—one was a secretary, another a waitress—who were quick to respond to the socioeconomic difficulties of rural-based living and who were eager to instruct other separatist-minded feminists in the complexities of everyday land cultivation. "Unless you have inherited money," readers are informed, "buying land means saving money—either one or two people saving a lot of money (several thousand dollars anyway) or a group of people saving smaller amounts."[53] Though it recognized that rural-based communality was not an affordable option for the majority of feminists, *Country Women* cultivated a non-urban reading public whom it felt offered a "living alternative" to dominant middle-class lifestyles that would influence *RFD*. And if its working-class readers could not finance a move away from cities (or if they questioned the political value of a back-to-the-land movement), some could afford a *Country Women* subscription that enabled them to imagine themselves as members of a non-urbanist collective.

As we see from the front cover of a special issue dedicated to "Living Alternatives," *Country Women* figured itself as a counter to supposedly "man-made cities" and all the aesthetic, socioeconomic, and narrative trappings that these environments were ideologically thought to entail for women, lesbian or not (fig. 2.7). Fighting what the editors saw as the aesthetic and socioeconomic norms of metropolitan leisure classes, this front page sketches an alternative to these concepts with idealizations of its own. First, what is most obvious about this front cover is its separatist erasure of men. Second, it is obsessed with the duplication of female rural bodies as a de-individuated collective. Four clustered scenes reproduce approximately four persons, none recognizable as male. Moving clockwise, we see one female who harvests hay; another reads in front of a wood-burning stove; another picks apples; another female sows a field. Though each is singular, these women are braided together through an illustrated border of grape and pumpkin vines. None of these females has a recognizable face since they are blank, though each is racially unmarked as white. None is particularly marked by "trendy" fashion. None participates in a capitalist economy. And none, to my knowledge, is beholden to ideals of "physical beauty" that stereotypically marked 1970s gay male cultures and that some strains of

Figure 2.7. Carmen Goodyear, front page of *Country Women*, June 1973. Courtesy of the artist.

lesbian-separatist critique fought against. They are instead opposed to and geographically distanced from a cosmo-urbanism that marks dominant homosocial publications like *Playboy*, dominant homophile publications like the *Advocate*, and dominant images like the metronormative *Advocate* subscription ads. This utopian scene presents potential subscribers with an alternative collective, a rusticity that "naturally" separates from the "man-made" "institutions" of urban gay print cultures by cloning white female anticlones. The print styles of *Country Women*, original founders Sherry Thomas and Jeanne Tetrault noted, "were simple and funky and plain crude."[54]

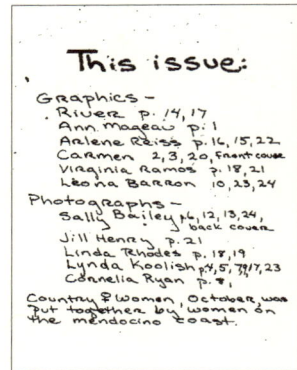

Figure 2.8. Contents page of *Country Women,*
October 1974. Courtesy of Carmen Goodyear and
Sherry Thomas for the *Country Women* Collective.

To rephrase these last claims, *Country Women's* simple, funky, and plain
crudity works against the bicoastal male sophistications of "Hollywood–
Madison Avenue" and the *Advocate* with a strategic aesthetic of womanly
ruralism. Though the journal did promote an emphasis on the white female
body, the front cover also shows two-dimensional pumpkins figuratively
overwriting the slick "Gay Lifestyle" designs that produced something like
the *Advocate's* AAAs. This is the textual reproduction of Jay's "woman/les-
bian culture" as "not gay male culture," and it occurs throughout *Country
Women's* paratextual "No Man's Land" during the mid to late 1970s. As
we see with the front page to "Living Alternatives," covers of the quarterly
were always hand drawn. Captions to articles were often scribbled or written in bubble letters. And its non-industrial, non-consumerist politics refused capitalist advertisements. Through such stripped-down imaginaries,
the journal naturalizes its critiques of cosmopolitanism through a woman-
identified eco-politics of coastal separatism.

Country Women also flouts these female-laden stylistics with invoca-
tions of graphic design that were more akin to a handwritten do-it-yourself (DIY) print (fig. 2.8). In lieu of the capitalized layouts found in the
Advocate or *Playboy, Country Women* consequently promotes a queer anti-
urbanism that collated a different imaginary of coastal living. As opposed
to the leisurely "fashionation" that saturated heterosexual mainstream and
middle-class gay "ghetto" U.S. print cultures, the journal offers a space
where metronormative stylistics—or a particular body type, if not a particular body's gender or racial identity—really don't enter into the picture. In keeping with these principles and its anti-capitalist critiques, the

quarterly published creative writings such as "A Fat Women's Journal" as well as how-to guides for collecting shellfish, sowing fields, raising sheep, chopping wood, bartering, welfare rights, building hotbeds, and raising calves. In the journal's first statement of purpose we are told: "Each issue will be regular columns plus articles about a central theme. Regular columns will include gardening, raising animals, how to use tools, building, food, country skills, alternatives (life styles), women's health, and reviews of women's literature."[55] In brief, *Country Women* ruralized a strain of anti-middle-class lesbian separatist critique into a distinctive version of radicalism. Though it may have enforced racial norms in its neglect of metropolitan or non-metropolitan third world/queer of color feminists, "the women on the Mendocino coast" nonetheless dismissed gay male metroprint norms.

Hence what this rural lesbian-separatist collective unleashed against the *Advocate*'s "male nudist colonies" was a stylistic anarchy opposite the graphic idealizations of gay male cosmo-urbanism. This anarchism—indebted to prevailing countercultural theories advanced in popular paperback anthologies such as David E. Apter and James Joll's 1972 *Anarchism Today*—was grounded in the collective body of rural radical separatism, in the individual body of the sexually non-normative though racially idealized country woman, and in the collective anti-bourgeois print culture that was *Country Women*. In lieu of the *Advocate*'s nationalizing imaginary, then, *Country Women* offered readers—who did not figure themselves as national consumers—a critical rusticity that encouraged a "lack of cultural sophistication and a preference for practical know-how."[56] By "critical rusticity," I follow anthropologist Gerald W. Creed and cultural critic Barbara Ching, who emphasize "the possibility of a culturally valuable rusticity" and note that "identities" stereotypically "based in the country can be considered *rustic* while those associated with the city are *urbane*, or, more vernacularly, *sophisticated*."[57] By this term, I refer not only to an actual geographic space removed from the metropolitan like Albion, California; I also refer to a dynamic mode of queer critique and a novel structure of feeling, a rhetorical and emotional engagement with U.S.-based metronormativity that critiques any representation of the rural as an "empty" space removed from racial, ethnic, and socioeconomic stress or inequality. Suspicious of metronormativity, such critical rusticity also functions as auto-critique. It would not only interrogate a leisurely print like the *Advocate*, but would also include the manifestos of collectives such as Combahee River and query the racial and ethnic presumptions of a ruralized journal like *Country Women*, as well as the faulty representations of Native non-urbanized populations and the racial primitivisms promoted by late-1990s radical faeries.

By accomplishing these tasks, such critical rusticity, notes one *Country Women* contributor in a self-reflexive "Retrospective" about an unnamed "rural commune in the northern Midwest," is an anarchic queer "state" that is adamantly not a commodifying urban gay nation-state.[58] "There is a lot of love and sensitivity in women—conditioned as we are to serve others, we must have developed some supersensitivity to other's needs," she tells her readers. "This allows us to live together in a state of what I'd call loving anarchy, and what a friend rephrased as 'responsible anarchy.' We need neither structure nor rules to live together. We find ourselves sharing work freely."[59] It is precisely this "responsible anarchy" that so intrigued *RFD* founder Stuart Scofield, who was disenchanted by the "cha cha palaces" and "trendy fashions" of the *Advocate*'s metronormativity, and who, "reading and loving *Country Women*" in the winter of 1973, was inspired to publish a complementary quarterly for "country men everywhere."[60]

Out of the Closets, Into the Woods

I shift our focus away from Albion's *Country Women* to *RFD*'s Grinnell, Iowa, where rural lesbian-separatist print culture helped set the stage for the quarterly's anti-national "faggot separatism." Published during the "Autumnal Equinox" in August 1974 with a print run of seven hundred copies, *RFD*, in its inaugural issue, made clear that the journal extended the rural stylistics of *Country Women*, that the working-class editors imagined themselves as non-normative alternatives to bicoastal U.S. gay lifestyle and as cross-identified anarcho-effeminists. The journal was published by the lesbian-run Iowa City Women's Press (begun as a collective in 1972) and strove to include lesbians of any color, separatist or not, in its pages. In the quarterly's first issue, the collective published an introduction titled "Rustic Fairy Dreams," which confessed that "no women have contributed material for this first issue, but we hope it is not so male-oriented/dominated to prevent Lesbians from using this magazine for communication with each other. And perhaps, with the Earth as our common ground, we can begin a much needed dialogue between gay men and women."[61]

RFD's critique of U.S.-based capitalism and its attention to racial representation complemented this emphasis on cross-gender alliance. Much like *Country Women, RFD* too advocated a critical rusticity as it offered readers an anti-cosmopolitanism that undid *Advocate* ideals of middle-class corporeality. Using language that mirrors *Country Women* "Retrospective" editorials, the first issue included a tongue-in-cheek advertisement for the Hop Brook Commune in rural Massachusetts:

> We share most of the values that you would expect from an alternative society—steering clear of consumerism, commercialism, T.V., A.M., affection, competition, intellectualized bullshit, egoism, role-playing, meritocracy and the rest of that bourgeois. We are multi-uni-racial. WE RECOGNIZE NOT LESS THAN ONE SEX AMONG HUMAN BEINGS.
>
> Rules. We have no rules. If we were to draw up a rule, it would be that no one here will objectify another (which is also to be objectified). We don't want this commune to be a crash pad—a homosexual motel—a place to bring the individual and collective falseness of "self"-hate and of "self"-love of either the major cultures or of the gay subcultures. But we have no fixed structures or systems for ourselves.[62]

With rhetoric that echoes *Country Women's* claim that one "needs neither structures nor rules to live together," *RFD* situates itself outside the "rules" of a dominant ("major") heteronormative culture and an increasingly homonormative gay male subculture. Refusing to become the print equivalent of a bourgeois "homosexual motel" or an armchair urban gay rural retreat, the journal distances itself from the consumerism, the commercialism, and "the rest of that bourgeois" thinking that epitomizes mid-1970s urban gay lifestyle publications. Though initially founded by white men, it refuses aesthetic norms characterized by what one contributor called "the 'gay-ghetto' with its agony under the tinsel, dealing out death to the spirit but surfaced with glamour."[63] It also tries to touch a different "you" than the one the *Advocate* hails, a "you" less settled in the "collective falseness" of homonormativity and less indebted to what was fast becoming a slick mainstream subculture.[64] "That was one of reasons we were moving to the country," one reader states when interviewed about his dissatisfaction, "not to move to a rural gay ghetto, but to get away from that, and to try to live in a more expanded community."[65] In this focus on "multi-uni-racial," gender, and capitalist oppression, *RFD* expands the political aims of metropolitan-based Gay Liberation Fronts as it also critiques U.S. "Gay Lifestyle." Recounting the journal's economic critiques of ghetto prints, one initial editor recalled that "we were poor and knew that many readers were poor, and 75¢ seemed the upper limit of what we personally could afford to spend for a magazine and it seemed what our collective political consciousness would allow."[66]

Thus the editors of *RFD*—a journal under perpetual financial strain— imagined themselves as an extension of anti-homonormative gay liberation magazines such as Boston's *Fag Rag*: "*RFD* was the last Gay Liberation magazine to begin, in many ways quite fittingly. Just as some of the counter culture people were choosing the quiet organic life, gay people began to see rural life as a real option to the urban ghettos."[67] But I also highlight that *RFD* did not participate in the rural-to-urban metronormativity that marked some of the most politically radical queer prints of the 1970s. Like its predecessor *Country Women*, *RFD* instead offered what one issue termed a "reader-participatory adventure" that details foraging for edible wild violets, paper cutting, goat dairy, water dowsing, basket making, and cooking with bark (not Auntie Lou's French stews).[68] It also functioned as a "de-isolating connection" for queer readers who could not afford a move to the U.S. city, or who could not participate in the imaginary metropolitan flight that I detailed earlier.[69] Such an anti-metronormative and anti-homonormative agenda builds off rural lesbian-separatism in particular, but it refuses isolation from lesbians in general, much as the statement of purpose for the first issue of *RFD* stressed. Explains one self-identified *RFD* queen: "I felt very alienated from the faggot scene and found myself constantly surrounded by Lesbians I was close to. I hardly used the city at all for things I had in the past."[70]

I emphasize that these queer anti-urbanisms do not fall under the rubric of a conventional and racist "white flight" from the city since they are literally "flights" from racially normative metropolitan gay culture. Like *Country Women*, *RFD* was more interested in defining itself outside these metro-norms, and its collective kiss-offs too occur within both the rhetoric of the journal and at the aesthetic level of the journal's printed pages (fig. 2.9). Compare the following 1974 subscription ad to the 1970 *Advocate* subscription previously shown. What is initially noteworthy is how the *RFD* composition lays itself out as a non-bourgeois "faggot separatist" offshoot of rural lesbian-separatist print culture and gay liberation by reprinting itself below a subscription to *Country Women*. What also stands out is how these two subscription notices are scrawled in chicken-scratch type rather than set in "Groovy Ga Ga" type. Unlike the *Advocate*'s imposing and crisp logo font in the bottom left hand of figure 2.3, here we have the aesthetic negation of such cosmo-stylization. In the *RFD* subscription,

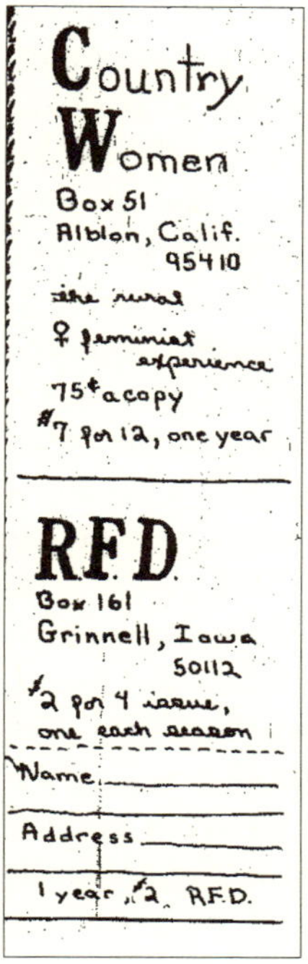

Figure 2.9. *RFD/Country Women* subscription advertisement, *RFD* issue 1 (Autumnal Equinox 1974): 11. Courtesy of Sr. Soami for the *RFD* Collective and the News and Microforms Library at Pennsylvania State University.

the typography slants. The initials are wobbly. Bold-typed abbreviations appear to tumble off their lines. There is no uniform typeface. The ad jerks from lowercase cursive to uppercase print. The spacing is skewed. That this double ad is not, in *RFD*-speak, "surfaced in glamour" cuts to the chase of the quarterly's anarchic attempt to undermine post-Stonewall U.S. metronormativity. It is not glossy. It is not beholden to universalizing standards of male physical beauty. It is not fashionable. It is instead critically rustic, a textual repetition of *Country Women's* hyper-feminized rusticity. Such an alternative literary public sphere functions as both a negative and a positive counter to the *Advocate's* mass-produced counter-public. It is "the rural feminist experience," the subscription suggests, which is also the radical rural experience of reading, writing, and participating in early *RFD*.

Indebted to *Country Women*, these stylistics also owe an unacknowledged debt to the working-class white rural cultures that refused to assimilate into the middle-class metronormativity of the mid-1970s (and that did not, could not, or would not participate in dominant "white flight" narratives of straights, lesbians, or gays). Given that some of the journal's editors were economically impoverished and resistant to self-identifications as urbanites, some also came to embrace not only the stigmatized slur of the "R.F.D. queen" but also the regional slur of the "hillbilly." As one *RFD* contributor from rural Massachusetts noted about Boston's metronormative climate in 1976: "Every time I go to the city, there's less and less there that I can relate to at all, even meeting people who are there. . . . I don't know what I'd relate to them about. It's really hard."[71] His boyfriend adds: "I just feel funny going into a bar in Boston and walking up to someone and saying, 'How's your bean plants, baby?' I don't have much to talk with people there, it seems. We've become such lovely hillbillies. When we go into town, we get dressed up, but it's not getting dressed up like people in Boston do. Like we put on a pretty flannel shirt."[72] Though the term "hillbilly" historically refers to the rural, impoverished white populations of Appalachia, this comment suggests that many *RFD* readers and writers in non-urbanized areas embraced (or, just as likely, re-appropriated) "hillbilly" working-class stylistics as a way to affirm the possibility of a culturally valuable—and culturally critical—rusticity that questioned normative post-Stonewall ideals.[73] A "pretty flannel shirt," that is to say, symbolically devalues the "trendy fashions of West Hollywood."

Though this "hillbilly" representation may be racially normative, *RFD* nevertheless deploys the stereotypical white working-class aesthetic to imagine something other than the masculinist "bar clone" style that saturates the *Advocate* and other nationalizing gay male slicks. The handwritten ad presents mirror-image calligraphy for both Albion's *Country Women* and Grinnell's *RFD*, which amounts to a duplication of the former's non-urban, non-consumerist aesthetics that extends into a unique form of queer anti-urbanism. Deploying the translocalities of Albion and Grinnell against the bicoastal U.S. metropolis, *RFD* resists incorporation—inscription—into the stylized aesthetics that is the *Advocate*'s nationalizing ghetto culture as it imagines itself to be what cultural historian Beth Bailey elsewhere terms "the antithesis of bicoastal sophistication."[74]

In so doing, disparaged "R.F.D. queens" transform into bumpkin-fied *RFD* faeries; Scofield, Engstrom, and other *RFD* editors conjure an alternative print culture for reading publics unimpressed by "the latest news of cha cha palaces in San Francisco, shows off-off Broadway, trendy fashions from West Hollywood, and Gloria Gaynor's latest album"; and *RFD* quarterly becomes an aesthetic reprint of *Country Women*, the quarterly, as well as a political reprint of "country women," the separatist rural

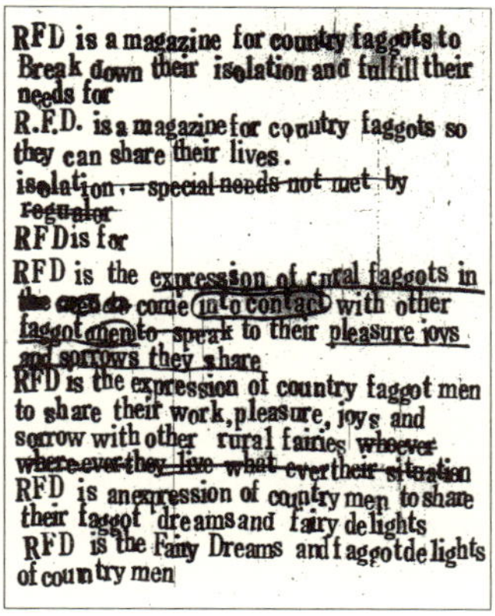

Figure 2.10. Richard Phillips, *RFD* statement of purpose, *RFD* issue 2 (Winter Solstice 1974): 1. Courtesy of Sr. Soami for the *RFD* Collective and the News and Microforms Library at Pennsylvania State University.

collective. As it seeks independence from the national norms of *America's Homophile Community*, what *RFD* imagines here is nothing less than a Gay Liberation Front—an aesthetic dislocation, so to speak—from the domineering stylistics of normative urban gay male print culture in the United States.

Much like the *Advocate's* insistent cosmopolitanism, this strategy of critical rusticity recurs throughout early *RFD* (fig. 2.10). Examine this somewhat ironic full-page statement of purpose, printed opposite the table of contents for a "Winter Solstice" 1974 issue that followed the first "Rustic Fairy Dream" edition of *RFD*. The graphic begins with a statement whose claim starts with certainty but fails to complete itself: "RFD is a magazine for country faggots to Break Down their isolation and fulfill their needs for." The statement following modifies this first claim: "RFD is a magazine for country faggots so they can share their lives." Supplementing this modification, the page then displaces these first two statements with a subsequent line. A lone word, "isolation," is inexplicably followed by a comma, then an equal sign, then the phrase "special needs not met by reguolor." After this, the line following the "isolation" statement begins with "RFD is for" but fails to finish itself. Beginning yet again, "RFD is" starts the following line, portions of which are underlined for no apparent reason, or encircled, or scrawled over with heavy black ink. Next, a line that ends with the claim "whoever whereeverthey live whatever their situation" is crossed out. The statement finally concludes with the claim that "RFD is the Fairy Dreams and faggotdelights of country men," yet it fails to properly punctuate this closing sentence with a period or an exclamation mark.

Overall, the page reprints "RFD is" seven times, each time undoing or overwriting previous versions of this copula.

In this exasperating yet playful statement of purpose—one harking back to the handwritten *Country Women* table of contents in figure 2.8— *RFD* again stands in chaotic opposition to the *Advocate's* crisp font; the *Advocate's* breezy assurance that it alone is the *Newspaper of America's Homophile Community*; and the magazine's confident self-presentation of bicoastal cosmo-urbanism in its various early 1970s subscription ads. In *RFD*, words such as "regular" are deliberately misspelled as "regua-lor." Capitalization is not standardized: "RFD is a magazine . . . to Break down." Punctuation appears for no particular rhyme or reason: "isolation , =. " Sentences fail to fulfill themselves: "RFD is for [for what?]." Like the previous image of the *RFD* subscription ad, margins in this statement of purpose are skewed. There is no set type. Lines bobble up and down the page. Spacing is sometimes unnecessarily doubled ("sorrow with other rural fairies"). Words are often smashed or cluttered or strung together rather than separated into neat linguistic components. The statement is a typographic nightmare. It is also textualized version of the stylistic anar-chy represented in *Country Women's* aesthetic layout. Through its attempt to "Break down" bicoastal norms, the quarterly becomes the antithesis of a clean-cut *Advocate* reader, as well as the antithesis of a clean-cut *Advocate* gray-scale graphic. It de-regulates an inchoate version of U.S. met-ronormativity and links us back to the "standardization and specialization in the gay world," and that "possibility of failing to identify with any of the particularities in the gay world as it was being parceled and its parcels were named" that Meeker diagnoses.[75]

Indeed, this mangled statement of purpose refuses to become a slick even though it slickly cultivates an aesthetic of anti-urbanity. It also refuses the aestheticization of bicoastal norms to offer interested readers what it elsewhere terms "country alternatives" to dominant 1970s U.S. gay print culture.[76] *RFD's* critical rusticity fails the easy boilerplate of the *Advocate* even as it boilerplates a slipshod version of itself. Its aesthetic is ceaselessly anti-normative at the level of the printed page since it strives to queer— to spoil, to disorder, to unsettle—an emergent stylization of "ghetto" met-ronormativity. Fighting the standardization of this U.S. urban type with skewed typographies, the "reader-participatory adventure" that is *RFD* refuses to become standardized at the precise moment that metro-norms do so on a national scale. Like its initial claims in "Rustic Fairy Dreams," and like its reliance on *Country Women's* non-urban aesthetics, *RFD* again presents its readers with a critical rusticity that overrides the "cha cha" ideals of the *Advocate* "ghetto."

To its credit, *RFD*'s statement of purpose acknowledges that this is a sloppy, often difficult task to undertake. Unlike the *Advocate*'s easy assertion in figure 2.5 that "our eyes would see as one, our minds would read as one every two weeks," *RFD* works against this insistent cloning by failing to properly clone itself, by leaving its program undecided. With this in mind, it is important to remember that the quarterly—unlike the *Advocate*'s venues on "Fashionation" and "Body Building"—was, like *Country Women*, a reader-printed, reader-written, and reader-produced magazine. This being the case, it makes sense that this *RFD* statement of purpose begins with a straightforward pronouncement on what its mission statement should be, but then undercuts itself by repeating what "RFD is," only to conclude, in the middle of the statement, with a blank space for what "RFD is for."

Such open-endedness, I want to believe, makes mid-1970s *RFD* an ongoing revision, a hands-on work-in-progress rather than a magazine that propels its readership into the *imaginaire* of the bicoastal U.S. city. Rather than an infinite set list of uniform AAAs, *RFD* presents "you" with a chance to revise a compulsory narrative of rural-to-urban migration or a compulsory clone narrative. At least in its earliest incarnations, the journal realized this negative vision of what one rural fairy, self-identified as Sunfrog, later termed "an anarcho-hillbilly intellectual bumpkinism"—a "bumpkinism," he did not hesitate to add, provoked by "the alienation of the city."[77]

RFD Country

As I noted in this chapter's introduction, *RFD*'s early efforts were soon complicated by a neo-primitivism that gradually overtook the journal once it was dominated by the radical faerie movement in the early 1980s. Its initial issue can still be historically recuperated. The first instances of *RFD*'s critical rusticity let us imagine alternative possibilities for belonging within the sexual boundaries of the geographic U.S. nation-state, as well as for extracting one's self from the metronormativity of *America's Homophile Society* at the moment of its historical inception in post-Stonewall queer print cultures. Though predominantly white men dissatisfied with the homo-norms of the bicoastal metropolis first deployed these strategies, the journal's tactics today reverberate for many queers regardless of where they might be geographically situated, metropolitan areas or not. As *RFD* moved its publication base from rural Iowa to the rural Northwest to rural North Carolina in the half decade following its first 1974 issue, we see how self-identified working-class "country men" aligned themselves with "country women" to replace an *Advocate*-inspired "gay nationality" with a small-town queer regionality, how *RFD* undercut queer urbanisms with a mimeographed insistence on the intra-national.[78]

As this hand-drawn 1974 image of transcontinental *RFD* readership suggests, the journal not only advanced *Country Women*'s aesthetics to counter the *Advocate*'s bicoastal cosmopolitanism (fig. 2.11); at times it also signified on the *Advocate*'s nationalist impulses to offer readers a regionalized queer country. Like much of the typescript and many of the images featured in early *RFD*, this drawing too is somewhat poorly drawn and crude. Missing the sleekness that defined concurrent metro-oriented gay lifestyle magazines, we instead have a map of the United States where many of the state lines appear scribbled or blurred. It looks to me as if the artist has traced the outline of the continental U.S. border from a standardized map and then loosely delineated the states. Printed over these boilerplate states are approximately 149 dots: some small, some large, some singular, some clustered, none uniform in size or shape. Each signifies a *RFD* reader or subscriber, with question marks around states of desire such as Mississippi, Kansas, Nevada, West Virginia, Arkansas, and Louisiana where readership cannot be verified.

Like the deliberate sloppiness of *RFD*'s statement of purpose, I think that this "cartographic carelessness" produces yet another image not set in bicoastal stereotype.[79] Though this map could be critiqued for its national emphasis (Mexico and other nation-states in North and South America are notably absent), we could imagine that the image takes the boilerplate of the United States to turn it into something other than a *Homophile Community*. This is one reading of the line below the nation-state, "RFD Country: each dot is a known reader." Again offering a resistance to the formulas of queer nationalization, the *RFD* image uses these handwritten dots to counteract the knowingness, the sophistication, and the cosmopolitanism of something like the *Advocate*'s clean-cut AAAs.

A brief remark on the success of this anti-urbane aesthetic: when compared to the *Advocate*'s "70,000" readers in 1970 alone, these dots may seem insignificant for political mass mobilization. They did not, we now know, halt the onslaught of cosmo-urbanisms that confirm U.S. gay cosmopolitanisms in the mid-1970s. But reading this "RFD Country"

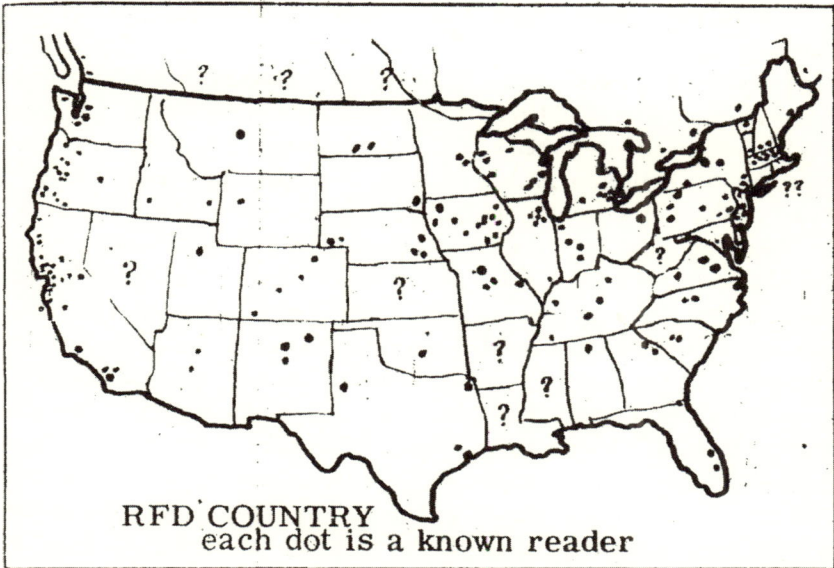

Figure 2.11. "RFD Country," *RFD* issue 2 (Winter Solstice 1974): 3.
Courtesy of Sr. Soami for the *RFD* Collective and the News and Microforms
Library at Pennsylvania State University.

morphology in a different light, we might follow Lisa Lowe and David
Lloyd's advice that "resistances are more and more articulated through
linkings of localities that take place across and below the level of the nation-state, and not by way of a politics that moves at the level of the national or modern institutions."[80] If such is the case, then these hand-drawn
dots might best be seen as tiny DIY pinpricks in the nationalizing U.S.
imaginary that was the *Advocate*'s visual and print culture; as micro-po-
litical interventions in the massive public literary sphere that the Los Angeles–based magazine came to exemplify; as a form of paper cut politics
nagging the urbanized queer nation that I theorized in my introduction.
Though *RFD* had only seven hundred or so subscribers by 1979, we might
read the cartography of this "RFD Country" as a small-scale intervention
that reintroduces the regional, the ruralized, and the nonmetropolitan to
blast open the bicoastal ideals of normalizing U.S. gay print culture. As the
Advocate obliterates supposedly insignificant U.S. places, "RFD Country"
insists on re-inscribing the local and regional geographies of feeling that
are rendered inconsequential in an ad such as figure 2.3.

It is for this reason, I think, that an anonymous caption below this sketch of "RFD Country" reads: "At this moment, RFD is being read in Vida, Nampa, Monona, Louisa; Philo, Solon, Malmo, Garnavillo; in River Rouge, Rogue River; Fall Creek, Clear Creek, and Cross Creek. . . . Camp Verde, Junction City, Liberty and Independence; Honeydew and Orange; Alpine, Bunceton, Caspar, Dearing and right where you're sittin.'"[81] Many of these small towns are located in the so-called U.S. hinterlands, and some are found in places far, far removed from *Advocate* subscription ads—Iowa, Missouri, Virginia, Arizona, North Carolina, Georgia, Wisconsin, and Ohio, among several others. When they are situated within the fantastic communal space of "RFD Country," however, the quarterly connects these disparate readers across disparate locales such as Talcotville, Connecticut; Somerville, Massachusetts; Lincoln, Nebraska; Carlinville, Illinois; Winooski, Vermont; Waukesha, Wisconsin; Grinnell, Iowa; Lexington, Oklahoma; Novi, Michigan; Concord, Alabama; Wolf Creek, Oregon; and, lest we forget, Albion, California. Reproducing localities erased in cosmo-urban print culture, *RFD* again offers a "country alternative" to an emergent East Coast–West Coast imaginary.

These localities are, I note in closing, the supposedly unsophisticated or rustic regions disavowed in the forging of 1970s U.S. gay male "ghetto" culture. They are not always the "hostile, hate-filled atmosphere of small-town America" that critics like Didier Eribon imagined queers "were running from."[82] They are instead spaces where a collective and critical anti-urbanism sometimes emerged, even as nationalized and urbanized prints were championing a bicoastal "flight to the city." As *RFD* readers reworked U.S. metronormativity with a consideration of queer spaces "right where you're sittin,'" the initial issues of the quarterly fought subscription with subscription, and the journal separated from the cosmopolitan typing and the ideological geographies of metronormativity with a typography that resisted urbane stylistics.

Through these counter-subcultural strategies, early *RFD* presented readers with the visual challenge of a regionalized literary public sphere that connected rural queers outside imaginary homonormative "ghettos" in New York City, San Francisco, and Los Angeles. It wrote over the *Advocate*'s national ideals with rural lesbian-separatist "living alternatives" inspired by *Country Women*. It circulated a negative imaginary of U.S. sexual citizenship and national belonging, one that might have been complicit in advancing a Westernized identity, but one that nevertheless thinks itself a regional alternative to the stylized homophilia found in urbane geographies. And while later *RFD* and early *Country Women* may have both instantiated racial norms, the journal's collectives nevertheless intended to be comprehensive and anti-assimilationist as they advocated a GLF-inspired critique for ruralized queers. With help from *Country Women*, *RFD* fantasized that it was a Rural Free Delivery from the stylistics of a U.S.-based metronormativity that, in countless regions, many refused to purchase, since the price of ghetto institutions was so notoriously high.

"At this moment" it still is. No matter where we all might be "sittin'," it has been our sheer dumb luck that the mainstream subculture confirming this identity continues to dominate, within and without U.S. borders. We traced the historical emergence of this cultural form in the last chapter, and we saw its ascendency in this one. Turning, respectively, to queer anti-urbanism in north-central Alabama, in eastern Michigan, in the Mississippi Delta, and in the mountains of central Pennsylvania, the following three chapters now follow the runoff of metronormativity's most unfortunate success.

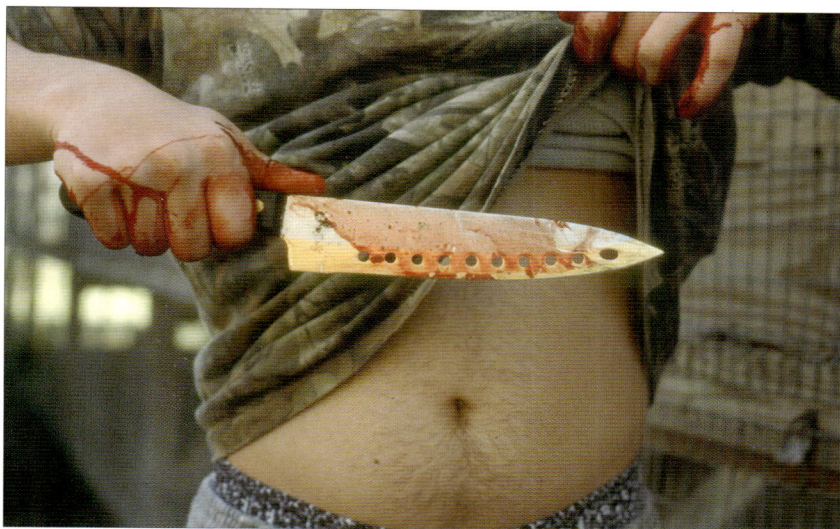

Figure 3.1. Michael Meads, *Pig Belly, 2003* (2003).

Figure 3.2. Michael Meads, *In My Studio: Still Life, 1992* (1992).

Figure 3.3. Michael Meads, *Allen: At the Old Confederate Bridge VI, 1996* (1996). Courtesy of the artist. All rights reserved.

Figure 3.4. Michael Meads, *Justin and Allen: In Allen's Bedroom, 1998* (1998).
Courtesy of the artist. All rights reserved.

Figure 3.5. Michael Meads, *Allen and Justin: On Marty's Bed, 1998* (1998).
Courtesy of the artist. All rights reserved.

Figure 3.6. (*opposite*) Michael Meads, *Justin and Allen: Naked Brand, 1998* (1998).
Courtesy of the artist. All rights reserved.

Figure 3.7. Baron Wilhelm von Gloeden, *Untitled* (ca. 1900).

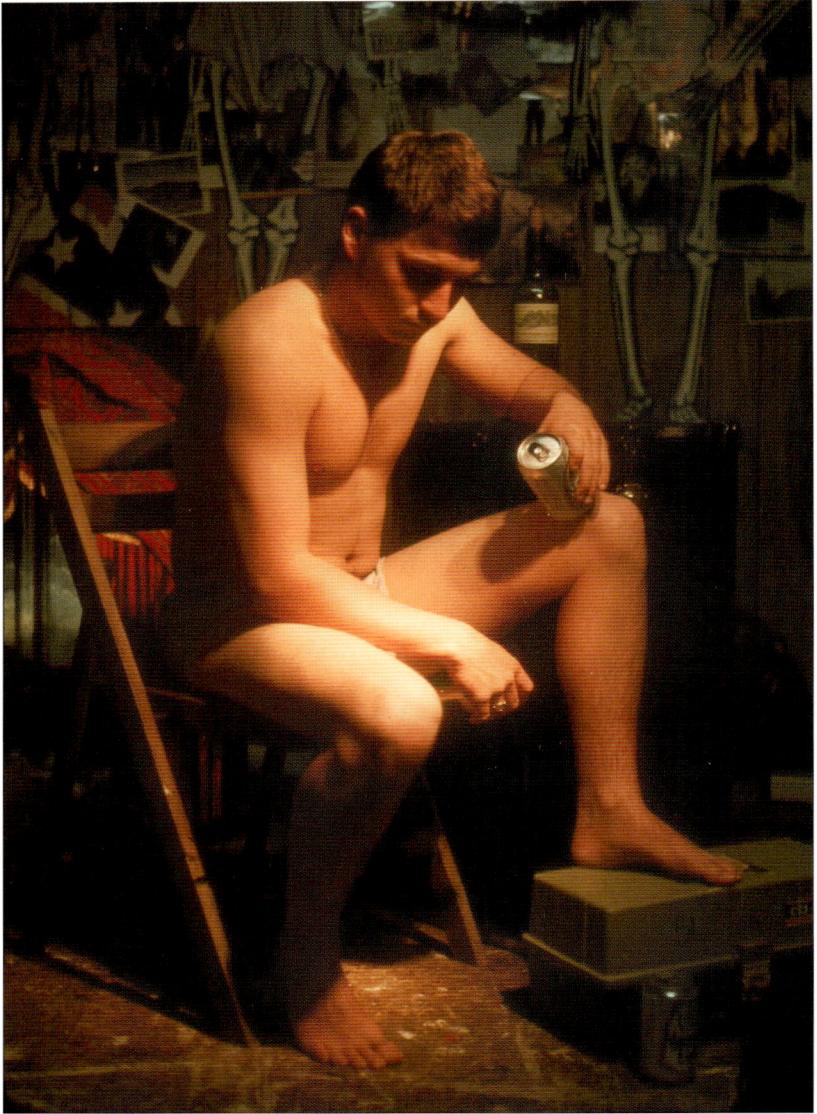

Figure 3.8. Michael Meads, *Aaron: As a Caravaggio VI, 1994* (1994).
Courtesy of the artist. All rights reserved.

Figure 3.9. Michelangelo Merisi, called Caravaggio, Italian (1571–1610), *Saint John the Baptist in the Wilderness* (ca. 1604–5). Oil on canvas, 68 x 52 in. (172.7 x 132.1 cm). Courtesy of the Nelson-Atkins Museum of Art, Kansas City, Missouri; purchase: Nelson Trust, 52-25; photograph by Jamison Miller.

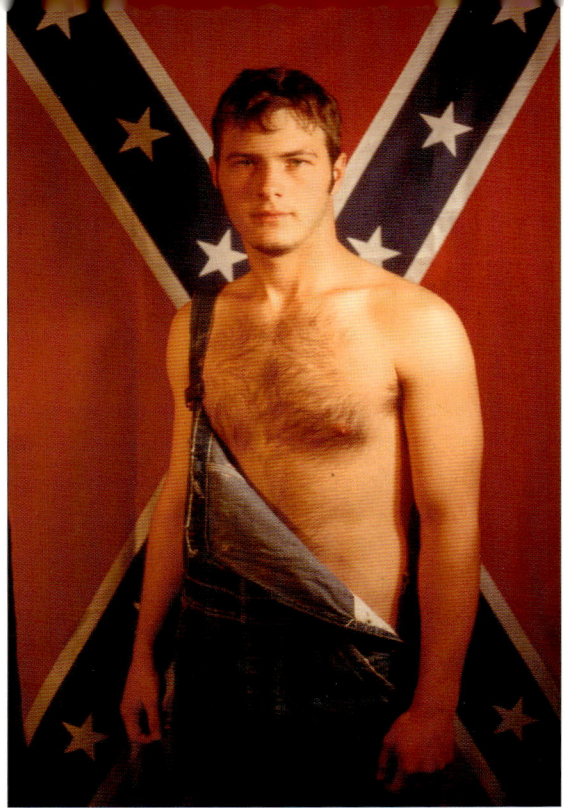

Figure 3.10. Michael Meads, *Jason the Bunny: In Overalls II, 1997* (1997). Courtesy of the artist. All rights reserved.

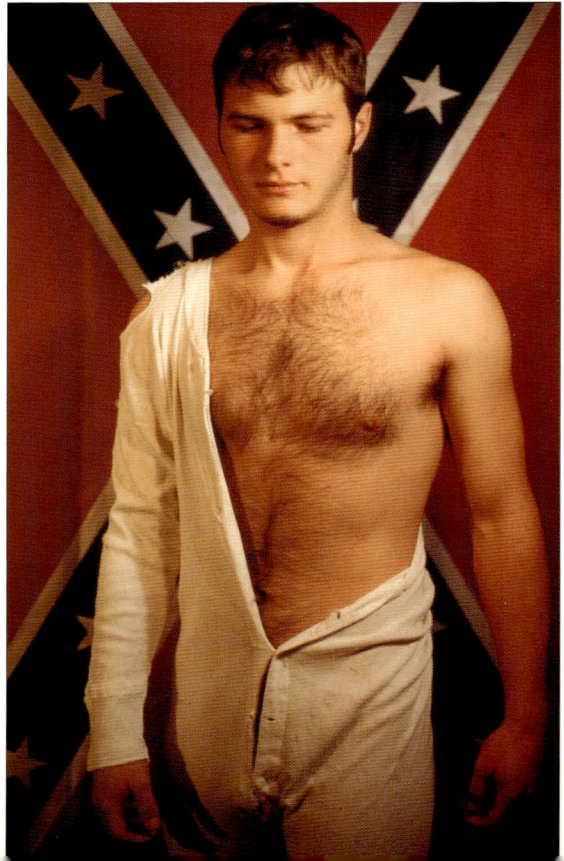

Figure 3.11. Michael Meads, *Jason the Bunny: In Longjohns IV, 1997* (1997). Courtesy of the artist. All rights reserved.

3

Southern Backwardness

Your Best Bubba

Online or off, nothing rattles metronormative gays more than the sight of "white trash" southerners cloaked in Confederate flags. In fall 2002 New York City's Nikolai Fine Art Gallery exhibited Michael Meads's *Eastaboga*, a series of photographs that had previously been shown in Paris; Rotterdam; Ghent; Albany; New Orleans; LaGrange, Georgia; and at a Sotheby's AIDS benefit. The title refers to a small, predominantly white, northeastern Alabama town of four thousand where Meads was born and raised, and the installation featured chrome color pictorials of Eastaboga residents taken from his extensive personal archive, one that spans from the early 1980s to the present. Most of the exhibition displayed documentary and studio portraits of the town's "redneck" boys that Meads took with a 35 mm camera—some former close friends, almost all in their late teens and early twenties.[1] *Eastaboga*'s subjects play cards, piss together, chug beers, hold cockfights, share pornography in the cramped quarters of a trailer home, embrace each other in the nude, brand each other with their initials, drape themselves in Confederate battle flags, mill about an art studio, and sit shirtless to eye the camera in poses that possibly index homoerotic desire, if not its actualization. Save for their first names, *Eastaboga*'s complex glorification and critique of these bodies revealed little else about these young white men, who are shown in intimate acts that suggest and surpass homosocial bonding.

Though the Alabama press has yet to comment on this archive, a variety of electronic and print media—coastal-based weeklies such as the *New Yorker, Gay City News*, and the *Village Voice*, to name a few—did make mention of *Eastaboga*, and Meads soon reproduced much of the installation in a digital gallery of his own making titled *Alabama Souvenirs*. I detail the mainstream media responses to these Web-based photographs later in this chapter. For now, I note that the spectacle of what Meads has described as Eastaboga's "weird area" generated a fair amount of online buzz in the DataLounge, a popular and somewhat standardizing lesbian and gay chat room devoted to arts, leisure, politics, and yammer run by a Manhattan-based software service company that calls itself, no joke, Mediapolis.[2] During one November 2003 forum, more than fifty men and several women—many metropolitan self-identified—discussed the pleasures and the frustrations that *Eastaboga* and *Alabama Souvenirs* induced, and many approached the images like a slumming venture below the Mason-Dixon line. Almost all of these responses fell under the subject heading "SO HOT!!!" to agree that the photographs were "disturbing," "amazing," and "vividly expressive."[3]

Unfamiliar with Meads's biography, a few were titillated by the sight of scantily clad southern ruralism and cast the photographs as urbanized performances of "trailer trash" twinkdom. "They look like imported Chelsea boys with a photographer in the background going 'come on give me your best bubba,'" states one respondent. Several others identified *Alabama Souvenirs*'s sexual preferences as similar to their own: "I think that Justin (my namesake) is totally hot, and . . . he is the top in the pair." Others, however, were far less certain, and were so affronted by the images that they denigrated the "redneck" males. "Ew," one respondent writes, "makes me glad I don't live in the redneck states. Those guys have nasty beer bellies by the time they hit 23. Sad."

Running alongside these aesthetic and corporeal judgments was social commentary obsessed with making sense of Meads's origins, his sexual relations to these images, his racial and class politics, and, most frequently, the sexual identity of his photographic subjects. Uncertain as to what these images might sexually denote, forum participants used a slew of metronormative interpretive strategies to crack open *Alabama Souvenirs*. Building on the assumption that the series was rural soft pornography, one puzzled viewer asks, "Did these fellas know they were doing gay jackoff pictures for their buddy?"[4] Another likens them to hustlers: "Jeez all these guys posing for dollars. SPAM [the luncheon meat] must be getting expensive." Yet another wonders, "Is he married to a woman so that these guys couldn't imagine he was queer despite the way he was asking them to pose? Or are these guys actually gay? Is this a glimpse into gay life in the rural south? The guys get heavier and heavier, turn into bears and radical fairy types and suck each other off during gay fishing or hunting trips? I mean, what gives here? I honestly want to know." One assumes with confidence that the photographs extend pre-Stonewall U.S. art practices as well as class imperialism: "These photographs are the direct descendants of beefcake photos of regular, poor men from the 1940s onward. Nobody would turn down being adored by somebody they respected, and the gay photographer/poor straight guy dynamic is a tried and true example of that." Another explains them through rural sociology: "Lots of country boys like to cornhole." And one lone male, disgruntled with all these explanations, relinquished his attempts at visual categorization—"What is this? Art? Kink? I don't get it"—only to exit the chat room.

While it remains unclear for many as to what sex-gender systems these ruralized males might adhere, it remains obvious that metronormative visual strategies fail to encapsulate *Eastaboga*. Time and time again, Data-Lounge members situate the soft-porn bodies within standard traditions of U.S. gay male art history, the economics of sex work, and the sexual binaries that inform closet logic, yet no one makes proper sense of these documents. Most commentators, in fact, seem dumbfounded in their interpretations. For the urbane queer, *Alabama Souvenirs* may gesture toward straight identifications ("poor straight guy dynamic"), but the kinky "way [Meads] was asking them to pose" then suggests otherwise: his focus on sustained same-sex intimacy belies a stable heterosexual reading. Similarly, when *Alabama Souvenirs* recalls gay male subcultural bodies such as the hustler, the bear, the radical faerie, or the urbanized Chelsea boy, Meads's images disappoint these "types" ("I mean, what gives here?"). Hence the images fail to realize successful heteronormative bonds as much as they also refuse to conform to the urbanity of late modern queer U.S. cultures. Meads's representations of rural Southern life, that is to say, cannot be classified under the terms and tales that currently give shape to homonormative gay U.S. cultures, since his visuals infuriate with their incoherence ("I don't get it") while they also deconstruct a stereotypical rural/urban binary.

In a parallel move, Meads nods to iconic pre-Stonewall art forms like a closeted "beefcake" photo, and, as I elaborate below, even earlier works; but he also disrupts his position within this tradition, given that *Alabama Souvenirs* cannot be encapsulated in visual codes stereotypically thought to signify (white) gay male desire. Trained in classical photography and well-versed in Western homoerotic art, Meads repeatedly invokes what art historian Thomas Waugh calls the "field of our [gay] erotic cultural heritage"—international "gay" icons such as Caravaggio, Walter Pater, Baron Wilhelm von Gloeden, and the "beefcake" pictorialist—only to queer it.[5] While the installation was shown in a hip Chelsea gallery that has since closed, the photographs reproduce an imaginary rural space opposed to collective visual ideologies that often ground what Waugh identifies as urban gay "imaginary homelands" like "New York City."[6] For metropolitan-based audiences both academic and popular, the contemporary photos of *Eastaboga* and *Alabama Souvenirs* may bring to mind forties muscle men, late-nineties Chelsea boys, and even earlier historical types, but these images also fail standard classifications of gay art and hegemonic U.S. gay male cultures. As the "redneck" photography courts a historical ur-narrative of erotic urbanized "heritage" only to undermine it, its anachronism challenges the imaginary of "homelands" such as New York City.

Such being the case, this chapter tackles Meads's queer (and queerly racialized) ambiguities to track how the photographs that make up *Eastaboga* and his Web site *Alabama Souvenirs* continue to vex the visual metro-norms that emerged in the decades after Stonewall. I am curious, that is to say, to understand how and why these icons are often boxed into an "erotic cultural heritage" that confirms a normative, urbanized gay male identity, and I'm eager to see how this "heritage" project often secures a collective sexual identity—a sense of belonging to an imagined historical community—for metro queers in the present that equates itself with the queer urbanities of the past. We saw some of this in chapters 1 and 2, and my readings here will build on these earlier findings as they face the post-Stonewall sprawl of metronormativity in new media such as the Internet.

I should thus state from the outset that my analyses will not concentrate exclusively on the sexual, racial, or socioeconomic circumstances captured in Meads's photography, though I do interrogate the sexual, racial, political, and socioeconomic confusions that this project produces for contemporary urbane spectatorship.[7] Without any doubt, there is much that could be said for the tiny town of Eastaboga, Alabama: its close proximity to cities such as Birmingham, Atlanta, and Anniston; its religious fundamentalism; its social conservatism; its economic dependence on the Anniston Army Depot; its high unemployment rate; its largely white racial demographic (hovering around 85 percent); its rampant racism and violent connection to the civil rights movement (in May 1961 a Freedom Riders' bus was firebombed and destroyed in Anniston); its largely blue-collar population; its homophobia; and, last but not least, its fraught relation to the urbanized sexual standardizations revealed in DataLounge commentary.[8]

It all adds up to a really ugly picture, and one far removed from the queer worldliness that marks the Chelsea gallery where Meads's photos were displayed. Yet while I acknowledge upfront the odious racial and gender politics that may structure the lives of some of Meads's photographic subjects, and while I agree with Judith Halberstam's recent suggestion that "some other epistemology than the closet [sometimes] governs sexual mores in small towns and wide-open rural areas," I present these photographic objects of *Eastaboga*—not necessarily of Eastaboga—as something more and something less than an authentic "glimpse into gay life" in the neo-Confederate rural U.S. South.[9] I want us to think alongside conventional readings of historical exclusion, inclusion, or excoriation for these visual bodies, since I believe Meads tries to do so as well.[10] As I show, his images negotiate, only to bewilder, both standard epistemologies of urbanized gay U.S. identity that anchor metropolitan/non-metropolitan contrasts as well as a collective heritage that anchors metronormative distinctions. The uneasiness that Meads's images provoke is best read as a reply to the taxonomic presumptions that inform many metronormative queer communities today, and the archive's illegibility can be seen as an affront to both the historicized narratives that structure U.S. queer urbanities in particular and a Westernized gay identity in general.

To support these claims, I showcase how these images produce gaps in sexual knowledge concerning U.S. rural bodies whose "backwardness" fascinates, repels, and aggravates spectators. To do so, I focus on the anachronistic stylistics that Meads's archive adopts to undermine the thrust of what one queer of color critic has termed "sexual assimilation."[11] First, I read *Alabama Souvenirs*'s late-1990s documentary photographs as an appropriative dialogue with earlier urbanizing gay icons such as the beefcake photo and von Gloeden's turn-of-the-century pictorials of southern Mediterranean males. I next turn to Meads's studio portraits to explore how his critique of this "erotic cultural heritage" distorts a visual history of white gay male art that, consciously or not, continues to affirm metronormative gay male cultures in the United States. Here I examine how Meads's studio photos use what the photographer calls "closet anarchy"—an anarchy that harkens back to the hillbilly stylistics of *RFD*—to undercut urbane cross-identifications with a major "gay" icon like Caravaggio. Finally, I close by turning to Meads's controversial images of queer "rednecks" and rebel flags, politically disturbing works that continue to propel viewers beyond the epistemologies of their citified gaze.

Alabama Souvenirs

At first glance, we might be tempted to situate Meads's photos within a familiar strain of contemporary American art such as New York–based photographer Larry Clark's *Tulsa* (1971), *Teenage Lust* (1983), and *Larry Clark: 1992* (1992); Nan Goldin's extensive record of East Villagers in *I'll Be Your Mirror* (1996); and Janine Gordon's photographic records of white male moshers such as *fuckshittup* (2001).[12] As critics try to make sense of his art, they frequently place Meads alongside these artists in mainstream reviews as well as in popular adolescent boy culture Web sites like that of the now-defunct *Pavement* (http://www.pavementmagazine.com/). *Eastaboga* photographs, one *Village Voice* reviewer argues, "look like a combination of Larry Clark's *Tulsa* updates and some white-trash porn shoot."[13]

In a personal interview, however, Meads is adamant that his connection to these artists and their realistic docu-projects is negligible. "On Larry and Nan I just wanted to add a few comments," I was told when I asked about their possible influence. "The more of his work that I see the less I think that there is any relation between what he does and what I do. . . . Remember that I was doing this long before I had ever heard of Larry Clark or Nan Goldin (of course they have been making photos much longer than I). It has only been in the last few years that I have really started paying attention to the work of other contemporary photographers."[14] By "this," Meads refers to his own extensive records of a male population far removed from a U.S. mainstream and one with which he, currently living in New Mexico, now has infrequent contact. And unlike an artist such as Goldin, who captures the quotidian lives of bohemian queers prior to the AIDS epicrisis, Meads implicitly suggests here that his work departs from a photographic tradition of making (urbanized) subcultural bodies visible to larger audiences. Given his self-professed distance from his contemporaries, it is clear that the artist is not nearly as invested in exposing queer underworlds as he is in how his images and their circulation undo recent projects of U.S. metronormativity.

To better acquaint ourselves with Meads's project, I walk us through several opening scenes in his collection, *Alabama Souvenirs,* which were exhibited on his Web site. The photographer's swipe at canonical forms of Western gay male painting and pictorial photography begins the moment the site's first window appears on the computer screen. Imposed over a pitch-black background is a stark photograph of a white working-class male wearing a long-sleeve camouflage shirt (fig. 3.1). No date is given, but the snapshot appears to be fairly recent. The image, which Meads titled *Pig Belly, 2003*, crops the unnamed male's body, and the viewer sees only a pale torso as the male partially lifts his shirt. In his right hand, parallel to his exposed stomach, he holds a hunting knife dripping with blood. The words "Alabama Souvenirs: Photographs from the Deep South" appear in white lettering underneath the photo, and it is hard not to imagine—as did many DataLounge members—that Meads invokes the stereotypical image of a menacing white "redneck," or that he invites you to stare at a homoerotic spectacle of southern "backwardness," or that he asks you to witness photographic "souvenirs" from an exoticized land since "narratives of rural regions like the 'Deep South' . . . have long explored the badlands of the rural; its sick, sordid, malevolent, *nasty* underbelly."[15]

Yet if you stare at the website's photograph for some length of time, something unexpected happens: the image of this unnamed male body fades through graphic animation into another image, which then appears to figuratively fade into another time that Meads has titled *In My Studio: Still Life, 1992* (fig. 3.2). Unlike the immediacy of *Alabama Souvenirs*'s first image and despite its dated title, this second image evokes a historical moment found in neither the late twentieth-century rural "Deep South" or its stereotypical counterpart, the queer cosmopolitanism associated with big city habitus. It instead appears to be deliberately antiquated. Three bronzed cherubs are shown hanging below a wooden shelf. Surrounding them are aged photographs of hunters as well as newspaper clippings. Above them is a partially illegible sign that ends with the words "LIFE," and next to this sign stand three miniaturized Confederate flags. In contrast to the bright colors that mark the first image, this shadowy second photograph is cast in sepia overtones, a color suggestive of a faded photograph. This retrogressive atmosphere is made even more explicit when one reads the quotation superimposed over this old-fashioned scene: "He was always a seeker after something in this world that is there in no satisfying measure, or not at all."

A line below this otherworldly reference informs viewers that the quotation is taken from Walter Pater's "A Prince of Court Painters (on the life of Watteau), from his 1887 book Imaginary Portraits." While no further mention is made of the proto-gay Victorian art critic, I believe that this citation is a key to understanding how Meads agitates visual traditions of metronormative gay male spectatorship.[16] The photographer informed me in a series of e-mail exchanges that he originally found the quote in a retrospective that New York City's Museum of Modern Art (MoMA) held for twentieth-century American painter Charles Demuth, whose queer anti-urbanist paintings I discussed in chapter 1. The exhibition was an homage to Demuth's now-classic watercolors of floral arrangements, working-class sailors, and the painter's 1918 illustration of Pater's "A Prince of Court Painters." By invoking these icons, Meads situates his work in relation to earlier queer art, yet he also seems less invested in extending a visual legacy that includes Pater and Demuth than in pestering this "erotic cultural heritage" altogether.[17] Unlike the MoMA's retrospective, *Alabama Souvenirs* is less homage to recognizable Western gay male art forms or an extension of their legacy than a retrospective sabotage of some major white gay male art icons. Rather than aligning himself with historical figures such as Demuth or Pater or even Jean-Antoine Watteau, Meads bypasses each to usurp the place of Pater's imaginary portraitist.

These dizzying inter-textual references could be tossed aside as trivia for art historians, but what fascinates me are the historical and identificatory confusions that Meads's ruralized media produces here and in later photographs. Thrusting Pater's imaginary eighteenth-century French painter into the Internet age of a sexually "backward" "Deep South," Meads confounds any linear trajectory that might suggest his deference to or his extension of traditional archives of Western gay male art that naturalize queer urbanism in a museum or on the Web. This process literally takes place before the viewer's eyes. Once the photograph of the unnamed "redneck" blurs into the photograph of the hanging cherubs, the latter then blurs back into the former ad infinitum. As it folds Pater's anachronistic recollection of Watteau onto Meads's anachronistic use of Pater into an appropriation of the MoMA's Demuth, *Alabama Souvenirs*'s introductory moments function as a leitmotif for the Web site's subsequent documentary and studio photographs: it rehearses the tense interconnections between the appropriations of Western gay art history and the "redneck" images that stump online spectators.

Such tensions become more apparent when we turn to a cluster of images that produced befuddlement on DataLounge—a series of homoerotic photos presented under the title *Allen*. After clicking on either the image of the "redneck" with knife in hand or the three cherubs, you are directed to Meads's "Photography Index." From this index, you navigate a list of titles such as *Toddy, Jason, Brent & Clint, Out & About,* and *In the Studio.* Hit another of these titles—*Allen*—and you are transported to a series of over eighty documentary-style photographs that show a young white blue-collar male in a variety of homoerotic poses (fig. 3.3). Many of these photos are taken, image titles tell us, in natural surroundings (e.g., *At the Old Confederate Bridge*), and each shows "Allen" in a homoerotic pose. In the majority of the images, he stares shirtless at the camera or looks beyond the photographic frame. In all, he wears tight-fitting cutoff blue jeans, or what are sometimes referred to as Daisy Dukes in fashion-speak. These photographs seem documentary, but given the camera's homoerotic gaze, an image such as *Allen: At the Old Confederate Bridge VI, 1996* appears to be less of a realistic portrait of white southern male ruralism found in, say, Walker Evans's portraits in *Let Us Now Praise Famous Men*. It instead looks like more of a recall or parody of a pre-Stonewall beefcake photo transported into 1996.[18]

Subsequent photographs that Meads posts in the "Allen" series further demonstrate how his anachronistic images trace the "fantasy echo" of an "erotic cultural heritage" not to pronounce an allegiance to this tradition, but rather to trouble it.[19] The forties physique pictorial poses that "Allen" strikes in the initial frames of *Alabama Souvenirs* are complemented by those in a third window, where "Allen" is featured with his friend "Justin" in images that supersede U.S. homosocial norms (fig. 3.4, 3.5, 3.6). In most of these photographs (DataLounge participants described them as "creepy," "frightening," and "disturbingly hot"), the two young white men are captured naked in scenes of affection, scenes that suggest same-sex intimacy and possibly signal a "jack-off picture for their buddy." In the first photograph that viewers see of the couple, "Allen" and "Justin" stand shirtless in the former's bedroom in front of a Confederate flag with a swastika pinned to it—an obvious signifier of what Meads stated was Allen's now-discarded white supremacist affiliations. When I asked Meads in email about the level of white supremacist participation among some of his photographic subjects, he replied: "In regards to the swastikas, only Allen had that on display. Why anyone would want to keep that horrible energy around is beyond me. When I first met him he was heavily into the 'white supremacist' thing. . . . Strange boy. I never asked him about what he did while involved with all that and honestly I never want to know."[20]

Next, Allen and Justin are shown viewing a straight porn magazine, an image that is then followed by the two lying on Allen's bed. Here viewers witness the males sitting nude together in what the photograph tells us is *Allen and Justin: On Marty's Bed, 1998*. The scene is overcrowded with fabrics such as bedsheets, pillow covers, jackets, and discarded clothes; and one faces the camera as the other sits at the edge of a mattress with his head bowed. The genitalia of both young men are visible, and the ruffled bed covers appear to suggest that sexual activity has happened—or will happen—sometime in the recent past or near future. Subsequent photographs show Allen with a hand draped over Justin; or Justin revealing the branding mark that Allen apparently just made; or Justin laying his head against Allen with his eyes closed.

While these intimate images might suggest Clark's "updated *Tulsa*," they nevertheless confound metronormative visual strategies since the photographic subjects fail to satisfy neat urban taxonomies like "imported Chelsea boys." And given the supremacist overtones of this series—overtones that Meads draws attention to by his framing—it's certainly not a "glimpse" into stereotypical "gay life in the rural South" in 1998 as Allen's affiliation with hate groups ties him to militant homophobia.[21] The images of "Allen" and "Justin," that is to say, complicate not only an assumed "gay photographer/poor straight guy dynamic" (Meads informed me that "no real cash ever traded hands," thereby debunking "the hustler" interpretation); the photos also disturb idealizations of the rural as a gay pastoral as well as the inverse of this sentiment—the rural as a space where queerness has no place.[22] To put this differently: just as *Alabama Souvenirs* queers urbanized types and a traditional gay pastoral, so too does it pastoralize white queer bodies to critique metronormative taxonomies. Meads states this strategy when one interviewer asks him to pinpoint the nature of the boys' sexual identities: "I could never get them to nail it down. I think that's what made it sort of magical. They never really tried to analyse it or qualify it or measure it. I think that's a problem that the whole gay culture is obsessed with—labeling."[23]

Meads's own idealizations aside, though it might be tempting to situate the photographs within cultural studies of queer southern male sexuality, we could just as well argue otherwise. In *Men Like That: A Southern Queer History*, historian John Howard contends that certain forms of queer male desire (like "cornholing") were condoned in predominantly rural localities such as the Mississippi Delta until at least the civil rights era, and he also suggests that these same-sex male activities are sometimes overlooked in the present-day Deep South.[24] While we might assume that the activities implied in *Alabama Souvenirs* would substantiate Howard's findings, it is important to remember that the historian sets an age limit on the social tolerance of such same-sexual interactions. Referring to southern white male adolescence, Howard claims that "homosex between boys was tolerated, expected even. To continue in homosexual activity as a teen or young adult, however, was more problematic."[25] Further: "as [southern white] males grew up, they approached the age at which same-sex play was frowned upon. Though imprecise, at some point in the teen years, sex between boys proved problematic, as the interests of many young men remained with or turned to young women."[26] Yet because "Allen" and "Justin" are presumably in their late teens or early twenties, both fall outside this period of sexual experimentation that Howard outlines. The images thus move beyond standard time frames of southern white male same-sexuality and into an anachronistic queer time, the same time that the viewer encounters in the introductory moments of *Alabama Souvenirs* and the "forties beefcake" photo of *Allen: At the Old Confederate Bridge VI, 1996*.

This is also to say that *Alabama Souvenirs* presents a rural queer space that is less an accurate historical reflection or a sociological document and more a social fantasy. It does not, as one reviewer assumed, "depict a rare portrait of Southern culture that uppity urbanites rarely glimpse."[27] Nor does it offer insight into "men in their natural state."[28] As it turns Eastaboga-based men into *Eastaboga* photographs, it goes beyond DataLounge claims such as that "lots of country boys like to cornhole." In lieu of the rural mimesis that first opens *Alabama Souvenirs*, it fades into "something that is there in no satisfying measure, or not at all." This indefinable "something," I believe, is a phantasmatic visual space that has little interest in any linear narrative of perverse modernity or U.S. gay male identity, metronormative or otherwise. To refine this last claim, when Meads rattles the securities of an urban/rural binary, the historical incongruities rampant in *Alabama Souvenirs* may be less the deliberate doing of a blue-collar white supremacist and his curious pal and more of a deliberate intervention by the photographer who cultivates these "creepy," racially charged scenes.

Eastaboga/Taormina

If such is the case, I draw our attention to how these images—apparently documentary in scope—reflect something other than sexy-scary snapshots of everyday rural gay supremacy for "uppity urbanites" in 1996, 1998, or today. When I first encountered the photos while thumbing through an *Attitude* magazine at a Barnes & Noble Booksellers in Champaign, Illinois, it struck me that Meads's photographs of "Allen" and "Justin" did not appear to be true to life; they instead seemed staged.[29] Upon further investigation, they not only seemed to anachronistically import "forties beefcake" poses into the early twenty-first century; they are each so highly composed as to reintroduce classical male nudes common to imperial white gay male pictorial photography at the turn of the twentieth century. Given Meads's prior training in classicism, this should have come as no surprise. He once told a reporter: "My eye has been trained. I [studied] at SUNY Albany and it's about as classical a training program as you can get in art. The classical standards for composition and colour and lighting are just drilled into me. I can't not think about those things when I photograph."[30]

Taking Meads's words here at face value (I'll inquire about a few others later on), and taking seriously his allusions to earlier icons like Pater and Demuth in the opening windows of *Alabama Souvenirs*, we could visually read these images as commentary on another queer scene of the rural South often considered "the first coherent licit artistic corpus of modern-day gay culture"—Baron Wilhelm von Gloeden's *Taormina*.[31] Meads cites "Baron von Gloeden, a German photographer of gorgeous Italian boys," as one of the icons in whom he was most interested, and many of the images in *Alabama Souvenirs/Eastaboga* appear similar to those featured in what art historians now term von Gloeden's *Taormina* series.[32] Hence just as Meads recalls and muddles the supposed heritage of modern white "gay" male art icons such as Pater, Demuth, and the physique pictorial, so too do the photographs of "Allen" and "Justin" gesture toward the initial moments of modern white gay male photography through their mimicry of von Gloeden. They inaccurately replicate the frames in which von Gloeden photographed his subjects to render this erotic historical heritage incoherent.[33]

Return to *Allen and Justin: On Marty's Bed, 1998*. As suggested earlier, the photograph appears to have the aura of documentary realism found in other contemporary boy culture photographers such as Larry Clark. But I also noted that what is striking about the photograph is its classical composition. What some DataLounge viewers considered an uploaded snapshot of blue-collar queer white southern culture—"they look like authentic bubbas to me"—instead appears to be a formalized appropriation of earlier white gay male art. As a matter of fact, the image dialogues with another classical composition, a pictorial photograph that von Gloeden took of two young Italian males in the Sicilian town of Taormina (fig. 3.7). Much like Meads's careful composition of "Allen" and "Justin," von Gloeden also has two men sit nude in an untitled photograph. The scene is overcrowded with fabric, and one male's face can be seen as the other lays on a mattress not with his head in his lap, but with his back to the viewer. The genitalia of one young man is visible, and the ruffled bed covers appear to suggest that sexual activity has happened—or will happen—sometime in the near future. Taken nine decades before *Eastaboga*, the *Taormina* image works as a precursor and an inversion of Meads's later photograph, and the artist repeats this dialogue throughout *Alabama Souvenirs*.[34]

I return to Meads's visual strategies of anachronistic appropriation momentarily. For the next few paragraphs, I detour into the history surrounding von Gloeden's untitled image because it offers another window into how *Eastaboga* debunks an American and a western/central European gay male visual "heritage," as well as the interpretive strategies that support these ideologies. A Prussian aristocrat who self-identified as a homosexual, von Gloeden moved to Taormina, Italy, in the early 1880s. Save for a brief forced relocation under Italy's fascist regime, he remained there until his death in 1931. Like other continental European imperialists, he found a non-urbanized southern culture accommodating to his same-sex eroticism, and he spent much of time photographing working-class Sicilian boys in sexually and racially charged scenes that late nineteenth-century male and female audiences considered classical nude portraiture and thus condoned.[35]

A fervid Orientalist and a devotee of Grecian ideals, von Gloeden was quick to use his economic capital to cultivate—through photographic images like the one featured above—an idyll that implicitly voiced his same-sex desire.[36] These individual images also help to forge an imaginary international community of like-minded spectators. As Waugh writes: "Homosexual subjects of the industrial North . . . projected their utopian male-male fantasies onto the homosocial Other of the Mediterranean littoral. . . . For those nineteenth-century subjects, situated within the heterosocial nuclear family and the industrial workplace, within the sociosexual regime which had just identified and pathologized the 'homosexual,' southern societies had distinct iconographical advantages: their preindustrial codes of gender segregation and male supremacy, their perceived pastoral intimacy with a Nature that northern societies had presumably left behind, and above all their ambiguity about the continuum of male friendship and male sexual exchange."[37]

For many metro-based European males, the spectacle of such southern Italian "backwardness" (another gay pastoral, if you will) paradoxically enabled them to announce their modernized homosexual identities in the city. "An international constituency of gay cultural practitioners" was realized through the circulation, exchange, collection, and the decoding of *Taormina's* photographic bodies.[38] As art critic Allen Ellenzweig writes, "[von Gloeden's] material was designed for and sold to adult [northern and central European] males seeking sexual arousal, confirmation, and pleasure by viewing images of nude youths."[39] To condense this imperialist history even further, von Gloeden's pictorial photographs evidence an emergent homosexual collective of turn-of-the-century metro-spectators in the West, a queer ruralism that formed the backdrop of an urban-based gay identity, and another example of the "international gay circuit" of cities such as Berlin, Rome, Paris, and New York City that we also witnessed in chapter 1's readings of Cather, Demuth, and Johnson.[40]

It is precisely how von Gloeden accomplished this imperial task of Sicilian homoeroticism that links up with my larger arguments about Meads's rural stylistics. Whenever he frames his photographic subjects, von Gloeden takes "iconographical advantage" of southern Italian bodies to situate them in spaces marked by what could be called anachronistic time, an anachronism that Meads borrows, negotiates, and dissects in the "Allen and Justin" series.[41] As we can see in this untitled photograph, von Gloeden's southern male bodies are photographed alongside relics such as a painted vase and a palm that are meant to transport the idea of a homoerotic ancient Greece into turn-of-the-century Italy. Hence just as Meads brings von Gloeden's "heritage" into the rural "Deep South," von Gloeden transports a "heritage" of antiquity into rural Sicily. Yet while Meads appropriates von Gloeden's anachronism to question metro-norms, the German photographer deploys anachronism to forge a collective gay body.

In one of the more incisive readings of the *Taormina* series, Roland Barthes picks up on von Gloeden's temporal strategies when he calls out von Gloeden's clashy ensemble: "These contradictions [in *Taormina*] are 'heterologies,' friction from diverse and opposing languages. For example, von Gloeden began with the laws of Antiquity, overloads them, parades them ponderously (with ephebes, shepherds, ivy, palms, olive trees, tunics, columns, steles), but (first distortion) mixes the signals, combining Greek flora, Roman statuary, and the 'classical nude' of Beaux-Arts academies: with no irony, it appears, he accepts any worn-out legend as a genuine article."[42] Barthes continues: von Gloeden's use of such anachronistic time—"the most 'classical' culture [mixed with] the most obvious [modern] eroticism"—is "splendidly bold."[43] Writing in 1978, the French critic finds that the temporal "contradictions" in *Taormina* only serve to confirm "the power of his vision, which continues to astonish us even now."[44]

Given Barthes' praise, it is clear that von Gloeden's anachronistic photographs not only helped to anchor modern urbanized homosexual communities in the early twentieth century; they also continue to secure urbanized homosexual communities in the century's later decades as well. With no apparent irony, the critic presumes that the overstuffed photos astonish "us" as he implicitly links anachronistic visual strategies of the early twentieth century to his own visual strategies in the late twentieth century. Through von Gloeden, Barthes (along with a host of other gay male spectators) forges an imagined transhistorical continuity that cements the collective sexual identity that Meads challenges. The Prussian pictorialist is, in brief, one of "our lascivious ancestors."[45]

As I have already suggested, *Alabama Souvenirs* works within the confines of this ancestral tradition only to scramble it for metronormative audiences both academic and popular. To do so, Meads repeatedly presents his 1996 or 1998 Eastaboga males in poses that reference a male physique pictorial from the forties or an imperial von Gloeden soft-core pictorial from the turn of the century. Yet while von Gloeden exploits anachronistic time to announce the historical emergence of imperial Western gay "types" located primarily in major metropoles such as Berlin, London, Paris, and New York City, Meads exploits von Gloeden not to advance a neo-colonial gay male identity, but to overhaul this master narrative with his rural stylistics in small-town Alabama. Though he, like his supposed ancestor, "mixes hillbilly and high art," he does not situate *Allen and Justin: On Marty's Bed, 1998* as a historical continuation of a standardized gay male pictorial tradition.[46] These young men, in other words, are not "direct descendants."

Instead, the temporal contradictions in *Alabama Souvenirs* question the contemporary compulsion to identify with this historical tradition, a narratological norm complementing the "flight to the city" tale that continues to provide many metronormative U.S. queer men with a sense of collective identity to this day. By doing so Meads grafts *Taormina* onto *Eastaboga* (and a forties beefcake pose onto a late-nineties "redneck" body) not to extend an ideology of so-called gay heritage, but to badger it. As he tells his viewers in a preface to the "Allen" and "Justin" series on his Web site: "These two had a bond that is rare these days, one that refuses analysis or classification. They were like brothers, not lovers, and the ease with which they found being in each other's company was fascinating if not aggravating."[47]

"Aggravating" is an interesting word choice. Trying to refuse "classification," *Alabama Souvenirs* too recalls preindustrial codes of gender segregation and white male supremacy, pastoral intimacies with a nature that northeastern metropolitan societies had presumably left behind, and ambiguities about the continuum of male friendship and male sexual exchange. But *Eastaboga*'s translocal—and simultaneously transnational— photographs argue with what an "erotic cultural heritage" of gay pictorial photography strives to make clear "these days," not with what this "erotic cultural heritage" should be or whom should be included in it. Each of the photographs "conjures places mysterious and unknown," one *Gay City News* reviewer writes, "yet not unknowable."[48] Aggravating a legacy that gives historical weight to metronormative imaginaries past and present, *Alabama Souvenirs* refuses to allow queer urbanites to find yet another version of their historical selves through his photography. As we saw in the Web site's opening frames, the "redneck" series entices metro spectators with approximations of canonical gay male art, but they also undermine any sense of continuity or cross-identification. By doing so, Meads' intimate stylistics could be said to perform what José Esteban Muñoz terms a "disidentification," "a mode of dealing with dominant ideology . . . that neither opts to assimilate within such a structure nor strictly opposes it; rather, disidentification is a strategy that works on and against dominant ideology."[49] Evoking several icons of white gay male art, Meads re-stages them in Alabama rurality only to mystify homonormative and heteronormative identification processes, past and present, altogether.

I think that Meads also plays on the idea of "southern backwardness" here, a term that I have been throwing around in this chapter without yet refining it. By "southern backwardness" I refer to a stereotypical characterization of the U.S. South—the state of Alabama an exemplar—as a geographic region that is socioeconomically, culturally, and politically lacking, one that is seemingly committed to ideals of an uncritical rusticity.[50] Such cultural lack also ties to a temporal "backwardness," most prominently expressed in the caricature of the U.S. South as a frozen region outdated by supposedly more progressive spaces across the nation (and one that supremacist notions of the U.S. South can and often do buy into). Likewise, such southern "backwardness" also links to temporal norms that structure queer metronomativity in the form of trendy fashions or being in the know. As Kath Weston notes in her discussion of compulsory queer urbanisms, there is often "a broader cultural tendency to map time onto space by characterizing inland locations as 'ten years behind' cities on the coasts"—to which I would include certain portions of the U.S. South.[51]

It is for this reason, I believe, that Meads likes to consider himself a "closet anarchist" when he photographs these males and presents his art in a Chelsea gallery on the coast.[52] Working with a metronormative tradition, he also works through some Western gay male iconography—Pater, Demuth, magazine physique photos, von Gloeden—to explode these traditions from within.[53] Along the way, he seeks after something other than what is already found in a standardized urban gay art scene, and the disidentificatory strategies of *Alabama Souvenirs* function as queer outsider art embedded within the heart of classic training and white gay male pictorial. Imaginary portraits from one of the poorest states in the United States, the seemingly documentary photos produce nothing less than "a sense of irreality" about southern "backwardness" in urbane spectatorship, a sense of anarchic confusion and "frightening" irritation that generates aggravation rather than successful identification—one form of the paper cut politics mentioned in this book's introduction.[54] In the words of one metropolitan commentator, "The tension between the erotic and the iconic in Meads' work make it difficult to tell what Meads' goal really is."[55]

Caravaggio's Rednecks

These queer configurations of "backwardness," disidentification, and anachronism intensify when we look at another *Alabama Souvenirs* series, Meads's studio portraits (1992–96). In retrospect, Meads recalls that his Eastaboga studio "was always a central meeting point and place to just hang-out. . . . I was always working on new paintings and would need someone to pose for this figure or that. Recording the pose on film was an easy transition for them to make. I could shoot what I needed and use it later for reference. . . . And more importantly, once one of them posed for me and gave me the seal of approval, the rest were more than willing to help."[56]

A complement to the documentary photos discussed above, the studio photos too situate *Eastaboga* "redneck" males in poses that suggest earlier icons of Western gay male art. In the first window of a series titled *In the Studio*, the viewer encounters six images of "Aaron"—a male previously shown in physique pictorial photos like "Allen"—that re-stage several of Caravaggio's late sixteenth- and early seventeenth-century paintings. To be even more specific, Meads restages *Boy With a Basket of Fruit* and *Saint John the Baptist in the Wilderness*, paintings that have appealed to post-Stonewall urban-based white gay male artists as they cross-identify with Caravaggio and his male bodies as "lascivious ancestors" (fig. 3.8 and 3.9).[57]

As we compare the two, we again see that Meads's appropriation pitches an earlier "gay" figure into a queer anachronistic time, here the southern "backwardness" of 1994. Just as *Allen and Justin: On Marty's Bed, 1998* undoes von Gloeden's *Taormina* series, so too does the photograph of "Aaron" invert Caravaggio's painting of *John the Baptist* from within. Both representations strike similar poses as they focus the viewer's gaze on semi-nude male bodies. In Caravaggio's *Saint John the Baptist*, the saint's torso is swathed in thick fabric and furs while the remainder of his body is displayed for spectators. In Meads's *Aaron: As a Caravaggio VI, 1994* the young male is clothed in white briefs while the remainder of his body too is spectacularized. But here any similarities between the two artworks end. Rather than hold a slim bamboo cross, "Aaron" holds an open aluminum can of Natural Light beer. Instead of lush green flora surrounding his feet, "Aaron" rests his legs on what appears to be a green fishing tackle box. *Saint John the Baptist* glorifies a white male body; *Aaron: As a Caravaggio VI, 1994* white-trashes it. While twentieth- and twenty-first-century spectators may read themselves into this homoerotic Caravaggio scene ("SO HOT!!!," so to speak), Meads troubles this identification by so playing up the "redneck" paraphernalia that it elicits an "Ew, makes me glad I don't live in the redneck states." He uses the stereotypical icons of southern rural "backwardness"—beer cans and tackle boxes—to disidentify with Caravaggio, a stereotypical icon of metronormative white gay male cultures.

Such self-professed closeted anarchy reaches its apex when Meads introduces the Confederate battle flag as a backdrop for these anachronistic studio photographs. We have seen references to this supremacist piece of cloth before in the opening frames of *Alabama Souvenirs* as well as in the "Allen" and "Justin" series. Following the initial *Aaron: As a Caravaggio* photographs, it becomes more ubiquitous and even more politically troubling. The remainder of the images compiled throughout *In the Studio* feature pictorials of shirtless white men (plus one woman, "Michelle," and one unnamed African American male) who face the camera brandishing shotguns, or guzzling bottles of wine, or handling snakes with the flag prominently displayed in the background. In some of these images, the photographic subjects are dressed in modern fashion. In most, the young men are costumed in unfashionable long johns or tattered overalls that again evoke a "backward" South in the late 1990s (fig. 3.10 and 3.11). *Jason the Bunny: In Overalls II, 1997*, for instance, frames a semi-nude white body against a backdrop that consists of nothing but an enormous

Confederate flag, and other "Deep South" photographs in the series follow suit.

Meads does not explicitly address why he uses this politically explosive icon on the *Alabama Souvenirs* Web site, but I believe that the flag's presence is central to further understanding the critique of these anachronistic photographs. In the introductory notes to the *In the Studio* series, viewers are only told that:

> the photographs of my friends in the studio were made for various reasons that included the creation of a continuing record of their visits, documenting changes in their appearance, or for use as reference materials for figures depicted in my paintings and drawings. When I would shoot portraits of them, they would usually choose what they would wear, or not wear, and how they wished to be presented. If I chose the garments it was usually for a specific piece of work I had planned. This included images of farm boys (long-johns and overalls), "rednecks" (old underwear, beer bottles), rough trade (leather), and athletes (football gear, wrestling singlets).[58]

Though Meads does acknowledge here that many of the studio photographs are staged, he makes no mention of how the flag might disturb urbanized gay spectatorship and its visual "heritage." Likewise, in the various interviews with international gay magazines and e-zines that Meads made to promote *Eastaboga*, he often repeats the claim that the flag is nothing more than a sociological record of white southern regionalism. "These flags are always present in their daily lives," he tells one critic in the e-zine *OUTspoken!*. "To include that flag in the photographs may seem provocative but it was actually rather matter-of-fact."[59] Downplaying his own pictorial staging, he insists: "I'm not trying to make a statement. . . . There's no intended social commentary or anything like that. . . . These are the people I knew and these are the stupid things we did."[60]

I think that Meads is correct to note that in many *Alabama Souvenirs* scenes—young white men sitting in the seat of their pickup trucks or reading porn in their bedrooms—the flag appears to be "matter-of-fact," but I also sense there is more to this claim when he undervalues his imaginary portraits of these "stupid things." Given the dense allusions to earlier gay art forms and Meads's deconstruction of this visual "heritage," I think he engages (as he does throughout his Web site) in a common southern practice of "dissembling" when he describes the icon for mainstream gay readers.⁶¹ It may take one queer Alabamian to know one, but sometimes even I couldn't tell what was truth and what was fiction in my interviews with the artist. In fact, when I pressed Meads in an e-mail exchange about his use of the flag and the racial, sexual, and historical politics of its display in his artwork, he contradicted his earlier published comments for gay glossies, replying:

> It doesn't take much to scratch off the polite patina that conceals the racial tensions that still exist in the South. You will find the flag all over the place—on belt buckles, on bumpers of cars, rear windows of trucks (right next to the "3" sticker), hanging above their beds etc. I think that RuPaul's entrance (God bless her!) in "To Wong Foo" is priceless! The Confederate flag can be used in unexpected, subversive ways. As I have said before I am a closet anarchist.
>
> I use the flag in the photograph as a way to:
> A. Create a strong graphic image that helps establish an honest sense of time and place, and adds a distinct level of menace.
> B. Shock and annoy the Hell out of the politically correct set (which is destroying honest communication and ruining this country).⁶²

Judging from this message alone, it is clear that Meads considers the flag to be something more than a "matter-of-fact" fixture of everyday rural southern life in the United States. With his references to "racial tensions," "anger," "hate," "menace," "shock," political correctness, and the flag's distribution across local and global media, he scratches off his interviewing patina to reveal an awareness of the pernicious racial politics that the flag often signifies in white southern cultures, rural or not—as well as how the flag has been used to provoke in expected and "unexpected" ways.

Indeed, in his recent history of the Confederate battle flag, historian John M. Coski notes that the flag usually connotes the "South as a distinctive region, individual rebelliousness, a self-conscious 'redneck' culture, and segregation and racism"—but sometimes these symbolic connotations get bent.⁶³ Coski rightly stresses that the white supremacy symbol is "associated with slavery," and he notes that in the late twentieth century "the flag assumed a powerful new meaning as shorthand for 'redneck' or 'good ol' boy.' For people outside the working-class southern culture from which this image emerged, a 'redneck' was a threatening figure to be avoided."⁶⁴ His exhaustive research details a history of the flag that spans the rise of the Ku Klux Klan in the late nineteenth and the early twentieth century, civil rights era initiatives, flag mania of the early 1950s, desegregation, southern nationalism, the Civil War centennial of 1961–65, debates in the U.S. Senate in the 1990s, bitter campus arguments at University of Alabama and the University of Mississippi, and its popularity at NASCAR racings as well as in television shows such as *The Dukes of Hazzard*. Yet the historian also notes that the flag has always been a highly controversial and highly re-appropriated symbol—so much so that Coski describes how "two Charleston, South Carolina, African-American men parlayed [the flag] into a successful clothing line" named NuSouth Apparel that has recently manufactured rebel flag-wear for their clientele.[65]

Despite his claim that he doesn't intend to provoke "social commentary," Meads's queer anti-urbanism enters into these fraught exchanges about the flag's symbolism and its connection to a painful history of U.S. white supremacy that too often facilitates a questionable "heritage" of white regional identity. And despite his public protests in mainstream media forums, it is also clear from his responses to my inquiries that Meads—like NuSouth Apparel and like the southern nationalists—uses this racialized icon to provoke spectators. "It gets people in general to think," I was told in one of our interviews. "My favorite thing is to be offended [by others' art]."[66] While Meads highlights the épater quality of his ruralized aesthetic in a claim that parallels what cultural critic Laura Kipnis has elsewhere termed a desire "to offend—anyone, of any race, any ethnic group," I also need to emphasize the ambivalence of the flag's racism in *Alabama Souvenirs*, and I pause over that "distinct level of menace."[67] I do not want to whitewash or erase the history of racial supremacy that the flag provokes, and I often find these images confusing in their political if not their cultural aims, a confusion that links us back to the ambivalence of the DataLounge metro-spectatorship ("I mean, what gives here?") as well as Meads's puzzling redeployments of queer time in the rural U.S. South. This may be one reason why it is "difficult to tell what his goal really is" as well as why the artist likes to self-identify as a "closet anarchist."

All this said, I also continue to believe that Meads's anarchic focus on the "subversive" potential of this offensive icon—an anarchy that, however unlikely, connects him to the "anarcho-effeminism" of *RFD* and *Country Women*—is crucial to his larger project of annoying "the Hell out of" the visual traditions that structure metronormative gay cultures. While the photographer does consider the Confederate flag to be a commonplace testament to white supremacy and white U.S. southern ruralism, I

Figure 3.12. *To Wong Foo, Thanks for Everything! Julie Newmar* still (1995).
Courtesy of Universal Studios Licensing LLP.

am struck that he also compares his particular use of the "strong graphic" and his particular awareness of "racial tensions" to African American drag queen RuPaul's performance in the 1995 film *To Wong Foo, Thanks for Everything! Julie Newmar*.[68] Filmed on location in Nebraska and New York City, *To Wong Foo* tells the tale of three sophisticated drag queens—one black, one white, one Latino—who take a cross-country trip from New York City to Los Angeles. Along the way, they find themselves stuck in a small midwestern town called Snydersville, where they unleash "Operation Decoration Storm" on the "fair hamlet" and attempt to aestheticize the town ("so Middle America," one states) with their cosmopolitan stylistics. In the New York City drag show that opens the film, a fellow drag queen beckons RuPaul to the stage so that she can announce the winners of "the Webster Hall Annual Drag Show." Rather than enter from the stage wings, however, RuPaul descends from a perch as "Miss Rachel Tension" (fig. 3.12). The name fits well since her full-body sequined dress doubles as a full-body sequined Confederate flag. The racially mixed crowd goes wild as they witness this spectacle, and RuPaul's fellow queens bow in deference as a queer of color disidentifies on an icon of white supremacy.[69]

However perverse and problematic, I want to close this chapter down by suggesting that Meads's closet anarchy puts *Eastaboga* men in Confederate drag to do more of the same with late modern U.S. metronormativity.

Though it is difficult to tell what his goal really is, I believe that Meads again pushes another visual artifact through historical authenticity and sociological document to muck up metro-stylistics, much like "Miss Rachel Tension" mucks up black and white "racial tensions." To re-frame this last point, just as he presents the white supremacist body of "Allen" to question the imperial "heritage" of dominant gay cultures in his inverted von Gloeden series, so does Meads use *Jason the Bunny: In Overalls II, 1997* to again critique the "dominant imprints" of a contemporary white gay urban body.[70] For a quick example of this normative model, we have only to remind ourselves of the DataLounge member's uncritical observations regarding *Alabama Souvenirs*: "They look like imported Chelsea boys."

"Look like" is key here. For the most part, the racist young white males that Meads photographs "in the studio" approximate an "erotic [gay] cultural heritage" as well as current metronormative types that also have their own racist histories. Yet as I have also suggested, they fail to satisfy these normative historical molds. If we examine closely *Jason the Bunny: In Overalls II, 1997*, we find that it too is an incoherent mess of queer iconography. Like "Allen" and "Justin," "Jason" has a slim, white, faintly muscular body, a body that one could find splashed on the monthly cover of urban-oriented gay magazines like *Attitude, Genre, Instinct*, or *XY*—extensions of the *Advocate* standardizations that we discussed in the previous chapter.

Yet the moment that Meads's images appear to participate in yet another tradition of pictorial iconography, he again performs a disidentification that pitches his photographs out of this discernable history of gay visual art. Though *In the Studio* may invoke contemporary metro types and contemporary metro cover boys, "Jason" also appears in staged attire that once more suggests the presence of an anachronistic rural body. Meads deliberately dresses him in the antiquated gear of what the artist categorizes as "farm boys (long-johns and overalls)" and "'rednecks' (old underwear, beer bottles)," types antithetical to urbane taxonomies that inform the sculpted, brand-named body of "the Chelsea boy." "Jason" is, in short, anything but a dominant historical imprint even as he recalls the dominant corporeal imprints of contemporary U.S. cosmo-urbanism. As one discerning critic suggests, Meads's images "disqualify them from [Bruce] Weber's Abercrombie and Fitch vision."[71] In so doing, *Jason the Bunny: In Overalls II, 1997* fails to fit proper molds as the photograph appears to be frozen in a queer anachronistic space. His body—like the body of Caravaggio's "redneck," like the bodies of von Gloeden's white supremacists, like the body of Pater's bubba, and like the forties pictorial body captured at the Old Confederate Bridge—could be said to reveal "the inadequacy of purely historical identifications" as it is "the insertion of nonhistorical [and anachronistic] modes of being in time," and as it announces a visual disaffiliation from late twentieth-century urban gay U.S. culture.[72] Pushed outside metro-gay heritage, "Jason" appears to be a literal icon of figurative and offensive "backwardness."

In a similar vein, Meads's appropriation of the Confederate flag—one that may also connect him to the redeployment of the Union Jack by "gay skins" in the United Kingdom—facilitates a "disidentificatory difference that help[s] toxic images expand and become much more than quaint racisms."[73] When it typically operates as a noxious marker of white supremacy, the rebel flag functions historically as an anachronistic marker of regional difference, a signifier of the white U.S. South's imaginary distinction from the white U.S. North. But in Meads's reworking of this collective visual "heritage," the artist transforms this too-present icon of racial hatred, regional exceptionalism, and alternate temporality into something else— an anachronistic symbol of critically queer anti-urbanism. Just as Jason's overalls and his long johns signal his "redneck" body's inability to comply with the dominant imprints of gay metro-norms, so does the retrogressive flag signal a refusal to sexually assimilate into the space or the time of contemporary urbane cultures. As he uses the menace of the Confederate flag to menace principal metro-norms, Meads turns an icon of racial tension into his own form of "Rachel Tension." Thrusting his models out of what can often count for gay visual culture, he again pitches his images beyond contemporary urbanized spaces and contemporary ruralized southern spaces into a fantastic locale, a souvenir of an impossible place.

Let's stretch my final argument but pray it doesn't snap: in online photographs such as *Jason the Bunny: In Overalls, 1997* the Confederate flag begins to disidentify not only on itself in "unexpected, subversive ways," but also on the racial norms of late modern queer urbanity and the cultural impetus to identity with its visual taxonomies and heritage on the Web or off. There is only one African American male and one female featured in *Alabama Souvenirs*, and such paucity seems deliberate coming from a knowing white artist who launches a queer critique through the "sick, sordid, malevolent, *nasty*" icons of white supremacy.[74] Substituting the Confederate flag for the rainbow flag throughout its anti-pastorals, *Alabama Souvenirs* consequently stages a frustrated—and, for me, politically frustrating—act of sedition from the metro-based queer nation. Determined to offend with a corroded racist icon, it means to shock you into thinking differently about the present tense of the U.S. gay metropolis. So we end where we began. Though the *Eastaboga* knife soon fades when it pops up on your computer screen, the Web site still cuts when you click, click, click into the new media that is Meads's working-class Taormina— a "something" in digitized queer urbanity "that is there in no satisfying measure, or not at all." This is just to say that somewhere in the cyberspace of *Eastaboga* (if not necessarily Eastaboga, Alabama), Meads's rural stylistics turned these backwoods bodies into an anti-urbanist queer avant-garde. The next chapter's turn to queer of color artist Sharon Bridgforth will similarly renegotiate the Deep South, while it firmly counters the white supremacy that *Eastaboga*'s soft-core flaunts before eager eyes.

4

Unfashionability

say a fashion prayer every night before falling asleep, lest you
    wake up without a style.

—Wayne Koestenbaum, Cleavage

Steel Boots of Leather

We are each fashion's victims. Take but two anecdotes from the previous decade. The first belongs to self-identified genderqueer crip activist Eli Clare who, in 1999, was "still learning the habits and manners of urban dykes" after she left her predominantly working-class hometown of Port Orford, Oregon, for the greener pastures of the Bay Area (135).[1] Settling uneasily in the lesbian communities of Oakland, California, she deemed herself an "exile," alienated from the "urban, middle-class queer activists" that surrounded her (30), unfamiliar with their "trust funds, new cars, designer clothes, [and] trips to Paris" (37–8), and often treated "like a country hick" (39). One day, at a moving party full of "friends, lovers, and ex-lovers, butch dykes, femme dykes, androgynous dykes," Clare cruises a woman named Leslie. More accurately, she cruises Leslie's steel-toed black leather boots, which trigger an involuntary memory that casts Clare back to a summer when she "was 15 working in the woods" at an Oregon lumber factory (135). Hungry for connection, nostalgic for Port Orford, and isolated from urbanized dykes, Clare strikes up a conversation with Leslie and inquires about her shoes after assuming a shared non-urbanized, non-middle-class upbringing.[2] To Clare's dismay, however, the conversation is over before it starts once Leslie admits that "I just bought them as a fashion statement." Horrified, Clare "felt as if I'd been exposed as a hick yet again, caught assuming she was someone I might have grown up with. *A fashion statement*. What did I have in common with Leslie?" (135).

The second anecdote belongs to literary and film theorist D. A. Miller, who, in 1992, penned a generous criticism of Roland Barthes' oeuvre, *Bringing Out Roland Barthes*. In the middle of this literary love letter to the

French critic, Miller slips in a lengthy paean to the proverbial "young man from the provinces" "familiar to readers of the nineteenth-century novel" (29).[3] A paragraph later, Miller then links this provincial figure to "those practices of post-Stonewall gay male culture whose explicit aim, uncompromised by the vicissitudes of weather or fashion, is to make the male body visible to desire" (30). I wrote "love letter," but I might just as well have typed "fashion statement." Miller's ode to gay urbanity continues: "The men of the Muscle System [in the Castro] or the Chelsea Gym, who valuing tone and definition over mass give as much attention to the abs and glutes as to pecs and lats; who array their bodies in tanks and polos, purchased when necessary in the boys' department, in Spandex and Speedos, in preshrunk, reshrunk, and, with artisanal care, perhaps even sandpapered 501s—let us hail these men" (30). To embellish his imperative, on the East Coast and the West, let us hail these metropolitan-based men their fashionability.

Will do. But before I get there I ask a not-so-obvious question: despite profound differences in sexual, socioeconomic, geographic, and gender identifications, what commonalities might Clare's self-professed "country hick" share with Miller's "young man from the provinces"? To the best of my limited knowledge, Clare and Miller have never shared the same page or party or exercise facility. Nevertheless, they are each intrigued with the vital role that fashion chic plays in contemporary urbanized U.S. queer cultures. Both might agree, as Clare elsewhere puts it, that "queer identity, at least as I know it, is largely urban" (37). And both are preoccupied with how this urbanized queer identity manifests itself via sartorial stylistics, how this group identity can function as a disciplinary regime that operates as identification, as communality, and, sometimes, as geographic stigma. For Clare, the Oakland dyke fashion of someone like Leslie reinforces a consumerist homonormativity that disavows the occupational styles of working-class queer regionality. Leslie's aesthetic sophistication makes her feel more like a hick, and less like a young woman fleeing the Oregon provinces. Hence it's all about the damaging shame factor of queer excess (the manual labor function of the boot forgotten by hip dyke couture) that clothing demands in a moment marked by the popularizing of lesbian chic. For Miller, by contrast, urban gay male fashion in Chelsea and in the Castro is nothing but celebratory. It's all about the pleasure of queer excess (the romp into the boys' department) that clothing enables for a scholar who also "discovered" the delights of stylish fabric during his "first year at Yale" (28). She feels cast out. He feels elected.

In lieu of their manifest differences, then, Clare and Miller are paradoxically connected by their discrepancies, since both suggest that fashionable chic is often central to the imaginary constructions of U.S. queer stylistics across both gender and, we'll later see when we turn to writings of Audre Lorde, racial difference.[4] In these comparative instances, fashion enables sexual recognition while it asks for sexual assimilation into an urbanized queer group identity. Together, steel-toed boots and Spandexed bodies add up to a hyper-awareness of how queer urbanity can normalize via a sartorial stylistic of fashionable chic, of how citified queers hierarchize themselves when they don what Clare calls the "habits and manners" of the trendy, the up-to-the-minute, the modish, and the sandpapered. And while I'm well aware that lesbians, gays, and trans of any color or class often have differing and diffuse stylistics, and while I'm well aware that queer clothing can and has often been deeply counter-hegemonic, I'm going to insist that these group identities often bathe in the guiding light of a homogenizing and supra-regional urbanity. While it may, at first glance, seem strange to couple Clare and Miller, situating them side-by-side reveals the vital role that chic plays in the ongoing urbanization of queer habitus—and how queer fashion castigates the remainders who fail its universalizing designs.

Facing these dire straits, this chapter focuses on how sartorial chic—as a style, as a statement, as a semiotic, as a public performance—is and has been a key component of metronormativity's ensemble. Given the historically entrenched relationship between urbanism and fashionability that is not going away anytime soon—what one scholar in fashion studies deemed the core "fashion worlds" of "Paris, London, and New York"—this should come as no surprise.[5] I suspect that for most of us it's not that hard to see how investments in the material imaginaries of queer chic, or how voluntary membership in any of its "fashion worlds," work by default to exclude those queer bodies who fail to fulfill fashion's guidelines, and who sometimes find themselves manufacturing attire for the bodies that exclude them.[6] As we witnessed in the *Advocate* subscription ads of chapter 2 and in the *Longjohns* photographs of Michael Meads in chapter 3, and as we see here in the anecdotes and the epigraph that open this chapter, this is a state of the union that many queers "without a style" must grapple with on a day-to-day basis.[7] It is also, I wager when I eventually turn to a queer solo performance that renegotiates queer chic, a sartorial fabrication that ruralized queers have long reproached with DIY aesthetics of their own making.

Rephrased: I reconsider Clare and Miller's fashion statements by think-ing alongside them. I want to recover regionalized responses to dominant U.S. lesbian and gay fashion systems that resist the perpetual investment in metronormative chic. To do so, I showcase how queers of the not-so-distant past embraced a ruralized stylistics of "unfashionability" to coun-teract the ongoing metronormativity of late modern apparel. To get at the work that "unfashionability" accomplished then and may accomplish now, I first revisit complementary theories of fashion chic and queer urbanism offered by two contemporaneous writers—Roland Barthes in Paris, and Audre Lorde in Greenwich Village—who each thought hard about the fabrications of an emergent metronormativity in the 1950s and 1960s. Building on their findings, I then apply their theories to *no mo blues* (1995), a "one-woman tone poem" by performance artist Sharon Bridg-forth. With an artisanal care that matched the men of the Muscle System, Bridgforth's queer anti-urbanism resisted incorporation into mid-nineties lesbian chic and exemplified the sartorial subversions I am trying to con-jure. Moving from Barthes' structuralism to Lorde's bio-mythography to Bridgforth's down-home rurality at a Michigan Womyn's Music Festival, I illuminate how a critical model of unfashionability can reconfigure the stigma of those "without a style." As both Clare and Miller note, such re-proach is often indivisible from the specter of a ruralized queer "from the provinces." We can assume this worn-out conflation, a fashionable trend for decades, to be a designer dud.

Style-less

What does it mean for a queer—any queer—to be unfashionable? One obvious place to look for an answer to this question is Barthes' encyclope-dic theory of Parisian fashion worlds, *Système de la mode*. First published in 1967 and set largely in the City of Light, *Système* is an exhaustive, obses-sive, and understudied account of how metronormative fashion and aes-thetic violence collude. Barthes' foreword states that "the object of this in-quiry is the structural analysis of women's clothing as currently described by Fashion magazines; its method was originally inspired by the general science of signs postulated by Saussure under the name *semiology*. Begun in 1957, this work was finished in 1963" (ix).[8] Behind his opening gambit lies another: to trace how urbanized fashion queerly elides into and aligns with urbanity through "only two magazines (*Elle* and *Le Jardin des Modes*), with a few forays into other publications (notably, *Vogue* and *L'Echo de la Mode*) as well as the weekly Fashion page to be found in some of the daily papers" (11). Exploring how designer clothing and its "qualities of matter: substance, form, color, tactility, movement, rigidity, luminosity" were linguistically transformed into fashion chic by these largely Parisian glossies from June 1958 to June 1959 (236), Barthes approaches the magazine descriptions of racially nondescript (read: white) middle-class women's apparel as a "worldly" system of sophisticated signs that contributes to a systematic world of urbane signifiers (winter woolens, mousseline formalwear, sporty furs, dressy shoes, and matching ensembles ready for "the docks of Calais" [196], to name a few standouts).

"Circulat[ing] Fashion broadly as a *meaning*" (10), Barthes finds this gendered print culture to be a universalizing fashion system dependent on minoritizing identification—what he shorthands as "a phenomenon of initiation" (14). Foreshadowing Clare and Miller, his findings systematize Parisian stylistics into a knowing rite of initiation for urbane readers, those familiar enough with fashion's rules to become what his acolyte Susan Sontag describes as "an improvised self-elected class, mainly homosexuals, who constitute themselves as aristocrats of taste."[9] With their capacity to recognize urban chic's "inventory of genera," these aristocratic tastemakers produce what Barthes vaguely terms "a normative whole, a law without degrees" that, like any good structuralist reading should, applies to all (22).

"Normative" is our keyword. Barthes shows how magazine subscriptions morph into a sartorial system whose formula is aesthetic standardization and interdiction. And despite his scientific structuralism, it's not too difficult to see how the writer outs (even as he often admires) the metro-norms of chic. Over *Système*'s pages readers witness how charts, graphs, and sentence trees of urban fashions in particular become urban fashion in general; how dress codes police via urbanity and knowingness; how chic turns juridical in a New York minute; and how the threat of unfashionability governs all these twists and turns. Barthes says so himself in the opening pages of his analysis: "The knowledge of fashion is not without its price: those who exclude themselves from it suffer a sanction: the stigma of being *unfashionable*" (14). This is not a dressed-up way of saying that last year's out and this year's in, though Barthes does emphasize this "*last year/this year, i.e., fashionable/unfashionable*" equation later on (49). Rather, he predicts what happens when you fail the cultural coding of urbanized outfits and exceed "normative" totality. Unfamiliar with chic's shared "knowledge," you find your unfashionable self this side of social recognition, sanctioned outside of fashion's like-minded imaginary community—and you know it.[10]

Amplifying the social stakes of this unfashionability, Barthes later charges that "under penalty of incurring the condemnation attached to the *unfashionable*, potential features which participate in the reservoir of Fashion are not noted (Fashion virtually never speaks the *unfashionable*), they form the category of the *forbidden*; finally, impossible features (which we saw were in fact historical) are *excluded*, shifted outside of the Fashion system" (179). Here we get a stronger sense of what we mean when we sentence something—and the someone who wears that something—to unfashionability. Fashion is and is not clothing, and it's not simply that an unfashionable someone is ignorant of the latest style. Worse, to their detriment this style-less person is also dated, "shifted," Barthes writes, "outside." To be outside of fashion is thus to be outdated, and, by extension, to be outdated is to be stigmatized and "*excluded*" as archaic or behind the times. It's not always what you wear (fashion, after all, can be anything). It's just as much when you wear it, since the "penalty" for wearing something at the wrong place and the wrong time is nothing less than social condemnation, the "*forbidden*" stigma attached to the non-urbane, the "impossible" features that result in social exclusion, the shame of being exposed by the chic as a hick yet again.

Metronormative queers are experts at this. Building on Barthes, I note that this forged link between behind-the-times penalization and unfashionability is integral to queer fashion's policing, since to be outdated by up-to-date urbanity is, more often than not, to be outside its time. To again cite Edmund White's epigraph on the New York–based "clothes and haircuts and records" that began this book, metronormative queers: "get to participate in whatever is the *latest*. We are never left out of anything; we know what's happening."[11] Barthes too notes this when he tells readers that chic legislates through a prohibitive temporal norm: "Every new Fashion is a refusal to inherit, a subversion against the oppression of the preceding Fashion; Fashion experiences itself as a Right, the natural right of the present over the past; defined by its very infidelity, Fashion nevertheless lives in a world it wants to be, and sees as, ideally stable, completely penetrated by conformist glances [and] the murder it commits of its own past" (273). Standardized and seasonal, naturalized and normalized, trendy and supra-historical, fashion is a gatekeeper of the present since its urban chic kills your past: "Long-term memory thus abolished, time reduced to the couple of what is driven out and what is inaugurated, pure Fashion, logical Fashion . . . is never anything but an amnesiac substitution of the present for the past" (289). With divine "Right," it produces a sartorial amnesia that obliterates any historical knowledge about what comes before as it advances an urbane knowingness of what your wardrobe should be right now. Thus "Fashion's *today* is pure, it destroys everything around it, disavows the past with violence, censures the future, as soon as this future exceeds the season" (289). This censure gets us closer to what it means when a queer in general—and a ruralized queer in particular—is dispatched as unfashionable, which, if not quite a social death sentence, certainly marks someone as socially contaminated by lack.

Barthes' *Système de la mode* teaches us that the chic of queer fashion, as it manufactures "a world it wants to be" and obliterates the historical worlds that have been, works by stigmatization, by presentism, by ideality, and by killer urbanity—conditions that will drive sartorial critiques made by his contemporary, Audre Lorde, and, later, by one of Lorde's successors, Sharon Bridgforth. His structuralism also shows us that queer fashion could care less where you come from. Its fidelity to worldliness has to obliterate the excesses of regional particularity on principle since its cosmopolitanism deracinates you by default. As it relays urbanism into urbanity, fashion stuffs geographic specification into an amnesic past that it "virtually never speaks" and tries to forget. We saw a couple of chapters above that metronormative stylistics has a deep history. To function optimally its urbanities need you to flatten this historical difference. Queers in the big city and the small town may share many events, but Fashion Week has never been one of them.

"Enemy Clothing"

If Barthes temporalizes the aesthetic norms inherent in urbanized fashion, then Audre Lorde widens this critique when she racializes chic and exposes the stigma of unfashionability as a participant in late-fifties Greenwich Village lesbian bar culture. Like Barthes, Lorde too is quick to de-naturalize the supposed timelessness of queer fashion in her writings. Yet while the French structuralist generalizes Parisian fashionability and provides us with a theory for better understanding the high stakes of the unfashionable, the working-class black poet/activist delves into the particulars of what happens when this standardizing queer theory meets historical praxis. Specifically, her 1982 bio-mythography *Zami: A New Spelling of My Name*—published one year before *Système de la mode* was first translated into English, and set in the same decades that Barthes conducted his research—offers us a less obvious but equally critical account of metronormativity as it recounts the worldliness of a pre-Stonewall lesbian fashion scene at a popular interracial watering hole, the Bagatelle. What Lorde found there was a racialized and gendered pecking order announced through what the author and activist would term "dyke-chic fashion": "In the bars, we met women with whom we would have had no other contact, had we not all been gay. There, Muriel and I were pretty well out of whatever was considered important. That was namely drinking, softball, dyke-chic fashion, dancing, and who was sleeping with whom at whose expense" (196).[12]

Lorde references her "queer" Afro hairstyle and her then partner Marion's "shaggy-bowl haircut" in an earlier version of *Zami* when she details her relationship to this "dyke-chic fashion,"[13] and such chic will be the focal point for our reading of Bridgforth's *no mo blues* when we turn to the mainstreaming of mid-nineties queer couture. For now, I want to track the late-fifties "dyke-chic fashion" that Lorde negotiated so that we can get a firmer grasp on the historical damage that Barthes' theories of queer apparel can do for non-metronormative queers, city-based or no. At the Bag, Lorde tells her post-Stonewall readers, nightly social engagements were land mines as the author suffered from the close-knit scene's inter- and intraracial metronormativity, one that still haunts her in the early eighties and one that broadcasts itself via a relentless fashion policing. Smarting from her years spent at the Village bar and working against queer fashion's sartorial amnesias, Lorde writes that "young america's growing pains, within the Bagatelle, were represented by the fashion conflicts between the blue-jeans set and the bermuda-shorts set. Then, of course, there were those who fell in between, either by virtue of our art or our craziness or our color" (221).[14] Cast out and thrust between these Cold War–era fashion conflicts, Lorde acknowledges that she is "part of the 'freaky' bunch of lesbians who weren't into role-playing, and who the butches and femmes, Black and white, disparaged with the term Ky-Ky, or AC/DC," terms that situate Lorde outside the binarized system of lesbian taxonomy and identification that she feels governed pre-Stonewall Village sociality (178). Stigmatized by this gender nonconformity as well as what she elsewhere terms her "raggedy-ass clothes," Lorde literally finds herself outside a Barthesian fashion system and incurs the condemnation attached to the unfashionable.[15] A kiki dressed in what she aptly names "enemy clothing," she just doesn't make sense in the Bag's butch/femme sartorial semiology (224).

Metronormative lesbians in blue jeans and Bermudas won't let her forget this, even as *Zami* elsewhere presents Lorde as a "citified little baby butch" (133).[16] In contrast to her "raggedy-ass" attire, Lorde is odd girl out at the Bag. The bar put "heavy emphasis upon correct garb," she recalls. "The well-dressed gay-girl was supposed to give you enough cues for you to know" (221). These women and their sartorial correctness "frightened me," she confesses, since they advance the same features of communality, knowingness, sophistication, and urbanity that we have seen from Clare to Miller to Barthes' fashion magazines (224). Through their "indigenous policing," these "well-dressed" lesbians manufactured ideals of sartorial and social exclusivity that forced on Lorde and her ilk the stigma of the unfashionable.[17] She writes: "It was hard enough to be Black, to be Black and female, to be Black, female, and gay. To be Black, female, gay, and out of the closet in a white environment, even to the extent of dancing in the Bagatelle, was considered by many Black lesbians to be simply suicidal. And if you were fool enough to do it, you'd better come on so tough that nobody messed with you. I often felt put down by their sophistication, their clothes, their manners, their cars, and their femmes" (224).

In this account, Lorde acknowledges that the socio-sexual politics of the Bag's pre-Stonewall lesbian urbanity are not fundamentally reducible to fashion chic since she cites how "manners" and "cars" put her down as much as "clothes." But like Clare's later emphasis on the "habits and manners" of some Bay Area dykes, Lorde nevertheless highlights the destructive potential that urbanized clothes and urbane sophistication can accomplish for queer-identified women outside dominant clothing systems in the late fifties, the early eighties, and, by extension, today. Her takedown of a Cold War lesbian habitus thus allows for affinities that connect structuralist theories of supra-historical fashion policing to pre-Stonewall dyke stylistics to later queer of color reappraisals of rustic unfashionability by performance artists such as Bridgforth.

It could also be said that Lorde recognizes this cross-racial lesbian metronormativity to be a *pharmakon* that many black women assumed to survive a potentially suicidal social climate. In her retelling, urbanized "dyke-chic fashion" is the end product of a rigid subcultural social order as well as the upshot of trickle-down U.S. racism, one dictated by "white-america's racist distortions of beauty" since "sometimes even [metronormative black butches and femmes] couldn't get in unless they were recognized by the bouncer" (224). Even so, while Lorde affirms that "the society within the confines of the Bagatelle reflected the ripples and eddies of the larger society that had spawned it" (220), no one really gets off the hook in *Zami*'s fashion critiques. Continuing her criticism of the bar's tendency to throw freaky women into an "anomalous no-woman's land" (224), Lorde observes that the Bag's black and white lesbians "were well-heeled, superbly dressed, self-controlled high-steppers who drove convertibles, bought rounds of drinks for their friends, and generally took care of business" (224). Her class critique also notes that these "superbly dressed" women "rejected what they called our 'confused' life style" in their commitment to couture (221). As if they each had a personal copy of *Système de la mode* on hand, these "well-heeled" women produce "the normative whole, the law without degrees" that segregates the Bag into "fashionable/ unfashionable" across and amid racial lines.

Likewise, it needs to be said that Lorde's recollections of the Bag in the fifties participate, consciously or not, in their own stigmatizations of a butch/femme identity in the eighties, even as these recollections call out the metronormativity that often enabled this ideal to emerge, and even as the memoir acknowledges that "butches and femmes, Black and white, disparaged with the term Ky-Ky, or AC/DC." During, prior, and following *Zami*'s 1982 publication date, Lorde drafted her memoir at a historical moment of intense scrutiny regarding butch-femme relationships in the United States. She states that neither she nor her partners promoted this relation, one that she held to be exclusionary: "For me, going into the Bag alone was like entering into an anomalous no-woman's land. I wasn't cute or passive enough to be 'femme,' and I wasn't mean or tough enough to be 'butch.' I was given a wide berth. Non-conventional people can be dangerous, even in the gay community" (224). Yet in an earlier draft of *Zami* published in 1979, Lorde also moves from ostensibly recollecting Bagatelle butch-femme sociability to outright damning these relations as antithetical to lesbian feminist politics:

> As a couple Marion and I were out of it a lot, since much of the role-playing that went on was beyond us. It seemed to both of us that butch and femme role-playing was the very opposite of what we felt being gay was all about—the love of women. As we saw it, only women who did not really love other women or themselves could possibly want to imitate the oppressive and stereotyped behavior so often associated

with being men or acting like men. Of course, this was not a popular view. There were butches and there were femmes, but *lesbian*, like
black, was still a fighting word.[18]

When Lorde dismisses "butch and femme role-playing" of the fifties
as detrimental to "the love of women"—an idealized activity that she files
under the identity category of "lesbian"—she betrays her own stigmatizations of the late-seventies and early-eighties butch-femme relations. Such
criticisms call to my mind an epigraph by her contemporary, Joan Nestle,
that was published in her edited collection *The Persistent Desire: A Femme-
Butch Reader*. I include it because I want to balance out Lorde's post-
Stonewall dismissals of pre-Stonewall urban butch/femme relations, if not
their metronormativity:

> April 24, 1982, marked the public start of what was to become known
> as the "sex wars" in the lesbian and feminist community. On that day
> several hundred women gathered to attend the Scholar and the Femi-
> nist IX Conference held at Barnard College in New York City. The title
> of the conference sounded innocent enough—"Towards a Politics of
> Sexuality"—but the night before, several members of Women against
> Pornography had called the college informing them of the unaccept-
> ability of several of the speakers. When I arrived at the campus that
> bright spring morning, I found a picket line walked by women wear-
> ing black t-shirts stating their position on certain sexual practices and
> handing out leaflets that named the unacceptable speakers and topics;
> butch-femme was included on the list.[19]

Nestle provides a subtle corrective to Lorde. She reminds us that butch-
femme relationships can and often do exceed metro- and homonormativities, and that these stylized relationships have, more often than not, borne
the brunt of subcultural stigma in many U.S. queer communities. Confirming Nestle's comments, Gayle Rubin has also commented in her ruminations on butch identity that, "despite theoretically embracing diversity,
contemporary lesbian culture has a deep streak of xenophobia. . . . Over
the years, lesbian groups have gone through periodic attempts to purge
male-to-female transsexuals, sadomasochists, butch-femme lesbians, bisexuals, and even lesbians who are not separatists."[20]

Yet while I would like to jettison Lorde's questionable depictions of
butches and femmes as "the very opposite of what we felt being gay was

all about," I also want to retain *Zami's* overarching class critique of urbane "dyke-chic" for the larger purposes of this chapter. Deprived of an assertive position in the Bag's metronormativity, Lorde perpetually finds herself this side of unfashionable stigma, shifted outside the bar culture's dominant fashion system, and shunted into a sartorially unspecified place (that "anomalous no-woman's land"). Recounting this space of social exclusion, she laments that "for some of us there was no one particular place, and we grabbed whatever we could from wherever we found space, comfort, quiet, a smile, non-judgment" (226).

Resisting sexual assimilation into the sartorial schemas of pre-Stonewall fashionability, Lorde would present her own counterpart to this fashion world at *Zami's* close with the larger-than-life figure of Afrekete, a lover from "Manhattan Avenue and 113th Street" who also goes by the name of Kitty (247). Kitty/Afrekete's erotic presence briefly provides Lorde with a phantasmatic non-urbane place for space, comfort, non-judgment, and pleasure as Lorde imagines that Kitty *"came out of a dream for me"* and *"brought me live things from the bush, and from her farm set out in cocoyams and cassava"* when her lover buys "magical fruit" from the local West Indian markets (249). Living in a "1 1/2 room kitchenette apartment with tall narrow windows in the narrow, high-ceilinged front room" (248), Kitty/Afrekete, we infer, may be metropolitan but she is not metronormative. She instead hails from a dream even while she resides in a New York tenement near "the high rocks of Morningside Park" (252). For Lorde, such bio-mythography—grounded in upper Manhattan streets—is one way to move beyond the temporal legislation and materialist constraints of the dominant fashion system in the Village.

Later queers like Sharon Bridgforth will heed this hard-earned lesson. In hindsight, we know that Lorde's critiques of hetero- and homonormativity influenced subsequent generations of queer activists, artists, and theorists (even as they hierarchized lesbian taxonomies).[21] We can now see how *Zami's* "raggedy-ass" stylistics also represents an influential counter to middle-class metronormative "dyke-chic fashion" in the late fifties and, perhaps, in the early eighties. I thus spotlight *Zami's* critique of Cold War dyke chic in this chapter because this metro-norm has all too often been presented as an ex nihilo invention of the mid-nineties, as a product solely of the mass media, and as a fad that faded along with the twentieth century.[22]

I'll expand these claims in the following section. For now I stress that the queer trends of metronormative chic—lesbian-identified or not—are always historically specific in their presentism and, if Barthes and Lorde are to be trusted, here to stay. Just as Barthes theorizes the destructive potential of queer fashion decades before the entrenchment of a U.S.-based metronormativity that we saw in chapter 2, so too does Lorde rebuke the historical underpinnings of metronormative dyke chic as early as 1956 when she testified against the "cutthroat" fashion systems that rivaled "the tyrannies of Seventh Avenue or Paris" (241). A decade before so-called lesbian chic would hit the national scene, *Zami* details how New York–based white lesbians—in fraught collusion with New York–based lesbians of color—produced varieties of Village fashion censure, stigmatization, sartorial ostracism, non-recognition, and temporal legislation that Barthes pinpointed in *Système de la mode*. Barthes's outdated semiotics gesture to the social lack inherent in his generalized theory of unfashionability. Lorde's urban exposé hammers this point home when she suggests that the iconic 1950s Village was interwoven with normalizing chic. Though far from perfect in their respective accounts, their findings nevertheless forecast how queers might begin to think outside metronormativity's fashion conflicts with an "anomalous no-woman's land" of their own creation, and both realize Bourdieu's maxim that "aesthetic intolerance can be terribly violent."[23]

In fact, this space of the unfashionable to which both Barthes and Lorde allude—this "no particular place" opposite a rigid Bagatelle habitus, this forbidden space outside *Elle*—may contain a pip of freedom. When you don enemy clothing, you are, like it or not, "given a wide berth." "Non-conventional people can be dangerous," to repeat Lorde, "even in the gay community" (224). As I have outlined, Lorde's memoir goes to great lengths to emphasize the social traumas of falling outside an urbane fashion system even as it instantiates its own social norms. But with this evocative phrase—"a wide berth"—Lorde not only confirms metronormative subcultural sanctions; she also nods to the fashion outlets that may be available when one tries on something else. This is perhaps one reason why U.S. unfashionability threatens with the stigma of ruralism but is also threatened by the possibility of a ruralizing stylistic. Moving from the fifties to the eighties to the nineties (less a historical hairpin turn than one might think), we make good on this last claim by turning away from the fashion epicenters of Paris and New York toward a performance that took place in the woods of western Michigan.

Outdated

Like Clare and Miller, Barthes and Lorde may seem like an odd pairing. But I situate these two together because they provide a stronger theoretical and historical basis for understanding the cultural and political stakes of contemporary queer unfashionability than if we treated them as separate. Read as counterparts, they enable us to better comprehend the material conditionings and historical repercussions of an urbane chic with which later works such as Sharon Bridgforth's *no mo blues* tried to grapple. Indeed, it is the carryovers of earlier sartorial conflicts found in the global fashion worlds of New York City and Paris that, intentionally and unwittingly, drive something like Bridgforth's mid-nineties "performance stories" of rural unfashionability.[24] Aware of the stigmatizing nature of queer sophistication that both precedes and informs her art, Bridgforth situates her piece outside the metronormativity of late modern U.S. fashion systems when she tells audiences that *no mo blues*, set in the 1920s, is a chance "to celebrate the rural / southern working-class Black bulldaggas / who were aunty-momma-sister-friend / pillars of the church," and who were anything but the standardizing "well-heeled, superbly dressed, self-controlled high-steppers" that marked Lorde's day—or Bridgforth's own.[25]

I don't know if she had read Barthes's *Système de la mode* when she wrote the prefatory line that I just quoted, but Bridgforth did read, admire, and augment Lorde's ruminations on "dyke-chic fashion." Her works, I believe, pick up where Lorde's left off. In a personal statement posted on one of her blogs, Bridgforth writes that "I have developed a method of facilitating creative writing that I call FINDING VOICE. This method focuses on identity-culture-memory-family histories-aspirations as a way to examine the spaces between and connecting autobiography and mythology/memory our stories. The personal then becomes a way to document oral traditions/herstory and poetic forms for the purpose of using literary-performance as a vehicle for community organizing social justice and Healing. Audre Lorde named the essence of this type of writing *bio mythography* (in her book *Zami: A New Spelling of My Name*)."[26]

In other online statements and interviews, Bridgforth informs us that her work was influenced by Lorde's critical "autobiography and mythology/ memory." Born in 1958, a self-identified "child of the Motown era," Bridgforth spent most of her early years in south-central Los Angeles.[27] She identifies herself as working class, her father hailing from the Algiers neighborhood of Orleans in Louisiana and her mother from Memphis, Tennessee. Looking for "financial freedom," her "mother migrated west (the promised land) but carried her southern sensibilities with her."[28] Urban-based but not urbanist-identified, Bridgforth thus found a regional, southern-based community in a predominantly African American district of Los Angeles and saw it "populated by people from the South, a southern town in many respects."[29] Growing up queer but removed from a normalizing lesbian identity that she coded as both foreign and white, Bridgforth eventually made her way to another southern-based metropolis, Austin, Texas, where she provided HIV outreach to the city's black community, concentrated on community building, and promoted an aesthetic that fails to match the compulsions of a nationalizing and racially normative urbanity. As of this writing, she spends her energies developing productions across the U.S., and has been awarded an artist-in-residency at Northwestern University.

By way of personalized bio-mythography, this is also to say that while Lorde did not live to see the mass production of queer chic, Bridgforth certainly did. I'm referring to that special standardizing moment in the mid-nineties. You may have arrived late to this scene, so here's a set list to remind you: fashionistas at the Clit Club, Melissa Etheridge on MTV, k.d. lang's barbershop duet with supermodel Cindy Crawford on the cover of *Vanity Fair*, Sandra Bernhard on the television sitcom *Roseanne*, the 1994 cinematic release of indie darling *Go Fish*, Madonna's Miami club hopping with gal pal Ingrid Casares, Ellen DeGeneres's outing, and Sharon Stone's glamour shots at each and every amfAR auction.[30] It is easy enough to dismiss this vogue as a star-studded and corporate-driven artifact of female same-sexuality made palatable for heterosexual consumption, and it was easily enough dismissed as soon as it appeared (I'm thinking of the Dyke Manifesto's 1993 command to "Fuck Lesbian Chic"). But it's still just as important to see mid-nineties lesbian chic as a hand-me-down of earlier instances of the fifties dyke chic that haunted Lorde, and as an alienating form of urbanism packaged to queer-identified women as a progressive cultural politics of fashionability. Reminding us of these hard facts, cultural critics Jodi R. Schorb and Tania N. Hammidi state that while "lesbian chic held the promise of putting lesbians front and center in both public and political life," it also managed to "create a class of 'deserving' versus 'undeserving' lesbians" that broke down along fault lines of clothing and hair style, racial normativity, socioeconomic status, and, they stress without naming it as such, a queer urbanity whose holdover continues to this day (259, 260).[31]

Like Lorde before them, Schorb and Hammidi ask us to remember that lesbian chic existed prior to and extended well beyond celebrity sightings. In their critique of lesbian urbanity, they emphasize that a populist "sho-lo showdown" operated on lower frequencies before, during, and after the short run of nineties lesbian chic to produce a *Zami*-like "fashion conflict" illustrating "a valuable lesson about the relation of style to community and the relation of beauty to community sustainability" (257). By "sho-lo," the two critics reference a popular haircut worn by many who identified with a post-Stonewall U.S.-based lesbian group identity in the seventies and eighties, a cut cropped short in the front ("sho") and left long in the back ("lo"). But despite the sho-lo's "long-standing iconic status in lesbian communities," Schorb and Hammidi also find that queers as diverse as working-class Latinas, Slovakian bisexuals, and South Asian lesbians began to dismiss the sho-lo in the 1990s as "backwater," "redneck," "not stylish," "very outdated," "lower income," "tacky," for "hillbillies," and "repulsive" (256–57). In its place, they increasingly identified with the sophisticated haircuts and fashions promised by a ground-level lesbian chic that, unlike the sho-lo, "elevate[d] white looks that highlight urban androgynous or butch aesthetics" (258) and "popularize[d] a vanilla representation" across mainstream and alternative representations of dyke couture (260).

In so doing, an aesthetic like the sho-lo "attains regional signification (as rural, country, or southern—and its derogatory counterparts, hick and redneck)" that establishes an imaginary urban/rural divide governing nineties U.S. lesbian stylistics across race, class, region, and fashion (261). The sho-lo signifies—and we've seen this before—"a rejection of the rural (favoring a tendency towards perceived urbanity)" (261) as much as it exemplifies an erasure of regional specification and an urbane assimilation that also characterizes the queer fashionability of Paris magazines, Village bars, Oakland parties, and Chelsea weight rooms. Yet to the horror of the self-appointed "lesbian style police," Schorb and Hammidi also insist that some still—*still*—continue to wear the sho-lo and wear it well, confirming that "the divergence from dominant beauty norms" featured in lesbian chic "has its risks, but it also has its rewards" (263).

I pause over the historical details of these mid-nineties lesbian fashion conflicts because Bridgforth's *no mo blues* stages its own kind of sho-lo showdown when it strives to resist, refuse, and reconfigure the sartorial abjection of regionally identified working-class black women through a rural-identified stylistics of unfashionability. *no mo blues* is, defiantly, out of date and unfashionable. Moreover, it enacts an outdated and unfashionable time and place in order to combat the regional, racial, and economic amnesias of 1990s chic. The episodic storytelling of *no mo blues* tells a tale of communality, identification, and sociability in an unnamed rural black southern town filled with butches, femmes, and kikis during the 1920s. Amid occasional breaks of jazz beats and blues singing, it tracks the roller-coaster love life of one woman, Bull-Jean; her noncommittal lover, Saffira; their on-again, off-again romance; and Bull-Jean's later entanglements with other women in and around the town. One commentator details:

> As performed by Sonja Parks, [*no mo blues*] is a one-woman tone poem about Bull-Jean, a rural black southern dyke, and her soul mate and lover Saffira. All the characters from Ms. Mama, the narrator, to Saffira and Bull-Jean, are played by Parks. These were not characters, stories, or lives from the white middle class, and the performance made no attempt to translate the characters for such an audience. What Bridgforth does do in her text (and Parks communicates through a virtuoso performance) is create such a complex, detailed, and exquisitely drawn reality that it allows communion across differences without their usual erasure; this is the kind of work that may make genuine affinity building possible.[32]

As much as *no mo blues* works as a jazz poem that makes "no attempt" to "translate" its ruralized working-class black idioms for the white middle classes, it works just as hard to provide theatrical release from U.S. fashion systems that dismissed regionalized styles like the sho-lo as a takedown of black and white middle-class lesbian glamour norms, and as a bittersweet commentary on the high and low fashion conflicts of the mid-nineties that repeat those of the late fifties and earlier. Bridgforth told me in an interview that "chic is not in my world, not a part of my consciousness. There were no references for me in that white world. I didn't see grounding in popular culture and for that I'm grateful. I didn't see myself."[33] With this in mind, we can concentrate on how the performance artist amplifies Barthes' and Lorde's sartorial theories through a deep commitment to ruralized unfashionablity, one faithful to her autobiographical and bio-mythographical Down Home roots.

With the aid of her Root Wy'mn Theater Company in Austin (founded in 1993 and directed by Bridgforth until 1999), Bridgforth produced and toured *no mo blues* from 1994 to 1998 in Columbus, Charlotte,

Minneapolis, Boston, Austin, Berkeley, and Houston, and the one-woman show would turn literary in her 1998 collection of "performance stories" titled *The Bull-Jean Stories.* I'm going to concentrate on the previously mentioned performance of *no mo blues* on the Acoustic Stage at the Michigan Womyn's Music Festival, itself a space that both disabled and confirmed certain metronormative prejudices given that the once gender-exclusive festival (now open to those trans-identified) is set on "650 beautiful acres of remote Michigan woodland," yet nevertheless tries to satisfy the urbanist orientations of some of its participants.[34] Begun in 1976 by Lisa Vogel and set on private land near Walkerville, Michigan, the Michigan Womyn's Music Festival (or MichFest) presents "a rural alternative to the bars, coffeehouses, and protest marches that were more readily available to East and West Coast urbanites"[35] as it attracts thousands to its musical and spoken word performances, films, arts and crafts, workshops, and "spontaneous woodland parties."[36] On one of its more recent Web site postings, the festival's organizers assure interested attendees that "you can hike into the interior of the land campsite far from the action, or settle into a fireside tent city with neighbors from around the globe. For the reluctant camper, we have plenty of comforts and conveniences to give a more urban flavor to your time in the woods."[37]

Facing the urbane norms of mid-nineties chic, the aesthetic violence of the queer urban past, and even the weak metronormativity of the rural-based tent cities of the Michigan Womyn's Music Festival, *no mo blues* took on all these ideological pileups when it was performed for an audience of about one hundred or so queer-identified women one summer evening. As a male-identified queer, I wasn't there to watch this performance, and I was living in Pleasant Grove, Alabama, when it occurred. But in 2007 Bridgforth mailed me a thick packet that included a VHS cassette tape of this *no mo blues* performance. I watched this grainy recording alone on my television set in my former residence of Bellefonte, Pennsylvania—a one-man viewing of a one-woman performance—and I want to speculate a bit about what the piece managed to accomplish, even though I cannot speak definitively about its audience reception.

With its primary focus on Parks's queer solo performance, the video opens to a spare stage.[38] There was no scenery in sight save for a backdrop of three makeshift pinewood walls, and the center stage was empty except for a pitcher, three unlit candlesticks, and a half-circle lined with salt. After Bridgforth walked out and introduced *no mo blues* to thunderous applause and left this stage, the performance's stripped-down aesthetic forced the audience to concentrate on Parks as the center of spectatorial attention. It also forced the audience to attend to the specifics of her costuming and her physical body, or, in Parks's case, the absence of such specifics, since she wore nothing more than "a simple black unitard, bare feet, no props or changes."[39]

This bare performance, I suggest, allowed *no mo blues* to exceed the presentism of dyke chic as the characters that Parks invoked from the rural 1920s were dressed in imaginary clothing from a decade far removed from the mid-1990s. Through her gestures and voice, the supposedly unfashionable characters that Parks conjured invoked what performance theorist Elin Diamond, following Bertolt Brecht, terms "gestus": "a gesture, a word, an action, a tableau, by which, separately or in a series, the social attitudes encoded in the playtext become visible to the spectator."[40] For Diamond, this "*gestus* signifies a moment of theoretical insight into sex-gender complexities, not only in the play's 'fable,' but in the culture which the play, at the moment of reception, is dialogically reflecting and shaping."[41] Hence Parks's performance, as it signified moments of insight into the cultures of mid-nineties lesbian metro- and racial normativity, also enabled what performance theorist Jill Dolan terms "a successful, transformative performance . . . that catapults an audience into a no-place of possibility."[42] Consequently, when Parks performed *no mo blues* on an acoustic stage in western Michigan, her presence functioned as both a critique of dominant "sex-gender complexities" as well as a catapult to a "no-place" that potentially removed the audience from the temporal norms of fashionability.[43]

This un-fashionable "no-place of possibility"—the 1920s Delta that Parks conjures, embodies, and performs through her voice, her comportment, her gestures, her narrative, and her unitard—is the phantasmatic setting of *no mo blues* that I mentioned earlier. Through Parks's gestus, an expressive culture outside middle-class black or white metronormativity is invoked, and *no mo blues* invites spectators to imagine a rural black gemeinschaft where the characters that Parks performs both precede and are indifferent to the "sex-gender complexities" of late modern U.S. metronormativity, "dyke-chic" included. For example, when she conjured Miss Mama, the narrator who introduces the audience to *no mo blues*'s world, Parks adopted a husky voice and a deep swagger, and she hooked her hands into her unitard straps to signify that Miss Mama wore denim overalls, a quintessential icon of ruralized American apparel and also a nod to Janie Crawford's Eatonville, Florida attire in Zora Neale Hurston's 1937 novel *Their Eyes Were Watching God*. While a pair of overalls may sometimes sneak into any urbanized fashion system, the temporal schema of *no mo blues* short-circuits such an interpretation, given that Bridgforth informed me that the characters Parks invokes always "sew, so though they are working class, fashion is not an issue."[44] In this interplay between a literal MichFest performance and the fictional world she performs (a U.S. southern imaginary that signifies much differently than the *Eastaboga* photographs discussed in the previous chapter) the rural-based characters that Parks presents occupy a time outside of fashionability and a space indifferent to the logistics of dyke chic. For Miss Mama and for the other bulldaggas embodied on stage, "fashion is not an issue," since narrative, voices, and gestures require the audience to dress Parks in their imagination, projecting onto her a pair of overalls. In doing so the imaginative gestus of hooking thumbs in overalls, like other unfashionable gests throughout this show, casts the audience out of 1995 and into the theoretical "no-place" that Dolan and Diamond highlight.

Distanced from the latest styles on Seventh Avenue or in Paris, we could call this performative no-place "Down Home," a southern staging that is not "repulsive" or "tacky" though it may be "not stylish" and "very outdated." For Bridgforth, for Sonja Parks ("who truly conjured all the people alive," critics noted),[45] and maybe even for *no mo blues*'s audiences, this is not a sartorial space of social lack, sanction, or regional shame. It is instead a space of social plenitude that works against the standardizations of dyke urbanity to introduce the gestus of a rural working-class black culture. Tacitly or not, this Down Home vernacular habitus—replete with overalls, crawfish holes, front porch gatherings, tall tales, a local church house, a general store, a swamp, and a watering hole that goes by the name Club Seeyaround—has often been derided as an "anomalous no-woman's land" within the hyper-consumerist urbanities of U.S. homonormativity. As opposed to any imagined community of metropolitan chic, Bridgforth conjures a non-urbanized, non-capitalist no-place and imagines the stage as an outmoded 1920s as opposed to a hyper-chic 1990s.

For Bridgforth, this folkish regionality is filled with "the chance to celebrate the rural/southern working-class Black bulldaggas / who were aunty-momma-sister-friend / pillars of the church."[46] The performance piece accomplishes this task as Miss Mama traces the erotic escapades of her friend Bull-Jean and Saffira. In this unimagined community where, one narrator tells the audience, "everybody else was southern / like me / Bull-jean and she aunty sassy b. gonn," Bridgforth tracks a bio-mythology much like Lorde's material fantasy of Kitty/Afrekete in *Zami*.[47] In *no mo*

blues's rurality, the central characters expound on the Deep South pleasures of queers that Miss Mama deems "seasoned-suzzies," "big-bettye,"
"tight-tammye," and "ready ripe-wrapped/donn-done-it wo'mn."[48] These
women of color who, we discover in *The Bull-Jean Stories*, go by the names
of Mina Stay, Big Briggette, Babett Johnson, and Mary Boutté, treasure
their southern dialects in a mixture of Delta blues and bayou anti-chic.
And while they may not be "urban androgynous" or "vanilla," they certainly do take up the stage in the production's hinterland aesthetics, itself
a far cry from the exclusionary sociability that marked Lorde's ventures in
the Bag or Bridgforth's own encounters with a nationalizing fashion world
that "was not a context [in which] to see" herself.

Interweaving "mythology/memory" with "autobiography" with "oral
traditions/herstory" with kinship geographies of the Deep South, Bridgforth goes out of style by outdating Parks, who incorporates herself and
her audience back into the 1920s—not a chic, sophisticated 1920s hall-
marked by the Anglo-sapphic sophistication that we witnessed in chapter 1, but a 1920s stamped with an ethos dated as indifferent to urbanized fashionability. Facing head-on the social and sartorial slights of the
mid-nineties, spaces that Bridgforth insists were "not in my world,"[49] the
performances allows audiences to move into a Down Home performance
that Parks, invoking Bull-Jean in one of *no mo blues*'s best received lines,
calls "southern comfort."

In this queer solo mythology of an outdated region, Bridgforth's neo-
agrarian ideal also resuscitates an obsolete queer of color identity—the
1920s Black bulldagga exemplified by Bull-Jean. It's safe to say that such
an icon has little place within the sartorial schemas of a late modern metronormativity committed to "vanilla representation." Opposed to the
bourgeois aspirations of a racially normalizing lesbian chic, figures like
Bull-Jean are also working-class and, in Bridgforth's performance schema,
ruralized blues women. Though historians and etymologists of U.S. sexual history agree that the working-class African American bulldagger was
most often associated with queer women of color in Harlem during the
1920s (the decade that the term began to receive wide currency in New
Negro Renaissance literatures and cabaret performances), and though
these scholars also agree that the term maintains vernacular prominence
well into the 1950s and beyond, Bridgforth nevertheless insists on locating Bull-Jean in the recesses of the early twentieth-century rural Deep
South.[50] And while this figure of the black bulldagger may have little place
within the metronormative fashion schemas of later twentieth-century

dyke urbanity, Bridgforth presents the regionally based working-class bulldagger as an integral component of her rustic imaginary. Bull Jean, we are told via Miss Mama, is one of the social "pillars"—rather than a social pariah—of *no mo blues*.

As the playwright stated in an interview: "Lesbians are white. Lesbians to me are white people. I still kind of move that way. My artistic aesthetic is grounded in a southern African American sensibility of the bulldagger (not the lesbian)."[51] Hence just as Lorde's "AC/DC" or "Ky-Ky" narrator fails to fit into the butch/femme semiotics of the Bagatelle in the fifties, so too does Bridgforth's Bull-Jean bulldagger fail the chic stylistics of the mid-nineties as well as the racially normalizing sexual identity marker "lesbian" itself. To date, there is no official history of the ruralized queer woman of color in the early twentieth-century United States.[52] *no mo blues* retroactively gives us one. A non-urbanized sexual group mythology for which there is no extant record, Bridgforth's "oral traditions/herstory" reintroduces late modern audiences to the rural bulldagger through a long-term "rememory" jumpstarted by a MichFest performance.[53] Fighting against Barthes' claim that every "Fashion is a refusal to inherit," Bridgforth states in her introductory notes to *no mo blues* that her "intention is to make . . . cultural documentation."[54]

This said, I don't want to idealize the theatrics of *no mo blues* as an unchanging pastoral of simpler times, an uncritically "utopian performative" of the ways of late modern black folk.[55] I heed Sharon P. Holland's claim that, regardless of their class identifications, the regional "quare" homes of the U.S. South are often four-letter words for African Americans, "bittersweet" imagined communities as much as they are spaces of "refuge and escape."[56] It's better, I think, to read *no mo blue*'s call for a Down Home bulldagga 1920s as an alternative sexual modernity (to build on Dilip Parameshwar Gaonkar's discussion of "the mystique of fashion" in Western urbanity),[57] and as another example of what I termed "critical rusticity" in my second chapter: an intersectional opportunity to geographically, corporeally, and aesthetically don non-normative sexuality that offers new possibilities for the sexually marginalized outside the metropolis as well as for those, like a MichFest audience accustomed to "urban flavor," inside it.

In the unpublished manuscript of *no mo blues*, Bridgforth supports this reading of her work. She is quick to situate one of her elder characters in the racial brutalities of the early twentieth-century Deep South, recollecting how "them hooded beasts burned da skin offa my man" (10).[58] And in another personal autobiography about her family's westward migration from Louisiana and Memphis published in *Curve* (a national glossy that recently published on "urban chic"),[59] Bridgforth writes that "i understood that the very conservative south they had all fled from / was present somehow within the confines of the female/male games they played. that these men had very little power outside of the homes they lived in and visited and that jim crow has preceded my family west / imposing continued separate but not equal housing education and employment opportunities."[60]

It is clear that Bridgforth recognizes the obscene pileup of physical and psychological violence that led to rural-to-urban migrations like her mother's in the fifties. It is just as clear to me that she records the aesthetic violence that sparked imaginary urban-to-rural migrations for queers in the mid to late nineties. When she launches her critique, she inverts the standardized flight to the city tale with what E. Patrick Johnson has termed the "resistant vernacular performances" of African American queerness.[61] So as much as voter coercion, perpetual economic underdevelopment, and the promise of better livelihoods prompted the Great Migration of millions of blacks from the rural U.S. South to the urbanized areas of Harlem, Detroit, Chicago, St. Louis, Washington DC, and Los Angeles in the early and mid-twentieth century, then fashion censuring, stigmatization, sartorial ostracism, non-recognition, and temporal legislation let Bridgforth conjure a return migration to *no mo blues*'s Deep South at the end of twentieth. This is a space of comfort amid a national climate where "people seeing me working class decided me not worthy of their time," and where rural working-class roots are re-signified as a Down Home fashion statement.[62]

Found "not worthy" of fashionability's "time," Bridgforth forcefully finds the time of another day, her resistant idealizations countering the ideality of the fashion system. While there may be something nostalgic about all these performative overalls and swamps and oral histories, we need only to recall—by way of conclusion—Barthes' line that "fashion is not without its price: those who exclude themselves from it suffer a sanction: the stigma of being *unfashionable*." And Lorde's: "For some of us there was no one particular place, and we grabbed whatever we could." *no mo blues* recognizes this social cost of falling outside the normative whole of queer fashionability. Yet it also makes good on Barthes' later charge that "to change Fashion is to depart from it; changing an utterance of Fashion . . . is to shift correlatively from Fashion to the unfashionable" (22). Departing from the established sartorial utterances of mid-nineties lesbian chic, Bridgforth envisions a nostalgic time of black queer folk. Along the way she counter-migrates from the inner circle of queer urbanity to the outer limits of an old-fashioned Deep South: "These are the stories they didn't tell me / the ones i needed most."[63]

So let's hail this woman and the 1920s bulldaggas who occupied an open-air stage back in the summer of 1995. Revisiting her regional roots, Bridgforth conflated the Michigan Womyn's Music Festival with an un-named southern working-class town to suffuse both with what we might call a local queer of color critique. Linking the non-metropolitan upper Midwest to a "no-place" of the rural Deep South, *no mo blues* performed an alternative to chic by staging a northern to southern counter-migration. Channeling this Great Migration of black folk into the urbanized migra-tions of contemporary queer folk, Bridgforth then returned her audience to a regional space within a historical moment hell-bent on the presentism of sartorial amnesia. If this space has too often been imagined as a dump-ing ground for queer urbanism, Bridgforth's performance stories trans-formed it into a historical repository for the démodé.

What this black dyke unfashionability of *no mo blues* offers, finally, is anything but "the latest" that may mark a Barthesian fashion system. It in-stead fashioned a queer anti-urbanism in excess of any fashion-laden urban system past, present, or future. It initiated a return migration to a social space that puts the vendettas of metronormativity into consignment. And it invites you to participate in what Eli Clare, her contemporary, dearly wished for but never found when she called out a few Bay Area dykes a year after *no mo blues* finished its national tour: "fantasies of a rural queer community" (37). Infusing metronormative worlds with some outdated rural flavor, Bridgforth's bulldagga performance art realizes Clare's dream-work when she staged her folk revival. Given a wide berth, Bridgforth's southern stylistics gave back just as good.

5

Queer Infrastructure

Pittsburgh to the East, Philadelphia to the West

Pennsyltucky: those sixty-odd counties that lie outside Pennsylvania's largest two cities and their accompanying suburbs. If a lack of inspiration strikes, you could also refer to it as Pennsylbama. The entire state then becomes—so the tired joke goes—Pittsburgh on the West, Philadelphia on the East, with Kentucky or Alabama in between. The dismissive allusion to these two southern states attests that Pennsyltucky is rarely held up as an epicenter of cultural sophistication. One recent post to the online Urban Dictionary agrees. It defines the region as "rural parts of Pennsylvania with large concentrations of country folk, noted for interest in Hunting, Country Music, NASCAR, trailer life, Wal-Mart, and working at the plant."[1] Another informs the curious that "you are required to own at least two off-road vehicles and if you have a firm grasp of the English language you are considered a homosexual."[2] Almost inadvertently, this latter post finds that Pennsyltucky also fails as an epicenter of queer urbanity. Others have come to the same conclusion. Save for the occasional Pocono cottage rental advertised in *Philadelphia Gay News*, this all-too-imaginary region receives all-too-little notice in lesbian and gay travel guides, history, or art. Often derided as another country, it's the queer equivalent to what a geographer would term nonecumene, one of the uninhabitable spaces that cover our planet.

I introduce the region in this harsh light because it provides a better sense of how one recent artwork—Alison Bechdel's 2006 *Fun Home: A Family Tragicomic*—renegotiates the urban legends swirling about Pennsyltucky to commemorate a speck of this vast terrain for queers. Bechdel sets her graphic memoir in the "narrow compass" of her childhood home of Beech Creek,[3] an economically distressed borough (current pop., 717; 99 percent white) nestled at the edge of the Appalachian Mountains that cut through the state (fig. 5.1).[4] An ambivalent depiction of small-town central Pennsylvania, *Fun Home* primarily recounts the relationship between Bechdel and her father, Bruce, a funeral director and English teacher who died (possibly by suicide) in 1980 when he was hit by a Sunbeam Bread truck while crossing Route 150. The book visualizes and verbalizes Bechdel's response to this deep loss as it dovetails with her gradual self-identification as a lesbian and the sexual mysteries of her ruralized father, who most likely had a series of affairs with young men throughout his short life.[5] Along the way, *Fun Home* courses through the mid-twentieth century to the twenty-first to provide a queer retrospective on Pennsyltucky's "misleading and accurate" provincialism. By proxy, it charts the metronormativity that supports this geographic slur, and its subtitle might well have been *A Study of Provincial Life*.

The memoir's focus on Beech Creek may, at first glance, seem like an anomaly for Bechdel. Prior to *Fun Home*'s publication, the artist was best known for her comic strip *Dykes to Watch Out For*. Influenced by earlier queer graphics such as Howard Cruse's *Gay Comix* as well as *Wimmin's Comix*, Bechdel introduced the strip in 1983 and in 1987 began to trace the lives of a racially diverse, largely urban-based group of women, men, and trans-identified persons that centered on the independent bookstore Mad-Wimmin Books.[6] Following the weekly activities of Mo, Harriet, Clarice, Toni, Jezanna, Thea, Ginger, Sparrow, and Sydney Krukowski, a women's studies professor, *Dykes* was written as Bechdel "watched our liberation movement flower into first a niche market, then a sitcom punchline, then a full-blown sitcom premise."[7] The strip followed all three devolutions and commented on a range of contemporary issues: radical lesbian feminism, gay marriage, AIDS activism, the corporatization of queer culture, suburbanization, the emergence of lesbian, gay, and queer studies in American universities, psycho-pharmaceutics, post-9/11 trauma, online sex, and urban homogenization.[8] Questions of rurality or ruralism, however, rarely appeared.

Nevertheless, my last item on the above list reveals that Bechdel has thought about urbanism and urbanity from the beginning of her published art. In an early vision of *Dykes* Bechdel sketched a strip critical of lesbian metronormativity titled "Look Out! It's Luppies," which was reprinted in 1986 (fig. 5.2). Luppies, an asterisk informs us, stands for Lesbian Urban Professionals, and "Look Out!" urges caution. The strip features three panels. The first presents two nameless women holding hands as one carries a "Bloomies" shopping bag. The ironic commentary to the left of these consumers reads: "Their leather jackets cost seven hundred dollars!!" Subsequent panels ratchet up the satire with sketches of luppies

HIS ULTIMATE OBELISK IS NOT CARVED FROM FLESHY, TRANSLUCENT MARBLE LIKE THE TOMBSTONES IN THE OLD PART OF THE CEMETERY.

MOM COULDN'T CONVINCE THE MONUMENT MAKER TO DO IT.

IT WON'T LAST. IN TEN, TWENTY YEARS YOU'LL HAVE LICHEN, EROSION. TRUST ME, YOU WANT GRANITE.

STRECK Monuments

THE GRANITE IS HANDSOME, CRISP... AND, WELL, LIFELESS.

BRUCE ALLEN BECHDEL 1936 — 1980

ON A MAP OF MY HOMETOWN, A CIRCLE A MILE AND A HALF IN DIAMETER CIRCUMSCRIBES:

(A) DAD'S GRAVE,

(B) THE SPOT ON ROUTE 150 WHERE HE DIED, NEAR AN OLD FARMHOUSE HE WAS RESTORING,

(C) THE HOUSE WHERE HE AND MY MOTHER RAISED OUR FAMILY, AND

(D) THE FARM WHERE HE WAS BORN.

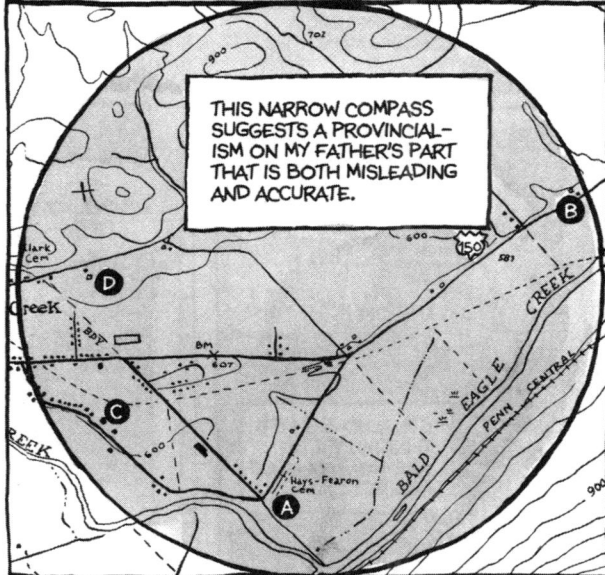

THIS NARROW COMPASS SUGGESTS A PROVINCIAL- ISM ON MY FATHER'S PART THAT IS BOTH MISLEADING AND ACCURATE.

Figure 5.1. Alison Bechdel, from *Fun Home* (2006). © 2006 by Alison Bechdel. Reprinted by permission of Houghton Mifflin Company. All rights reserved.

Figure 5.2. "Look Out! It's Luppies" by Alison Bechdel, from *Dykes to Watch Out For* (1986). © 1986 by Alison Bechdel. All rights reserved.

discussing bond issues over a chilled bottle of wine or conferring about the necessity of a fine-toned gym body: "But what good is the revolution if I'm out of shape when it happens?!"

Eleven years later, Bechdel would feature a panel titled "Demographic Rift" that mapped the metropolitan layout of *Dykes* and its characters' residences (fig. 5.3). Two matters of note about this playful cartography. First: gridded streets on an unnamed city honor prominent queer women such as modernist photographer Berenice Abbott, Djuna Barnes, Sally Miller Gearhart, Joan Nestle, Willa Cather, and Dolores Klaich (author of *Woman + Woman: Attitudes Toward Lesbianism*), as well as public figures such as Eleanor Roosevelt and her companion, Lorena Hickok. Second: travelling westbound through the urban grid of "Demographic Rift" is Interstate 92, a road that, like Cather Avenue or Klaich Avenue, does not yet exist. The numbered interstate was once a proposal for an east-west highway that would run from Burlington, Vermont, to the Canadian border near Calais, Maine, but the Federal Highway Administration shelved the project in 1970.[9] While "Luppies" makes hash of post-Stonewall metronormativity, "Rift" reveals the concrete streets of queer urbanism to always be a mythic fabrication. When readers ask Bechdel, "What city is the comic strip set in? It reminds me so much of Oakland/Jamaica Plain/Seattle/Pittsburgh/ Chicago/Grand Forks," she replies, "I keep the location of *Dykes to Watch Out For* intentionally nonspecific so that readers in Grand Forks can imagine it's happening right there."[10] To supplement this Q & A, *Dyke's* benign urban variation refuses to privilege one geographic space or street over another. It implicitly acknowledges how quickly an instance of urbanism can tip over into a hierarchy of metronormativity.

Fun Home doesn't take swipes at present-day luppies in California (or in North Dakota), but the memoir does continue these gentle critiques to prod the tensions between queer urbanism and devalued social spaces such as Pennsyltucky. Like the "Demographic Rift" panel, it offers numerous allusions to the narratives of modernist and late modern metronormativity—the cruisy gardens of Proust's *Remembrance of Things Past*; Raclyffe Hall's *The Well of Loneliness*; Isabel Archer's cosmopolitan flight in Henry James's *The Portrait of a Lady*; E. M. Forster's pastoralized *Maurice*; and the New York production of Larry Kramer's *The Normal Heart*, among many others. Like *Dyke's* take on Interstate 92, it too thinks critically about the queer uses of infrastructure as they came to bear on the standardization of imaginary lesbian and gay geographies in the post-Stonewall United States.

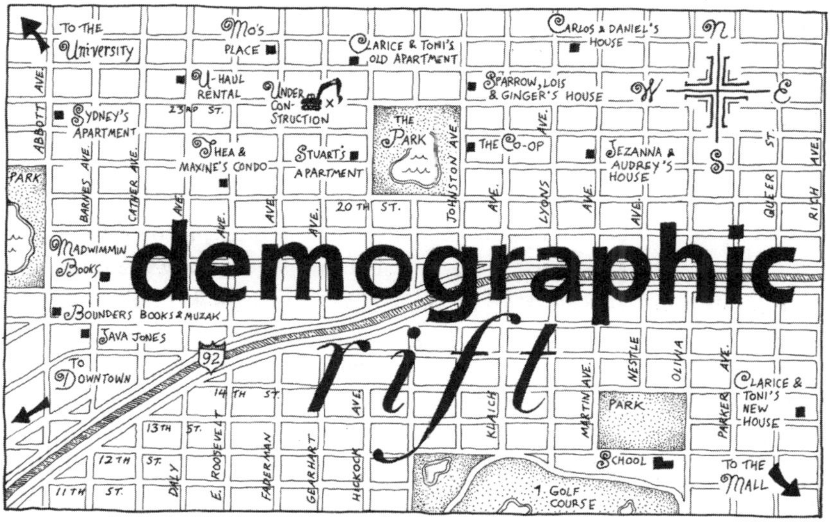

Figure 5.3. "Demographic Rift" by Alison Bechdel, from *Dykes to Watch Out For* (1997). © 1997 by Alison Bechdel. All rights reserved.

In a recent interview, Bechdel notes that: "*Fun Home* is very much about place: this particular part of rural central Pennsylvania, on the edge of the Allegheny Front, where Route 80 got blasted through the isolated valleys in the sixties and seventies. The construction of the interstate during my childhood felt kind of mythic. It was just over the ridge from us, and it ran from New York to San Francisco. Of course I didn't think then of New York and San Francisco as gay poles, but now I see that was part of it."[11]

When Bechdel references New York and San Francisco as "gay poles" linked by Route 80, she recollects ("now I see") the literal and figurative reverberations that infrastructure brought to bear on supposedly "isolated" spaces like "rural central Pennsylvania." Placed in conversation with her earlier *Dyke* drawings, her comments suggest that roadway lore is vital to her takes on queer urbanities past and present. Even the half-page splash panel that "circumscribes" the limited geographies of her father—a mere "mile and a half in diameter"—highlights the importance of Route 150 for Bruce's truncated life narrative, and the memoir's repeated links between put-down Pennsyltucky roads and exalted thoroughfares such as I-80 do more of the same. At these critical junctions, *Fun Home* becomes a rural transit system that grapples with the mythology of metronormative flights as well as the idealized routes (not to mention those much-maligned "in between" places) that these treks too often rely on.

By focusing on a closer reading of this memoir, I thus hope to make some inroads into how "queer infrastructure"—the six-lane highways, the cloverleaves, the county roads, the suspension bridges, the no passing zones, the alleyways, the tollways, the stop signs, the exit ramps—has often formed the base to metronormativity's stylistic superstructure. We have spent a good deal of time in these pages theorizing, historicizing, and countering these stylistics across a variety of media. But I also sense that as much as high modernist books or nationalizing newspapers or Internet chat rooms enable dominant forms of urbanism, so too have the forgotten materials of infrastructure (the gravel, the tar, the asphalt, the buckets of yellow and white paint) enabled imaginary and realized practices of metronormativity to proliferate. Often, critics who question these overbearing forms of lesbian and gay urbanity (myself included) concentrate on the social and aesthetic practices of inclusion or exclusion in an urbane habitus. Here I'd like to use *Fun Home* as a springboard to see what it took to get these spaces, to briefly trace a history of metronormativity's mobility as it dovetailed with evolving forms of U.S. infrastructure, and to finally develop an alternative route as I bring the last chapter of this book to a close.

Roads to Nowhere

When Bechdel finds that the "narrow compass" of Beech Creek "suggests a provincialism on my father's part that is both misleading and accurate," it's misleading because Bruce, in many respects, is a metronormative white gay man who just doesn't live in a city. Though he's "not rich," he enjoys a comfortable middle-class existence and doesn't identify with the straight working-class masculinity that surrounds him (he may, however, deeply desire it) (5). He rural gentrifies with what he considers impeccable taste, "the gilt cornices, the marble fireplace, the crystal chandeliers, the shelves of calf-bound books," the flagstones, the mirrors, the Chippendale furniture, the wallpaper, the gold leaf trim, and the pristine outdoor gardens that help to restore their dilapidated Gothic revival house and its yard (5). He is well-read in Western queer classics by authors such as Colette, and his travels to cities such as Paris, New York City, Cannes, and elsewhere lend him an aura of worldliness. Given these accomplishments, he links up with the pre-Stonewall white gay men mentioned in chapter 2, urbanized males that one Gay Liberation Front activist derided for their "Wedgwood tea cups and chandeliers and . . . fancy clothes and home furnishings."[12] His knack for home décor leads his daughter to wonder: "But it's puzzling why my urbane father, with his unwholesome interest in the decorative arts, remained in this provincial hamlet" (31).

Yet to suggest a provincialism on her urbane father's part is accurate because Bruce doesn't always fit into pre- or post-Stonewall metronormative schemas. First, he's not really urbanized by the surrounding geographies of Appalachia. With Pittsburgh, Philadelphia, and New York City miles away, the largest city in the vicinity is State College, a cosmopolitan university town with a population of about thirty-eight thousand nestled in what locals like to refer to as the Happy Valley. Alongside numerous boroughs and townships, another city (Lock Haven) also neighbors his home in rural central Pennsylvania, yet Bruce nevertheless resides in a region that the narrator believes "historically discouraged cultural exchange" (126). Second, though the artist discovers that her father had male lovers in the army, at school, in Beech Creek, and perhaps in New York, he may not be gay-identified. He was married—unhappily—to his wife until his death, and Michael Moon has hypothesized that Bruce "may have been leading a secret life as an ephebophile (a lover or would-be lover of adolescent males)."[13] Third, even if he was gay-identified, while he may be aesthetically self-standardized into a queer urbanity, he certainly is not linguistically. Bechdel's father may have an urbane style and may surround himself and his family with urbane stylistics signified by chandeliers and shrubs, but he does not have what a linguist might term an urbane stylistic variation.[14] To be crass, he talks like a hick. Bechdel picks up on this when she replays a cassette tape of her father recording a "guided tour of a museum run by the County Historical Society" (133). With the sound of her father's voice playing next to his framed portrait, she recalls: "Listening to the museum-tour tape, I'm surprised by his thick Pennsylvania accent. Despite the refined subject matter, he sounds bumpkinish" (144) (fig. 5.4).

A bumpkin is vernacular for a "simple person from the country."[15] Coined in the eighteenth century to describe rural English laborers, "bumpkin" can also refer to an "awkward country fellow," an "unsophisticated rustic," or a "yokel" who is "not interested in culture."[16] With the adjective "bumpkinish" Bechdel encapsulates her father into a devalued rural stylistic. Given his family background, his "thick" accent resonates with what a dialectologist probably would identify as Scotch-Irish mixed with a touch of the Pennsylvania Dutch, but Bechdel's assessment of his speech is also not that far from the Appalachian stereotypes that have often attached themselves to some residents of Pennsyltucky: hillbilly, ruralized, isolated, culturally illiterate, uncouth.[17] Note two social linguists: "Appalachian English is associated with a rural, stigmatized vernacular at the same time that it may be associated with people's sense of cultural identity."[18] Bechdel's recollection of her father's "bumpkinish" accent thus reveals how "dialect features that were formerly markers of regional speech have been transformed into markers of social class, ethnicity, or urban-rural distinctions,"[19] and Bruce's museum guide infuses itself with the taint of derided backwardness and rusticity that we have seen far too many times in this book. His is a scandalously thick Pennsylvania accent that recalls the scandalously thick Kentucky accent of Robert Reid-Pharr's lover encountered in *Another Country*'s introduction—minus the eroticized adoration or the critical usage. The recording confirms Beech Creek (on the tape Bruce speaks as president of the Clinton County Historical Society) as a "provincial hamlet" or, worse, an unsophisticated "relic area," a geography "where older language features survive after they have disappeared from other varieties of the language."[20]

It's no coincidence that Bechdel, with years of hindsight, places her father's linguistic non-urbanity in close proximity to a yearned-for migration to the city.[21] On the same page above the panel where she identifies her father's voice as "bumpkinish," she sketches Bruce and his family in

IN A SIMILAR KIND OF LANGUAGE FAILURE, IN THE LOCAL DIALECT THE BULLPEN WAS SAID TO BE SITUATED SIMPLY "OUT ON THE MOUNTAIN," THAT IS, ON THE PLATEAU. IN THE PRIMEVAL WILDERNESS BEYOND THE FRONT, SPECIFICITY IS ABANDONED.

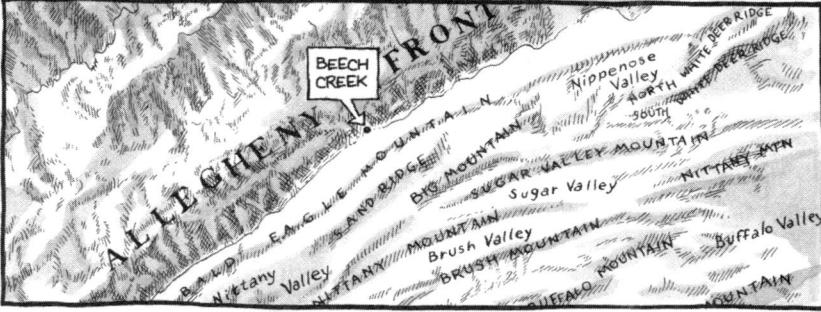

AND HURTLING TOWARD NEW YORK CITY ON ROUTE 80, SPEED AND PAVEMENT ERASED NOT JUST THE NAMES OF THINGS, BUT THE PARTICULAR, INTIMATE CONTOURS OF THE LANDSCAPE ITSELF.

IN THE END, ALTHOUGH THE ANONYMITY OF A CITY MIGHT HAVE SAVED MY FATHER'S LIFE, I CAN'T REALLY IMAGINE HIM ANYWHERE BUT BEECH CREEK.

LISTENING TO THE MUSEUM-TOUR TAPE, I'M SURPRISED BY HIS THICK PENNSYLVANIA ACCENT. DESPITE THE REFINED SUBJECT MATTER, HE SOUNDS BUMPKINISH.

IN THE BACK DISPLAY ROOM IS A FINE, CHERRY HEPPLEWHITE CORNER CUPBOARD OF ABOUT 1790. THIS WAS DONATED BY THE KLECKNER FAMILY OF SUGAR VALLEY. ON THE WALL ARE KITCHEN TOOLS USED BY EARLY FARM FAMILIES IN THE NINETEENTH CENTURY.

Figure 5.4. Alison Bechdel, from *Fun Home* (2006). © 2006 by Alison Bechdel. Reprinted by permission of Houghton Mifflin Company. All rights reserved.

their station wagon driving over the asphalt of Interstate 80. Behind them are diagonal cuts into the Appalachians that mark where the roadway was "blasted through." The caption in the gutter above this panel reads: "And hurtling toward New York City on Route 80, speed and pavement erased not just the names of things but the particular, intimate contours of the landscape itself" (144). The panel's presumption is that Bruce (with wife and children along for the ride) is making a trek to the metropolis, one that could potentially erase the contours of a ruralized Appalachian identity. Hence a tiny illustration-free panel placed beside this one states that "the anonymity of a city might have saved my father's life." Route 80, that is to say, offers her father the opportunity to sidestep regional stigma, eradicate local particularity, and get out of Dodge. As hillbilly vernacular (what the top panel of this page layout terms "language failure") becomes "bumpkinish" recording, it's the new technology of "speed and pavement" that enables a queer to leave the mountains behind. In quick succession, these four interdependent panels reveal successful standardizations to happen via a rural-to–New York City road trip. A trek to the City That Never Sleeps becomes mythologized as a lifesaver. A place like Beech Creek turns into a social death sentence.[22]

Given these graphic associations between automotive flight and freedom, it's worth spending a few paragraphs to rehearse how a brief history of the U.S. interstate—specifically, a brief history of Interstate 80—illuminates the memoir of metronormativity that *Fun Home* tells. We were granted a clue with the introductory block quote, where Bechdel notes that her book is about a place where "Route 80 got blasted through the isolated valleys in the sixties and seventies." Inspired by the German autobahn built before the Second World War (a roadway system that helped rationalize the nation-state and facilitate its genocidal programs), a nationalized U.S. interstate system had been in the works since the first third of the twentieth century. After much wrangling, Congress passed the Interstate Highway Act as well as the Federal-Aid Highway Act under the presidency of Dwight D. Eisenhower in 1956. Both measures provided billions in federal funding for the development of major roadways under the official rubric of an Interstate Highway System. Incorporating other major highways and infrastructures such as the Lincoln Highway, the Ohio Turnpike, and the San Francisco–Oakland Bay Bridge, the system eventually accrued tens of thousands of miles of inter-regional and trans-continental railway, and it continues to expand annually (fig. 5.5).[23] Many of these miles join with the National Highway System, and in 1990 the infrastructure was

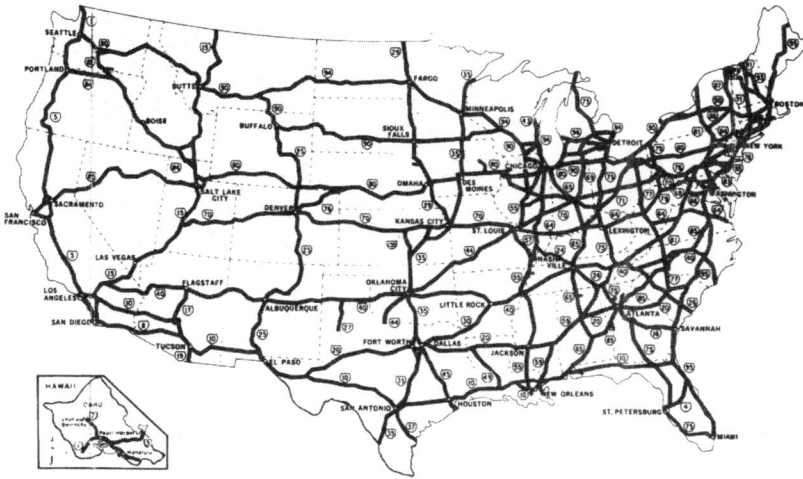

**The Dwight D. Eisenhower System
of Interstate and Defense Highways**

Figure 5.5. Dwight D. Eisenhower National System of Interstate and Defense Highways (1993). Courtesy of the Federal Highway Administration, U.S. Department of Transportation.

renamed the Eisenhower System of Interstate and Defense Highways. An integral part of this system, Interstate 80, was begun in the late fifties and only completed in 1986.[24] Running 2,909 miles, it connects San Francisco, California, to Ridgefield Park, New Jersey. It was, and still is, central to the national mythos as a premier coast-to-coast route, a monument of "speed and pavement" that has yet to receive a historical marker.

Just as mythic for many Pennsylvanians was the state's portion of Interstate 80—officially named the Keystone Shortway—that was begun in 1959.[25] Running west-east from Sharon to East Stroudsburg and paralleling the Pennsylvania Turnpike, the 313 miles of Interstate 80 promised economic prosperity for impoverished rural populations, decreased their supposed isolation, and promoted swift connection to major metropoles. According to a congratulatory brochure distributed by the Keystone Shortway Association in 1970 that touted the road as the fastest route across the state, "the Keystone Shortway opens vast areas to industrial development, provides direct access to previously inaccessible fish and game lands and recreation facilities, and stimulates tourist and vacation travel, particularly in the Pocono Mountains region, 'Pennsylvania's Playground.'"[26] Another proselytizes the Shortway's "inclusion in the Interstate system as a vital link in Interstate 80, a transcontinental highway which one day would be a ribbon of concrete between the nation's two ocean coastlines."[27] Still another exclaims that "the Keystone Shortway after 15 years becomes a reality and an important link in the 3,000–plus non-stop Freeway between the George Washington Bridge in New York and the Golden Gate Bridge in San Francisco."[28]

Likewise, just as mythic for many rural central Pennsylvanians was the Clinton and Centre County portions of I-80 that were officially dedicated on September 17, 1970. Held fifteen miles from Beech Creek at what is now the Milesburg Exit 158, a grand "Highway Week" celebration was organized to commemorate the interstate's completion in the region. A picture taken by the Federal Highway Administration documented the festivities and shows a smattering of individuals who hover around a guardrail (fig. 5.6). The participants stand behind two enormous signposts that signify the nation's poles of East Coast and West. One sign reads, "Interstate 80 West San Francisco 2675 miles;" the other, "Interstate 80 East New York City 230 miles." An observer at the scene later recounted that "when Governor Raymond Shafer fires a flare gun, an electronic signal in the Goodyear blimp overhead is activated, officially opening the Milesburg interchange and the highway."[29] These celebrations were accompanied by local Continental Trailways ads in college newspapers, such as one printed on October 24, 1969 for The Pennsylvania State University, that promised speedy bus trips ("the easiest travel on earth") to New York City (and Boston, Chicago, and Cleveland) with inexpensive "1–way" tickets (fig. 5.7). Together these visuals showcase how "local, county, state and federal" institutions—as well as ruralized towns such as Beech Creek and urbanized areas such as New York City—were thought to conjoin, converge, and conflate via a ribbon of concrete.[30] In the popular imagination, 80 made "accessible" terrain that "historically discouraged cultural exchange." Simultaneously, it directed residents of rural central Pennsylvania toward a paved way to the coasts.

Let's emphasize that "1–way" ticket to New York available for purchase four months after the city's Stonewall riots. This brief history of U.S. interstate infrastructure suggests the imaginary possibilities—when roads like Interstate 80 were akin to a road like Bechdel's I-92—that could realize connections across geographic divides by thrusting queers into a post-Stonewall inter-regional community. And while it may seem strange

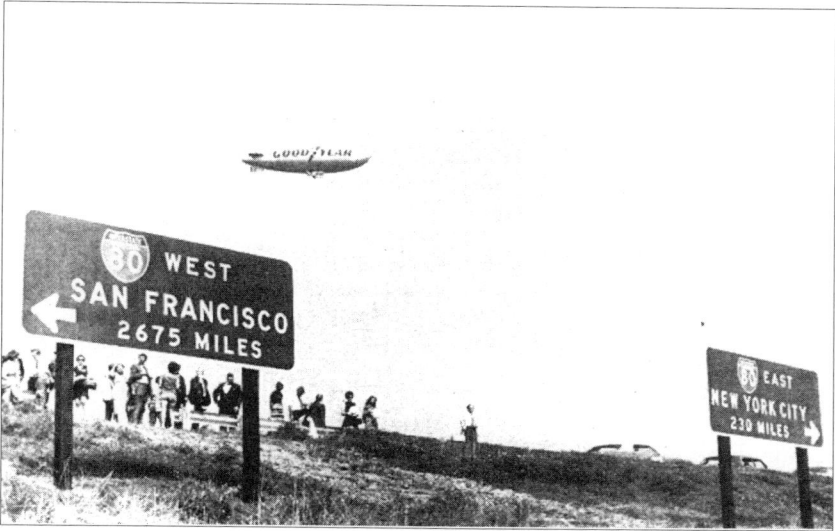

Figure 5.6. (*above*) "Highway Week" celebration at Milesburg, Pennsylvania (1970). Courtesy of the Federal Highway Administration, U.S. Department of Transportation.

Figure 5.7. (*left*) Continental Trailways advertisement. *The Daily Collegian,* October 24, 1969. Courtesy of Collegian Inc. and WH & L Associates LLC.

to think of a road as having a sexual orientation, some of this I-80 my-thology—the mythology of local and regional infrastructure that fed into a nationalized street scene—did lend itself to metronormative iconogra-phies across the nation in the sixties and seventies, and quickly thereafter. I don't want to neglect other forms of transportation such as train, ship, subway, foot, or plane, but I follow Bechdel to highlight that the Inter-state Highway System was part of a larger mythos of coastal and urban-ized connection for many U.S.-based queers.[31] When she recalls that "the construction of the Interstate felt kind of mythic" as it connected the "gay poles" of San Francisco and New York City, her observation suggests how queer infrastructure could facilitate a sense of bicoastality and subcultural standardization that fused "the nation's two ocean coastlines" into a de-sirable destination. It's a material connection of roadways that rivals the newspaper as an Andersonian imagined community, though I'll show in a second that the two also went hand-in-hand.

Though she "did not see then" that the East Coast and the West Coast were "gay poles," this link is no figment of her later imagination: other queers fostered such memory making as the Interstate System was realized over the decades. In fact, Route 80's constant associations with New York City as its easternmost endpoint implicitly linked the interstate to what *Fun Home* sees as another "mythologized flashpoint": the National His-toric Landmark that is the Stonewall Inn, or, to call it by another name, 53 Christopher Street (104). This mythic street address of the 1969 Stone-wall riots was and remains just as important to urbanized U.S. lesbian, gay, and queer mythology (and tourism) as the bar itself, and I do not want us to forget how vital the roadway, its offshoots, and its piers continue to be for queer kids of various colors.[32] Yet for our purposes I highlight that some of the first "gay pride" parades—initially called the Christopher Street Liberation Day March—idealized not just the revolutionary acts that took place at the Stonewall Inn, but also the road outside the water-ing hole.[33] As much as the Stonewall Inn, New York City's Christopher Street and its associated parades were integral to mythic connections be-tween sexual liberation, queer urbanity, and celebrated infrastructures like Route 80 that bound the almost-mile-long Greenwich Village road to the national Interstate System (even though the 80 thoroughfare doesn't cross into New York City or even into the state of New York).

To get a quick sense of how some of these forged links might have oc-curred, consider this 1970 *Advocate* image featured a year or so after the Stonewall riots. The sketch commemorates the first annual Christopher

Figure 5.8. Artist unknown. "Christopher St. Parades East and West." *Advocate*, July 22–August 4, 1970.

Street parades, precursors to later celebrations that would take place across the United States as well as to other Christopher Street Day celebrations in European cities such as Berlin, Frankfurt, Vienna, and Warsaw (fig. 5.8). The drawing features scores of predominantly white men and women waving U.S. flags and carrying posters with titles such as "Gay Is Good" and "1 Out of 6 of You Are One of Us" as they march toward the viewer. On the sidelines of these festivities are well-wishers varying in age and gender. Two "gay poles" rise above these smiling faces. One reads "Hollywood Blvd." and the other "7th St. Christopher St." A banner connects these two street signs with the phrase "Christopher St. Parades East and West." In the background of this action-packed parade are numerous skyscrapers, water towers, balloons, and signs for Greenwich Village shops that urge readers to "Buy Gay." The detailed drawing imagines a queer consumer citizenship that links West Hollywood–Los Angeles to Greenwich Village–New York City–Stonewall, and it is an early hymn to lesbian and gay pride that is also a subtle paean to U.S. metronormativity.

Like the "Highway Week" celebration signs near Beech Creek, this image links spectators to the nationalized (note the stars and stripes) sense of east-west bicoastality that we theorized in chapter 2. Despite their specifics, Los Angeles–West Hollywood and New York City–Greenwich Village appear interchangeable in a sketch that prominently connects two gay-identified roads: as the drawing recedes into the background, these distinct urbanized spaces fuse into one uniform parade. Thus when I study the drawing's crowds, I don't just see a historical record of lesbian and gay empowerment or visibility or liberation; I also see a celebration of two roadway signs that celebrates post-Stonewall urban standardization.[34] Behind this cosmopolitan celebration of urban pride I also see a commemoration of the national infrastructures, such as I-80 or I-44 or I-70 or I-40 or I-10, that connect these two roads together.

What I highlight about this iconic image of queer infrastructure is that its urbanized emphasis on "Parades East and West" offers no legend to account for other travels or expressive roadways. The sense of promise matches the sense of foreclosure, making good on anthropologist Anna Lowenhaupt Tsing's claim that "roads create pathways that make motion easier and more efficient, but in doing so they limit where we go. The ease of travel they facilitate is also a structure of confinement."[35] Here "East and West" roads become "East and West" pride parades become the "gay poles" of Los Angeles and New York City. As it queers U.S. infrastructure into Hollywood Boulevard and Christopher Street, it expels—even as it absorbs and evacuates—other not-so-mythic geographies like a Beech Creek, or a Milesburg, or a Sharon, Pennsylvania. Certain coast-to-coast erasures start to accrue beyond the frame of the drawing, and celebrated streets start to support the stereotype of the rural as a place of isolation, "suspicion, persecution, and secrecy."[36] This is how an intra-regional road like I-80 becomes a supra-regional gateway becomes a one-way ticket to urbanized sexual liberation, and this is "part of" what *Fun Home* is getting at when Bechdel says her memoir is "very much about" a "place" where an interstate "got blasted through in the sixties and seventies."

These verbal and visual histories of mythic East Coast–West Coast infrastructure enable *Fun Home*'s portrayal of Bruce in Beech Creek. We saw this when the memoir links her "bumpkinish" father with the image of a "blasted through" I-80. An earlier series of panels make the connection even more explicit (fig. 5.9). In a minor moment in the narrative, Bechdel features a panel with four captions that mimics an aerial photograph of rural central Pennsylvania topography. The first square balloon states that "Interstate 80 had just been blasted through the ridge beyond ours." The second panel states, "Our house," with an arrow pointing to a dot near Route 150, and the third panel states, "Route 80," with an arrow pointing to two lines that symbolize the highway. These two small panels are placed one on top of the other, as if to suggest their potential proximity. The fourth panel informs readers that "on its way from Christopher Street to the Castro, it passed only four miles from our house—albeit on the other side of Bald Mountain." It's telling that Bechdel uses the "gay poles" of "Christopher Street" and "the Castro" as stand-ins for "San Francisco" and "New York City." Like the *Advocate* cartoon, the panels in toto collapse coastal cities into two roadways that signify the supposed freedom of queer urbanity. Like the Continental Trailways advertisement, the panels see I-80 as the "easiest travel on earth" by idealizing the "glorious thoroughfare" thought to connect San Francisco to New York and the East to the West. In the meantime, however, roads like Route 150 are relegated to the corners of this imaginary frame.

Bechdel often wants her "bumpkinish" father to participate in this narrative of standardized flight, to hop on a bus and make a permanent pilgrimage to Christopher Street. Recall that she feels Interstate 80 "erased not just the names of things, but the particular intimate contours of the landscape itself." Why the "mythologized flashpoint" of 80 "erases," rather than, say, connects, is an interesting word choice. When it is thought to "erase" the Appalachian landscape, the roadway—along with its close associations with Christopher Street and the Castro—levels the idiosyncrasies of ruralized geography that Bruce sometimes typifies. Yet while Bechdel wants her father to make the leap from a devalued social space (call it "Pennsyltucky") to a vaunted one (call it "the big city"), Bruce can't easily extirpate since he seems encircled by the "narrow" compass of a rural central Pennsylvania habitus. Bechdel rationalizes that "perhaps the peculiar topography really did exert some kind of pull" (126), and by voice, inclination, and a resistant topography her father seems stuck despite easy access to a Route 80 flight.

The last panel on the page that presents Interstate 80's "Christopher Street to the Castro" connection to Bechdel's hometown heightens this observation. It features a gutter caption that states: "This massive earthen

Figure 5.9. Alison Bechdel, from *Fun Home* (2006). © 2006 by Alison Bechdel. Reprinted by permission of Houghton Mifflin Company. All rights reserved.

berm [Bald Eagle Mountain] effectively deadened any hint of noise from the glorious thoroughfare . . . " Below this caption is a drawing of Bechdel, her father, and her brothers playing cards as they scan the horizon for the sound of an interstate that they can't hear, "except on still, hot nights when the humidity was particularly conductive" (127). Glancing out to Route 80, Bruce appears to be a bystander to the "glorious" possibilities of an urbanism that pass him by, a queer socially "deadened" by the "massive" Appalachian terrain. For this reason Bechdel later admits that "I can't really imagine him anywhere but Beech Creek" even though she often wants him to treat the borough like a deserted village (144). In sum, he's "stuck in the mud" of the seemingly isolated valleys (54).

If Only

That said, *Fun Home* gradually comes to terms with an urbanist perspective that can only see her father as a rural pity. When Bechdel—who describes herself and Bruce as "inversions of one another"—says that his ruralized stylistics sound "bumpkinish," and when she's stumped by her father's permanent address, her comments imply a value judgment informed by her own ingrained metronormativity (98). Yet much like her critical takes on Route 80, Bechdel seems well aware of these ruralized representations as well as her own urbanized self-characterization. In fact, she points to their origins. On the page opposite her drawing of the museum-tour tape, the artist positions two panels side-by-side. The first shows her as a young woman opening a letter as an unnamed college friend asks, "Who's that from?" She replies, "My dad." The second then shows her university friend heckling Bechdel for her own "bumpkinish" speech ("Your Day-ud?!") when she makes a diphthong out of the word "Dad." She replies curtly, "My Daaad, okay? My DAAAHD." The self-reflexive caption above the first panel informs readers that "by the time he died, I had nearly succeeded in scrubbing those elongated vowels from my own speech" (145). The caption above the second states with bitter irony that "my deracination was kindly abetted by various friends at college" (145). Etymologically, "deracination" means "uprooting," and the word calls to mind the erasures and losses of local particularities as well as the promise of a regionally non-specific cosmopolitanism that universities and colleges too often exemplify. Losing her local accent at college, Alison here recalls the larger erasures of a ruralized Pennsyltucky habitus.

This migration is not, however, only a transplant into a college setting that uproots the artist from Beech Creek. *Fun Home* also suggests that the loss of "those elongated vowels" complements Bechdel's deracination into a self-identified lesbian identity that is just as much a deracination into a queer urbanity "kindly abetted by various friends at college." Significant sections of the memoir record her sexual liberation as a young lesbian feminist at college, and these same-sex explorations also function as assimilations into an urbane queer identity that acculturates the author into what she calls the sexual "underworld" of her university (209). Such assimilations then carry over into New York's queer social spaces where Bechdel moves "after college expecting a bohemian refuge" (107). Her linguistic standardization ("My Daaad, okay?") thus parallels her sexual standardization as the narrator eventually makes her own flight to the city. As she portrays herself, Bechdel is acculturated into what Bourdieu terms a dominant "linguistic habitus," one that the memoir links to a dominant queer habitus denigrating her rural central Pennsylvania dialect.[37] As Bourdieu explains and as Bechdel sketches, this incorporation happens once "the linguistic differences between people from different regions cease to be incommensurable particularisms"—and this practice, I add, is always an acquired taste.[38] "Measured *de facto* against the single standard of the 'common' language," Bourdieu continues, "they are found wanting and cast into the outer darkness of *regionalisms*, the 'corrupt expressions and mispronunciations' which schoolmasters decry. Reduced to the status of quaint or vulgar jargons . . . popular uses of the official language undergo a systematic devaluation."[39] Put otherwise, Bechdel is standardized into an urbane discourse of sexual liberation (of the kind if not the degree that we saw in the above *Advocate* image and others featured earlier in this book) that distances her from the devaluation of Pennsyltucky regionalism—or, to be more accurate, that she learns to distance herself from at college.

We might theorize this education as a regional shame. We might, following the slurs in Urban Dictionary, say that if you have a firm grasp of the standard English language you are considered an urbanized homosexual. It stands to reason, then, that Bechdel narrates much of her memoir as an urbanized queer linguistically and geographically displaced from the "outer darkness" of Pennsyltucky, as a self-identified lesbian whose metronormativity propels her to homogenize her father into the same post-Stonewall narrative that she learned to embrace even as she distances herself from his corrupt geographic expressions. When she leaves her college and returns to Beech Creek for her father's funeral, an older man shakes her hand in condolence and tells her that "the Lord moves in mysterious ways." Bechdel thinks to herself, "I'd kill myself too if I had to live here" (125). Above this panel, she fantasizes acting out at the service and yelling to everyone in attendance: "There's no mystery! He killed himself because he was a manic-depressive, closeted fag and couldn't face living in this small-minded small town one more second" (125). In the pit of grief, she sees Beech Creek as a dead end and Bruce as lost to urban sexual liberation.

Other scenes do likewise as *Fun Home* visualizes how Bruce might have taken up a queer flight to the exalted city and survived, either a pre-Stonewall road trip following his participation in World War II or a post-Stonewall trek following his unsuccessful marriage.[40] Given that Route 80 "passed only four miles" from her home, both stories seem within reach to the narrator as she imagines what might have been done to keep her father alive. A panel below the two funeral scenes tells us that "when I think about how my father's story might have turned out differently, a geographical relocation is usually involved" (125). Idealizing Greenwich Village, she finds New York's urban streets "reduced, like a long-simmering demiglace, to a fragrance of stunning richness and complexity" (103); and she points to "the contact high" of the weeks following the Stonewall riots (104). She tells us that "I imagine my father taking the bus up from college to visit my mother, walking down Christopher Street in his borrowed Brooks Brothers finery"—and all the while cruising a man outside Li-Lac Chocolates store (105).

Likewise, another heartbreaking caption placed over a replication of her father's obituary with the words "Beech Creek" highlighted seven times reads, "If only he'd been able to escape the gravitational tug of Beech Creek, I tell myself, his particular sun might not have set in so precipitate a manner" (125). Though she elsewhere notes that "the Village in the early eighties was a cold, mercenary place" (107) and that "there were many such humiliations in store for me as a young lesbian" (107), she still wants to place her dad in an Interstate 80 mythology that ends at the celebrated Christopher Street, to assimilate him into an urbane social space, and to set him on the road to a gay migration that incorporates him into a tale of metropolitan liberation. But in so doing she again repeats stereotypes of ruralized Appalachia as stagnant, depopulated, and underdeveloped, of "the country a locus of persecution and gay absence."[41]

As Bechdel the narrator sometimes sees her father as a lost opportunity of urban promise, much of her affective labor here hinges on that subjunctive mood "if only." "If only" is sort of like the inverse of a wish fulfillment, "I wish" being another form that the phrase often takes. A wish unfulfilled, it's another way of saying that "what could have been" may have possibly turned into "this would have been." It is a hope for the past that may accompany a faith in the future (as well as a touching wish to keep her father alive), and its grammatical tense technically takes on the apt title of the past perfect. While it may not be future-oriented, "if only" can nevertheless function as a retroactive idealization of the past that is similar yet distinct from nostalgia, an affective state that imagines how things *were* better back then rather than how things *could have been* better back then.

"If only" is thus the photo negative of a melancholic claim such as Michael Warner's that "the sexual culture of New York City serves people around the world, even if only as the distant reference point of queer kids growing up in North Carolina or Idaho, who know that *somewhere* things are different"; but his "if only" statement and Bechdel's "if only" get at the same impulse.[42] Both are displaced mythologies; both allow for possibility production; and both can overlook not what could have been but the opportunities of what was and is. When "if only" is invoked, it's like you're stuck in a land of lost opportunities. While I recognize that this counterfactual can be highly productive, it can also be repetitive in its social generations (cross-reference an urbanized Bechdel's numerous relocations, flights, escapes, road trips, and street scenes for her deceased father in Beech Creek). Though it may implicitly acknowledge what could not have been, "if only" keeps you going but it can get you nowhere fast. It can be the equivalent of a narratological roundabout, or what Bechdel elsewhere terms the "peculiarly literal cul de sac" where she repeatedly finds herself trying to fantasize "if only" Bruce had "been able to escape" into a standardized Route 80 flight (197).

I've also hinted that there's something going on about loss and mourning—and the accompanying theme of being stuck in incorporation—when *Fun Home* tries to entertain the failed promise of "if only" for Bechdel's father. I mean incorporation in three interrelated senses: civic, communal, and psychoanalytic. By civic, I refer to the incorporation of a town that grants a geographic space its own municipal government and is recognized as such by its citizenry and by state and federal agencies such as the U.S. Census Bureau (which we discussed in this book's introduction). By communal incorporation, I refer to the gathering of many into one. Specifically, I refer to incorporation as a form of collective standardization into a national imaginary via queer infrastructures such as Interstate 80. I finally refer to incorporation as a psychic process. According to psychoanalytic critics Jean Laplanche and Jean-Bertrand Pontalis, incorporation is a "process whereby the subject, more or less on the level of phantasy, has an object penetrate his body and keep it 'inside' his body. . . . Incorporation provides the corporal model for introjection and identification."[43]

It is here that *Fun Home* connects the social histories of U.S. queer infrastructure with the psychic histories and unacknowledged losses of pre- and post-Stonewall U.S. metronormativity. It puts the artist's "if only" in dialogue with other theorists of lesbian, gay, and queer incorporation, particularly Judith Butler, who has built on Freud to theorize the queer operations of "melancholic *incorporation*" (134).[44] In classic psychoanalytic theory, melancholic incorporation is the antithesis of mourning. According to Freud, mourning involves the conscious and unconscious recognition that an object has been lost and is no longer in the external world. This external object may, however, be incorporated into a person's internal reality through the labor of grieving. In this act of grief, the ego phantasmatically consumes the lost object, incorporates it into the psyche, and invests in other external objects over time. In what the psychoanalyst calls "a withdrawal of libido from this object and the displacement of it on to a new one," you eventually move on after "the command of reality-testing."[45]

In melancholia, however, you're stuck in the mud. The subject never consciously or unconsciously recognizes the loss of this external object. I again turn to Freud: "But the free libido was not displaced on to another object; it was withdrawn into the ego. There, however, it was not employed in any unspecified way, but served to establish an identification of the ego with the abandoned object. Thus the shadow of the object fell upon the ego, and the latter could henceforth be judged by a special agency, as though it were an object, the forsaken object."[46] In this set-up, melancholia is the absence of mourning, a narcissistic refusal to let go as the subject self-identifies with the lost object in what Freud normalizes here as "pathological mourning."[47]

Freud himself would later complicate and revise his thesis on frozen grief;[48] and Butler too advances these theories by finessing them, arguing that melancholia may be a pit stop to mourning rather than its botched kin. She contends that in mourning, "giving up the object becomes possible only on the condition of a melancholic internalization or . . . a melancholic incorporation" (134). She then applies this premise to gender theory to suggest that a heterosexual identification—which for her can include a stubborn masculine or feminine identification—is melancholic in nature since it refuses to mourn "the loss of homosexual objects and aims" even though this identification may achieve a melancholic incorporation with the homosexual object (139). Hence "we might expect a culturally prevalent form of melancholia, one which signals the internalization of the ungrieved and ungrievable homosexual cathexis" (139). Notably, for Butler, this psychic process can also apply to queers. She cites a "gay melancholia, a loss which cannot be recognized and, hence, cannot be mourned" with regards to heterosexual incorporations (149), yet she also insists that "gay melancholia" can collectively produce affect "that can be translated into political expression," featured in public memorials such as the NAMES Project Quilt (147–48).[49]

Or an *Advocate* ad. Or a quote from Edmund White. Or a Christopher Street Liberation Day March. Or a Keystone Shortway. Or a graphic memoir. Or a book on queer anti-urbanism. Butler remarks that "melancholy spatializes. One might profitably read the Freudian topography that melancholy occasions as precisely such a spatialized landscape of the mind" (174), a landscape that she elsewhere terms "psychic topography" (196). This "spatialized landscape" of queer mourning and melancholia returns us to the theme of incorporation as a keystone of subcultural geography and collective identification with national standardization. It brings to mind the urbanization and incorporation of a dominant queer habitus (always a conscious and unconscious process for Bourdieu) that Bechdel repeatedly portrays when she presents scenarios of the "if only." A "spatialized landscape"—which could describe a psyche, a small town, a big city, an interstate, or a work of art—also enables us to see that queer identifications are often just as dependent on geographic identifications that involve phantasmatic forms of opportunity lost and gained, disavowal and displacement, conscious and unconscious renunciation. If heterosexual and homosexual identity formations are "not dispositions" but "indeed accomplishments," then so too are the urban and rural identifications of someone like Bechdel and her "Day-ud" (or the flag wavers in an *Advocate* Christopher Street East and West parade) (135). This is especially so if we accept Kath Weston's claim that "urban/rural contrasts have structured the very *subjectivity* that allows people [in the United States] to think of themselves or others as gay" (emphasis added).[50]

At the beginning of this book I claimed that ruralized U.S. geographies are the potentially unincorporated (and often positively disavowed) queer spaces in any spatialized story that lesbian and gay urbanity likes to tell itself. Playing with this theoretical set-up of a "gender melancholy" that Butler introduces (140), could we also imagine a geography melancholy and risk speaking of the collective incorporations of urbanized queer life? Throughout these pages I have concentrated on the cultural poetics and practices of queer anti-urbanism that inhibit metronormativity: the paintings, the photos, the journals, the novels, the performances. With my end in sight, I want to briefly suggest that these concepts also have psychic lives. If place and personhood are as much psychic experience as they are concrete and steel, deep hollow and shallow creek, what disavowals have to take place to perpetually imagine U.S. queer life as an urbanized landscape? Has an urbanized queer made an unconscious and foreclosed identification with whatever counts for the rural once the rubber meets the asphalt?

While I am wary of seeing such questions as a royal road to any queer unconscious (Butler notes that her own theoretical scenarios are "hyperbolic" [147]), I have to wonder if someone who has assimilated their "very subjectivity"—in whole, in part—into metronormativity has also incorporated the rural into an interior landscape that they must strive to disavow. This may be but one reason why the rural is often fetishized as much it is dismissed (see the 2005 tearjerker phenomenon of *Brokeback Mountain* for one example; see the spike in urban cowboy motifs at the height of lesbian and gay urban migrations in the 1970s for another), and it may enable us to see an urban gay pride celebration like the Christopher Street Parade or a roadway like I-80 in a new psychoanalytic light. Scenes of myth making for U.S. queers since the 1970s and now for many across the globe, these "mythologized flashpoints" may be unconscious wakes for the lost possibility of rural queer identification. They may be structured and haunted by "if only."

When I put matters this way, I'm trying to return us to how fantasies structuring "the psychological journey" to a big city tie into fantasies structuring "the physical" dimensions of metronormativity mentioned by Halberstam at the beginning of this book.[51] I don't want us to neglect the psychic processes of those who pivot between—or who stand outside—a ruralized and an urbanized identification; those who haven't completely succeeded in "scrubbling those elongated vowels" from their speech; and those who may live in an urbanized area yet consciously fail to incorporate themselves into a metronormative milieu. Others besides Butler have thought about these psychic variations, notably genderqueer and disability activist Eli Clare, who wonders if "it is as simple as still feeling like a country hick—with all of its class implications—in the city? In any case, it leaves me feeling queer in the queer community" (39).[52] Join the club. Moving from the town of Port Orford, Oregon, to Oakland, California, she confesses that "I hate the cost, hate the kind of exile I feel" when she assimilates herself into the middle-class milieu of urbane lesbianism (43). She also observes that a "commercial extravaganza" such as the twenty-fifth anniversary of the Stonewall riots "strikes me not so much as a celebration of a powerful and life-changing uprising of queer people, led by transgendered people of color, by drag queens and butch dykes, fed up with the cops, but as a middle- and upper-class urban party that opened its doors only to those who could afford it" (39).

With this class critique launched, Clare thinks that maybe it's best to approach the complexities of late modern queer urbanization with "a sense of allegiance and connection—however ambivalent—to the place left behind, an attitude of mourning rather than of good riddance" (32). For Clare, such ambivalent mourning takes the form of two unanswerable questions. First: "Is queer identity worth the loss?" Second: "How do we deal with the loss?" (37). Given its keen focus on the traumatic loss of Bechdel's "bumpkinish" father, the loss of her Appalachian accent, the loss of her incorporated town, the loss of her rural central Pennsylvania habitus, and the spatialized landscapes of Greenwich Village and Beech Creek, these may also be the central questions that *Fun Home* begs us to consider.

Alt-Routes

I think that Bechdel—no stranger to queer studies, as references to *Social Text* and the Modern Language Association in *Dykes to Watch Out For* attest—has thought long and hard about these theoretical matters, so let's conclude this book with those two set pieces of urbanized standardization that the memoir introduces: the linguistic "scrubbing of elongated vowels" at college and the infrastructure erasures of "the particular, intimate contours of the landscape itself." I earlier argued that both forms of leveling foster post-Stonewall metronormativity. But there's another way to read them as testaments—rather than as disavowals—of deep loss. As *Fun Home* moves to its close and as Bechdel presents a closing image of her father ready to catch a leaping Alison in a swimming pool, it increasingly ponders "the complexity of loss itself" (120). It also starts to sense that Bruce may not easily fit into any physical or psychological rural-to-urban flight.

A string of images in the memoir's last chapter depicts this working through (fig. 5.10). Over the course of one full page, Bechdel features herself in four panels. In each she rides her bike through the streets of lower Manhattan. In the first panel, readers witness her lock her bike next to a pole wheatpasted with posters for a Public Theater performance of *The Normal Heart* and a notice for an AIDS Candlelight Memorial March. Above this sketch Bechdel writes, "Or maybe I'm trying to render my senseless personal loss meaningful by linking, however posthumously, to a more coherent narrative." The next sketch shows Bechdel riding her bike on a street in the city and features no caption. The third sketch reveals her destination—the Christopher Street piers—and provides readers with an illustrated long shot of the piers with Bechdel and other visitors in silhouette. The caption above states, "A narrative of injustice, sexual shame and fear, of life considered expendable," with another caption at the bottom of the sketch that reads, "It's tempting to say that, in fact, this is my father's story." The final panel shows Bechdel smoking on this spatialized landscape and glancing across the Hudson River into New Jersey. The caption above states: "There's a certain emotional expedience to claiming him as a tragic victim of homophobia. But that's a problematic line of thought." Another caption admits that "for one thing, it makes it harder for me to blame him." Arriving at the end of Interstate 80, so to speak, Bechdel ponders what her father's life was rather than how "my father's story could have turned out differently." At these moments she unhinges her father's narrative from the larger tale of a liberating rural-to-urban flight.

At the edge of the Christopher Street piers Bechdel liberates her father from the "more coherent narrative" of metronormativity that we've being developing for several chapters: she can't easily incorporate her dad into the nationalized narratives that queer infrastructure typically demands. At the tail end of *Fun Home*, the narrator writes: "'Erotic truth' is a rather sweeping concept. I shouldn't pretend to know what my father's was" (230). She then follows this revelation—one that inverts her earlier fantasy that "There's no mystery! He killed himself because he was a manic-depressive, closeted fag"—with one of the memoir's most important lines: "Perhaps my eagerness to claim him as 'gay' in the way I am 'gay,' as opposed to bisexual or some other category, is just a way of keeping him to myself—a sort of inverted Oedipal complex" (230). "Keeping him to myself" is one way of incorporating her father into a larger melancholic narrative of queer urbanity, and it resonates with a younger Bechdel's claim

OR MAYBE I'M TRYING TO RENDER MY SENSELESS PERSONAL LOSS MEANINGFUL BY LINKING IT, HOWEVER POSTHUMOUSLY, TO A MORE COHERENT NARRATIVE.

A NARRATIVE OF INJUSTICE, OF SEXUAL SHAME AND FEAR, OF LIFE CONSIDERED EXPENDABLE.

IT'S TEMPTING TO SAY THAT, IN FACT, THIS **IS** MY FATHER'S STORY.

THERE'S A CERTAIN EMOTIONAL EXPEDIENCE TO CLAIMING HIM AS A TRAGIC VICTIM OF HOMOPHOBIA. BUT THAT'S A PROBLEMATIC LINE OF THOUGHT.

FOR ONE THING, IT MAKES IT HARDER FOR ME TO BLAME HIM.

Figure 5.10. Alison Bechdel, from *Fun Home* (2006). © 2006 by Alison Bechdel. Reprinted by permission of Houghton Mifflin Company. All rights reserved.

that "there's no mystery!" when it comes to making sense of her father's death on Route 150 in Beech Creek.

This is a perfectly understandable and often vital way of moving through queer worlds. Yet when Bechdel the narrator returns to her father's "senseless personal loss" almost twenty years later (196), she sees another way of keeping Bruce to herself that does not violate her father's particularity or place him in a standardized rural-to-urban flight. With an ambivalent "perhaps," she recognizes that this other way involves a complicated form of mourning. Hence her sadder but wiser recognition that an urbanized identification with her father may be unfeasible pitches her past earlier attempts at metropolitan reclamation, and it provides us with a different take on her previous observation that "in the end, although the anonymity of a city might have saved my father's life, I can't really imagine him anywhere but Beech Creek" (144). Moving through the psychic repetitions of "if only" that structure her previous melancholic representations, she senses that Bruce may have also belonged in Beech Creek, not only at the celebrated piers of lower Manhattan's Christopher Street.

This inability to envision a ruralized queer anywhere else may seem like a deep failure of imagination. It's not. Losing her grasp on this lost object may be disappointing, but it's not devastating. In place of a standardized narrative, Bechdel offers readers something ambivalent and something new: the chance to witness a queer wrestle with the aftershocks of assimilation into post-Stonewall metronormativity—and then try to wrestle out of it. Through word and image she thus stages "the processes that are needed to *undo* introjection, idealization, or identification" when it comes to the urbanities that often center around New York City.[53] What's remarkable, then, is how the book learns to tolerate the uncertainties of why people live where they do. This is what I meant when I earlier wrote that *Fun Home* grapples with metronormative flights and the idealized routes that these treks rely on. Since her father can't be incorporated into the psychotypography of queer urbanity, her object of study goes off in a different direction than planned. She soon lets go of the temptation "to say, that, in fact, this is my father's story," and she mourns not just Bruce, but the urbane foreclosures that cast ruralized areas like Beech Creek as the outer darkness.

I don't think in any way that these losses are equal, and I don't want to present them as such in my reading, but I do nevertheless want to stress the geographic unconscious of the memoir that often associates them together. Hence when the overall arc of *Fun Home* return-migrates to "rural central Pennsylvania" and revisits life with her father (and her other family members) in Beech Creek, the story stops entertaining the idealized bounty of the queer metropolis that has been typified by Christopher Street for the past four decades. Its disenchantment comes to terms with the "stunning richness and complexity" of other geographic narratives and stylistics; and, like a second-growth forest, other supposedly inaccessible scenes begin to crop up (103). Perversely, it is Bechdel's father—a specialist in salvage and a high school teacher—who may have coached his daughter into this urban de-idealization before his death. In a letter from Bruce to Alison that *Fun Home* reproduces verbatim, he responds to his daughter's coming out at college and writes: "You ɑknow I was never even in New York until I was about twenty. But even seeing it then was not quite a revelation. There was not much in the Village that I hadn't known in Beech Creek" (212). In this double back, he teaches her how to recoup those left by the proverbial roadsides of U.S. metronormativity, to memorialize those disparaged subjectivities—so often figured as unconscious afterthoughts—that didn't or couldn't or wouldn't make the revelatory migration.

A visual act of mourning the loss of her father as well as the loss of geography, *Fun Home* is a record of this struggle to reoccupy "in between" space. As it cuts through the 1950s to the twenty-first century, it is as much a response to the present as it is a remembrance of things past, and the metro-norms that enable it are the very ones that it tries to shuck. This is not to over-sentimentalize or romanticize or to neglect the memoir's keen attention to U.S. social history and socioeconomics. Bechdel never forgets that the streams of Beech Creek are polluted by years of unbridled coal mining; she emphasizes that Bruce was a neglectful father; and her critically queer anti-urbanism acknowledges that a place like her distressed hometown, though somewhat conducive for her dad, is certainly by no means for other races, ethnicities, genders, and classes.

But in the graphic's "tricky reverse narration" where her "bumpkinish" father—not Interstate 80—becomes "kind of mythic," *Fun Home* detours through "glorious" infrastructure and tries to get back to something like an alternate route. It then starts to pick up other objects besides a Christopher Street or a Stonewall, and it visualizes a bypass for an interstate so integral to Bechdel's burgeoning sense of the "gay poles" that continue to haunt queerness in the United States. This is to say that Beech Creek's Route 150 doesn't necessarily have to catch up with I-80 (fig. 5.11). It can go north, cross into Lock Haven, and then connect with Route 220 North

Figure 5.11. I-80/Route 220 signpost outside Bellefonte, Pennsylvania (2009). Photograph by author.

up through New Albany to end at Waverly, New York. With the Keystone Shortway crossing over "the massive earthen berm," it can also go south to hook up with ALT Route 220 and cut through other towns such as Harper, Virginia; Roanoke, Virginia; Cumberland, Maryland; Greensboro, North Carolina; and Rockingham, North Carolina, for approximately 537 miles.

You might read this as a road to nowhere, a dead end, a cul-de-sac. You might also see it—along with the countless other highways and byways that have received scant mention in an urbane queer topography—as a much-needed detour. There are many push-pull factors here. There is every which way. Some people have to leave; some folks never do; some come back; some don't. It's the disavowal of these supposedly out of the way spaces and the foreclosure of their associated stylistics that will continue to warrant my concern. I know full well that there will never be a Route 220 Day to celebrate every sweltering summer. I doubt there will be a Route 150 Parade anytime soon (so does *Fun Home*). I also know that while a sliver of New York State—once two by thirteen miles of Native field and marsh—was the start of this book, such a sweeping concept does not have to be its end. This may involve the slightest twist of your compass. By design more than necessity, a change in fault need not be a seismic shift.

Coda

On the Borderlands of the Midwest

SOMEWHERE IN A small town in the Midwest—let's call it Plainville, USA—there is a mobile home park near an interstate exit. Among the many working-class whites, there is a trailer rented out by a young Mexican migrant from a town "two hours south from Mexico City. It's a very, very small town. It's not like the city. I'm not sure how many people, but it's a very, very small town." He lives with his friend and both work in a local service industry. They've been doing this for over a decade, as have so many others: "There's fifteen to twenty gay and lesbian Mexicans, and I'm very surprised because every time you find out somebody else is a gay Mexican and they're like 'our group is getting bigger and bigger' because all of us know that it's now okay for other people, other gay Mexicans. We support each other. All these people that we know, like, we have our group. We go out. We all go out all together and have fun. We take care of each other, and we support ourselves. We feel like we're growing a little population."

Once a month, he and his friends drive to a midwestern metropolis for *Noche Latina* at a big gay club in what some would call a big gay village. But when they dance, they don't dance metronormative: "We're so many. We are so many. At that time, our music, our culture, everything from us is in a bar. You could feel everything—the music, the culture, the people. You had no problems to talk to anybody if you wanted to meet them. It's your own language, its people, your town, even your town." Once a month, a small piece of this big gay club turns into a very small Mexican town. It may or it may not be "your town," but for a few short hours the shock of recognition makes it his. Sometimes he and his friends stay in the city overnight, sometimes not. Most have to be back by noon for work in Plainville. This is where Mexican *ambiente* rusticates a few square feet of the nation. For these specialists in rural-to-rural, rural-to-urban, and urban-to-rural migrations, it's less an arrival on any queer urban scene than its exploit. Call it work in progress.

I want to tell you more, but human subjects ethical guidelines prohibit me from revealing further details about undocumented or "clandestine" laborers in the United States for rightful fear of an Immigration and Customs Enforcement raid. Suffice it to say that when a big city club turns into something less than a *zona rosa* and something more than a small town gay bar, the aims of this book are realized—and then some. Throughout *Another Country*, I gleaned metronormativity from modernist literatures and paintings; nationalizing newspapers and glossies; fashion schemas of Cold War lesbian bar cultures; online chat rooms; and pre-Stonewall interstates that dead-end at post-Stonewall Christopher Street parades. I listened to the queers who debunked these urban legends, and I highlighted a few devalued spaces such as the central Pennsylvania Appalachians; a northern California commune; the rural Midwest of Nebraska, Kansas, and Iowa; northeastern Alabama; and the Mississippi Delta bayou. I focused on how these imaginary geographies engaged with several geographies in Los Angeles, New York City, San Francisco, Paris, Berlin, and southern Italy. And while I concentrated primarily on the intra-national, the regional, and the intra-regional aspects of these spaces, locales such as Paris and a "very, very small town in Mexico" suggest that queer ruralization both underlines and extends beyond U.S. borders. A national frame, I mean to say, is indispensable and sometimes insufficient. Moves between nations will always complement internal migrations, and scholars have been paying attention to the interplay between the two for quite some time.[1] I want to add that not all these movements end or have to end in whatever may count for a city, and I hope that the resistances to dominant forms of urbanism that I have presented contribute to these discussions.

This is just to give ourselves a gentle reminder: there are countless "ways of falling off the gay-world map without actually dying."[2] I opened this book with a quote by Edmund White on the "clothes and haircuts and records and dance steps and decor" that he believes a certain kind of New Yorker typifies. It was clear that White saw urbane stylistics as cultural ambassadors importing metronormativity to ruralized queers once "our restlessly evolving style" "soon enough becomes theirs."[3] But the fellows in Plainville (an Army of Lovers, no?) stall out this standard story. The above anecdote—and the preceding chapters—showcase the many ruralized stylistics to be found in raggedy-ass clothing, in RFD queendom, in sho-lo haircuts, in bumpkinish memoirs, in not-so-slick oil paintings, in molasses-thick Kentucky accents, in plain and crude do-it-yourself journals, in downtown nightclubs, in hillbilly farmhouses, and in the double-wide trailers that pockmark the Deep South, the Midwest, the valleys of Appalachia, and well beyond.

For a century plus, these innovative cartographies have been making every space—not always the metropolis—a Lesbian and Gay space. Every street a part of our sexual geography. A city and a country of yearning and then total satisfaction. Another city and another country were we can be safe and free and, well, I dunno, more.

Notes

Introduction

1. Michael Warner, *The Trouble with Normal: Sex, Politics, and the Ethics of Queer Life* (New York: The Free Press, 1999), 190.

2. Warner, "Tongues Untied: Memoirs of a Pentecostal Boyhood," in *Curiouser: On the Queerness of Children*, ed. Steven Bruhm and Natasha Hurley (Minneapolis: University of Minnesota Press, 2004), 216.

3. Queer Nation, "An Army of Lovers Cannot Lose," in *The Queer Nation Manifesto* (New Haven, CT: Beloved Disciple Press, 1997), 5.

4. Didier Eribon, "The Flight to the City," in *Insult and the Making of the Gay Self*, trans. Michael Lucey (Durham, NC: Duke University Press, 2004), 19.

5. Elizabeth Lapovsky Kennedy and Madeline D. Davis, *Boots of Leather, Slippers of Gold: The History of a Lesbian Community* (New York: Penguin, 1993), 35.

6. Warner, "Something Queer about the Nation-State," in *Publics and Counterpublics* (New York: Zone Books, 2002), 210, 211.

7. "Urban," *Webster's New World College Dictionary*, ed. Michael Agnes, 4th ed. (Foster City, CA: IDG Books Worldwide, 2001).

8. "Rural," *Oxford English Dictionary*, http://www.oed.com/ (accessed July 31, 2007).

9. "Urban," *Oxford English Dictionary*, http://www.oed.com/ (accessed July 31, 2007).

10. "Census 2000 Urban and Rural Classification," http://www.census.gov/geo/www/ua/ua_2k.html (accessed August 16, 2007).

11. "Alphabetically Sorted List of UAs," http://www.census.gov/geo/www/ua/ua2k.txt (accessed August 16, 2007).

12. This observation builds on earlier findings by Michael M. Bell, "The Fruit of Difference: The Rural-Urban Continuum as a System of Identity," *Rural Sociology* 57.1 (1992): 65–82; and R. E. Pahl, "The Rural-Urban Continuum," *Sociologia Ruralis* 6.3 (1966): 299–329. Both argue that any urban/rural divide is no less material even as it functions as social fantasy. Such claims allow us to negotiate repeated attempts to define the historical shifts and definitional alterations in concepts such as "the metropolis," "the metropolitan," and the "non-urban" across decades of interdisciplinary scholarship. For but five accounts of these endeavors, see Joel Garreau, "Edge Cities," *Landscape Architecture* 78.8 (1988): 51–55; John

Fraser Hart, "The Perimetropolitan Bow Wave," *Geographical Review* 81.1 (1991): 35–51, on the concept of "the fringe city," as well as Hart, *The Rural Landscape* (Baltimore: Johns Hopkins University Press, 1998), 328–30; Robert Bruegmann, *Sprawl: A Compact History* (Chicago: University of Chicago Press, 2005), on the concept of "exurbia," or "the very low-density region beyond the regularly built suburbs that is still economically and socially tied back to the central cities" (80); and Mike Davis, *Planet of Slums* (London: Verso, 2006), on "megacities" with populations over eight million and "hypercities" with populations over twenty million (5).

13. The term "queer urbanities" was first coined by Michèle Aina Barale, "Queer Urbanities: A Walk on the Wild Side," in *Queer Diasporas*, ed. Cindy Patton and Benigno Sánchez-Eppler (Durham, NC: Duke University Press, 2000), 204–14. See also David Bell and Jon Binnie, *The Sexual Citizen: Queer Politics and Beyond* (Cambridge: Polity Press, 2000), 84.

14. Robert McRuer, *The Queer Renaissance: Contemporary American Literature and the Reinvention of Lesbian and Gay Identities* (New York: New York University Press, 1997), 69; and Kath Weston, *Long Slow Burn: Sexuality and Social Science* (New York: Routledge, 1998), 32.

15. See McRuer, *Renaissance*; Weston, *Long Slow Burn*; Michael Moon, "Whose History? The Case of Oklahoma," in *A Queer World: The Center for Lesbian and Gay Studies Reader*, ed. Martin Duberman (New York: New York University Press, 1997), 24–34; John Howard, *Men Like That: A Southern Queer History* (Chicago: University of Chicago Press, 1999); Lisa Duggan, *Sapphic Slashers: Sex, Violence, and American Modernity* (Durham, NC: Duke University Press, 2000); Judith Halberstam, *In a Queer Time and Place: Transgender Bodies, Subcultural Lives* (New York: New York University Press, 2005); José Esteban Muñoz, "Impossible Spaces: Kevin McCarty's *The Chameleon Club*," *GLQ* 11.3 (2005): 427–36; Robert Reid-Pharr, *Black Gay Man: Essays* (New York: New York University Press, 2001); E. Patrick Johnson, *Sweet Tea: Black Gay Men of the South—An Oral History* (Chapel Hill, NC: University of North Carolina Press, 2008); Elizabeth A. Povinelli, *The Empire of Love: Toward a Theory of Intimacy, Genealogy, and Carnality* (Durham, NC: Duke University Press, 2006); Beth Bailey, *Sex in the Heartland* (Cambridge, MA: Harvard University Press, 1999); Sharon P. Holland, *Raising the Dead: Readings of Death and (Black) Subjectivity* (Durham, NC: Duke University Press, 2000); Craig Womack, *Red on Red: Native American Literary Separatism* (Minneapolis: University of Minnesota Press, 1999); Jasbir K. Puar, *Terrorist Assemblages: Homonationalism in Queer Times* (Durham, NC: Duke University Press, 2007), 69–71; Mary Pat Brady, *Extinct Lands, Temporal Geographies: Chicana Literature and the Urgency of Space* (Durham, NC: Duke University Press, 2002), 90; and Sherrie A. Inness, "Lost in Space: Queer Geography and the Politics of Location," in *Queer Cultures*, ed. Deborah Carlin and Jennifer DiGrazia (Upper Saddle River, NJ: Pearson Prentice Hall, 2004), 254–77.

16. See *Carryin' On in the Lesbian and Gay South*, ed. John Howard (New York: New York University Press, 1997); *Reclaiming the Heartland: Lesbian and Gay Voices from the Midwest*, ed. Karen Lee Osborne and William J. Spurlin (Minneapolis: University of Minnesota, 1996); *De-Centring Sexualities: Politics and Representations Beyond the Metropolis*, ed. Richard Phillips, Diane Watt, and David Shuttleton (London: Routledge, 2000); James Baldwin, *Another Country* (1962; New York: Vintage, 1992); Randall Kenan, *A Visitation of Spirits* (New York: Grove Press, 1989), and *Let the Dead Bury Their Dead, and Other Stories* (New York: Harcourt, Brace, 1992); Dorothy Allison, *Bastard Out of Carolina* (New York: Penguin, 1992), and *Trash: Stories* (Ithaca, NY: Firebrand Books, 1988); Toni Morrison, *Sula* (New York: Knopf, 1973); Eli Clare, *Exile and Pride: Disability, Queerness, and Liberation* (Cambridge, MA: South End Press, 1999); Alison Bechdel, *Fun Home: A Family Tragicomic* (New York: Houghton Mifflin, 2006); and Gloria Anzaldúa, *Borderlands/La Frontera: The New Mestiza* (San Francisco: Aunt Lute Books, 1987).

17. Samuel L. Delany, *Times Square Red, Times Square Blue* (New York: New York University Press, 2001), traces the stereotype of the rural as a geography of hate, violence, and hostility to discuss the "provincial and absolutely small-town terror of cross-class contact" (153). See Arlene Stein, *The Stranger Next Door: The Story of a Small Community's Battle Over Sex, Faith, and Civil Rights* (Boston: Beacon Press, 2001), for a reparative reading of a rural Oregon town ("Timbertown") and its relationship to these issues in the 1990s. And see Osha Gray Davidson, *Broken Heartland: The Rise of America's Rural Ghetto* (Iowa City: University of Iowa Press, 1990), for a discussion of rural poverty in the U.S. Midwest from the Second World War onward.

18. Duggan, *Sapphic Slashers*, 124.

19. Povinelli, *Empire*, 3.

20. Reid-Pharr, *Black Gay Man*, 9. For more on Reid-Pharr's complex regional identifications to the U.S. South (particularly North Carolina), see *Once You Go Black: Choice, Desire, and the Black American Intellectual* (New York: New York University Press, 2007), 172–74.

21. There is, of course, a third term that both disrupts and stabilizes the rural/urban binary, one that plays a vital role in queer representational life in the United States: suburbia. While I do not concentrate on suburban-identified queers in this book, I hypothesize that many of its theories regarding urbanity and rurality may potentially apply to suburban negotiations of lesbian and gay metro-norms. For book-length accounts of queer suburbia outside the established vicinities of Los Angeles and New York City, see Karen Tongson, *Relocations: Queer Suburban Imaginaries* (New York University Press, 2010); and Wayne Brekhus, *Peacocks, Chameleons, Centaurs: Gay Suburbia and the Grammar of Social Identity* (Chicago: University of Chicago Press, 2003).

22. Weston, *Long Slow Burn*, 41.

23. Reid-Pharr, *Black Gay Man*, 9.

24. Ibid.

25. Ibid.

26. Thomas Jefferson, "Letter to Benjamin Rush (September 23, 1800)," in *The Writings of Thomas Jefferson*, ed. Paul Leicester Ford, 10 vols. (New York: G. P. Putnam's Sons, 1892–94), 7:459. For an account of Jeffersonian rural pastoralism, see Leo Marx, *The Machine in the Garden: Technology and the Pastoral Ideal in America* (1964; Oxford: Oxford University Press, 2000), 117–44.

27. Thomas Dixon Jr., "From the Horrors of City Life," *World's Work* 4.6 (October 1902): 2604. Quoted in David B. Danbom, "Why Americans Value Rural Life," *Rural Development Perspectives* 12.1 (1996): 17. Danbom also provides an extensive history of American anti-urbanism's historical development, which I draw on here.

28. For detailed analyses of "white flight," see William H. Frey, "Central City White Flight: Racial and Non-Racial Causes," *American Sociological Review* 44.3 (1979): 425–48; Eric Avila, *Popular Culture in the Age of White Flight: Fear and Fantasy in Suburban Los Angeles* (Berkeley and Los Angeles: University of California Press, 2004); and Steve Macek, *Urban Nightmares: The Media, the Right, and the Moral Panic Over the City* (Minneapolis: University of Minnesota Press, 2006).

29. Warner, *Trouble*, 188.

30. Ibid. These two neologisms are mentioned in Michelangelo Signorile, *Life Outside: The Signorile Report on Gay Men: Sex, Drugs, Muscles, and the Passages of Life* (New York: HarperCollins, 1997), 207.

31. Signorile, *Life Outside*, 206.

32. Lisa Duggan, *The Twilight of Equality? Neoliberalism, Cultural Politics, and the Attack on Democracy* (Boston: Beacon Press, 2003), 50, 65.

33. Leo Marx, "The Puzzle of Antiurbanism in Classic American Literature," in *Cities of the Mind: Images and Themes of the City in the Social Sciences*, ed. Lloyd Rodwin and Robert M. Hollister (New York: Plenum Press, 1984), 165.

34. Weston, *Long Slow Burn*, 45.

35. Ibid., 40.

36. Omise'eke Natasha Tinsley, "Black Atlantic, Queer Atlantic: Queer Imaginings of the Middle Passage," *GLQ* 14.2–3 (2008), critiques the metro satellite—here, Rehoboth Beach—as it informs the "cosmopolitan" foundations of queer theory (206). See also Lionel Cantú, "*De Ambiente*: Queer Tourism and the Shifting Boundaries of Mexican Male Sexualities," *GLQ* 8.1–2 (2002): 139–66, on "satellite gay space" (145).

37. Halberstam, *Queer Time*, 190. Others who have noted this include Weston, in *Long Slow Burn*, who states that urban/rural distinctions produce "a symbolic space that configures gayness itself by elaborating an opposition between rural and urban life" (55); Gerald W. Creed and Barbara Ching, in

"Introduction: Recognizing Rusticity: Identity and the Power of Place," *Knowing Your Place: Rural Identity and Cultural Hierarchy*, ed. Ching and Creed (New York: Routledge, 1997), who maintain that "the experiential significance of the rural/urban distinction still holds" (2); and Mark Lawrence, "Heartlands or Neglected Geographies: Liminality, Power, and the Hyperreal Rural," *Journal of Rural Studies* 13.1 (1997): 1–17.

38. Halberstam, *In a Queer Time and Place*, 36–37.

39. Ibid., 37.

40. José Esteban Muñoz, "Dead White: Notes on the Whiteness of the New Queer Cinema," *GLQ* 4.1 (1998): 129.

41. Marlon Riggs, dir., *Tongues Untied* (Frameline Distribution, 1989).

42. Eric Michaels, *Unbecoming* (Durham, NC: Duke University Press, 1997), 128.

43. By "cosmopolitanism," I refer less to the heterogeneity of racial, ethnic, or national populations than to a leisure-oriented vantage of worldliness—compounded by the socioeconomic privilege of self-mobility—that produces an uncritical globality liberated from any particular nation-state yet nevertheless rooted in an urban bias if not necessarily an urbanized locale. This is not to neglect that cosmopolitan embodiments cannot be countered or have not been critiqued by more socially expansive versions of the concept. Theories that have influenced my thinking on this matter include: Jacques Derrida, *On Cosmopolitanism and Forgiveness*, trans. Mark Dooley (London: Routledge, 2001), where the philosopher finds cosmopolitanism to be "a novel status for the city" (3); and Gayatri Chakravorty Spivak on planetary identifications that too often feast on "the spectralization of the rural (altogether distinct from ruralism) . . . as the forgotten front of globalization for which the urban is an instrument" (92–93), in *Death of a Discipline* (New York: Columbia University Press, 2003).

44. "Popular Tags: Out.com Stylelist," *Out Magazine: Fashion, Style, Celebrity, Opinion for the Modern Gay Man*, http://stylelist.out.com/ (accessed September 10, 2007).

45. For critiques of globalizing lesbian and gay "lifestyle" in commodity capitalism, see Rosemary Hennessy, *Profit and Pleasure: Sexual Identities in Late Capitalism* (New York: Routledge, 2000); Sharon Zukin, "Urban Lifestyles: Diversity and Standardisation in Spaces of Consumption," *Urban Studies* 35.5–6 (1998): 825–40; Ann Pellegrini, "Consuming Lifestyle: Commodity Capitalism and Transformations in Gay Identity," in *Queer Globalizations: Citizenship and the Afterlife of Colonialism*, ed. Arnaldo Cruz-Malavé and Martin F. Manalansan IV (New York: New York University Press, 2002), 134–45; and Donald M. Lowe, *The Body in Late-Capitalist USA* (Durham, NC: Duke University Press, 1995), 135–37.

46. Susan Sontag, "Notes on 'Camp,'" *Against Interpretation, and Other Essays* (New York: Picador, 2001), 290.

47. Alfred C. Kinsey, Wardell B. Pomeroy, and Clyde E. Martin, *Sexual Behavior in the Human Male* (Philadelphia: W. B. Saunders, 1948), 457.

48. Or, as Anthony Freitas, Susan Kaiser, and Tania Hammidi ("Communities, Commodities, Cultural Space, and Style," *Journal of Homosexuality* 31.1–2 [1996]: 83–107) argue, "citizenship in the G&L communities, like in any community, may be marked through the deployment of style" (85). Likewise, I align myself here with Karen Tongson's necessary interventions to recuperate the concept of style and queer taste from racially normative gay men. Her essay "Metronormativity and Gay Globalization," in *Quer durch die Geisteswissenschaften: Perspektiven der Queer Theory* (Queering the humanities: Perspectives in queer theory), ed. Elahe Haschemi Yekani and Beatrice Michaelis (Berlin: Querverlag, 2005), calls for "the centrality of style as a concept constitutive of metronormative queer discourses, as well as alternate spatial genealogies for queer life" (47), and for a "model of queer style that asserts its rural and suburban roots" (52). She further develops this line of thought in "JJ Chinois's Oriental Express, or, How a Suburban Heartthrob Seduced Red America," *Social Text* 84–85 (2005): 193–217; and in "The Light That Never Goes Out: Butch Intimacies and Sub-Urban Sociabilities in 'Lesser Los Angeles,'" in *A Companion to Lesbian, Gay, Bisexual, Transgender, and Queer Studies*, ed. George Haggerty and Molly McGarry (Malden, MA: Blackwell, 2007), 355–76. For other considerations of style, stylistics, and queer communal identity—most not in agreement on the value of these terms—see Michel Foucault, *The History of Sexuality, Volume 3: The Care of the Self*, trans. Robert Hurley (New York: Random House, 1986), on "the subject's 'style of activity' and on the relation he [*sic*] establishes between sexual activity and the other aspects of his familial, social, and economic existence" (35); Judith Butler, "Agencies of Style for a Liminal Subject," in *Without Guarantees: In Honour of Stuart Hall*, ed. Paul Gilroy, Lawrence Grossberg, and Angela McRobbie (London: Verso, 2000), 30–37; David Halperin, *Saint Foucault: Towards a Gay Hagiography* (New York: Oxford University Press, 1995), 72–75, on gay male style; Andrew Ross, "Uses of Camp," in *Camp Grounds: Style and Homosexuality*, ed. David Bergman (Amherst: University of Massachusetts Press, 1993), on "the operation of taste" (55); and Dereka Rushbrook, "Cities, Queer Space, and the Cosmopolitan Tourist," *GLQ* 8.1–2 (2002): 183–206. Finally, for more on "'rural' style" as "a cultural value attached to rural places and people," see Creed and Ching, "Introduction," 21.

49. Edmund White, http://www.edmundwhite.com/ (accessed March 17, 2008).

50. Unless otherwise noted, all citations from Edmund White can be found in White, *States of Desire: Travels in Gay America* (1980; New York: Plume, 1991).

51. See http://www.southernvoice.com/ (accessed September 10, 2007).

52. Unless otherwise noted, all citations from Pierre Bourdieu can be found in Bourdieu, *Distinction: A Social Critique of the Judgement of Taste,* trans. Richard Nice (1979, 1984; Cambridge, MA: Harvard University Press, 1996).

53. For complementary readings of Bourdieu's applicability to queer studies, see Katherine Sender, "Gay Readers, Consumers, and a Dominant Gay Habitus: 25 Years of the *Advocate* Magazine," *Journal of Communication* 51.1 (2001): 73–99; Sender, *Business, Not Politics: The Making of the Gay Market* (New York: Columbia University Press, 2004); Sara Ahmed, *Queer Phenomenology: Orientations, Objects, Others* (Durham, NC: Duke University Press, 2006), 56, 129; and Elizabeth Freeman, introduction to "Queer Temporalities," *GLQ* 13.2–3 (2007): 159–76.

54. Esther Newton, *Mother Camp: Female Impersonators in America* (Chicago: University of Chicago Press, 1972), 29.

55. Ibid.

56. "Rusticity," *Oxford English Dictionary,* http://www.oed.com/ (accessed September 22, 2007).

57. For an elaboration of felt experience, see Phillip Brian Harper, "The Evidence of Felt Intuition: Minority Experience, Everyday Life, and Critical Speculative Knowledge," in *Black Queer Studies: A Critical Anthology,* ed. E. Patrick Johnson and Mae G. Henderson (Durham, NC: Duke University Press, 2005), 106–23.

58. These stylistics and those they counter, I add, are not the sole property of anti-metronormative queers or, for that matter, the sole property of queers. See Laura Kipnis with Jennifer Reeder, "White Trash Girl: The Interview," in *White Trash: Race and Class in America,* ed. Matt Wray and Annalee Newitz (New York: Routledge, 1997), 113–30, on hetero-identified rural counter-stylistics; and David Coad, *The Metrosexual: Gender, Sexuality, and Sport* (Albany: State University of New York Press, 2008).

59. "Style" and "Stylistic," *Oxford English Dictionary,* http://www.oed.com/ (accessed September 18, 2007).

60. Ibid.

61. Michel Foucault, *The History of Sexuality, Volume 1: An Introduction,* trans. Robert Hurley (New York: Vintage, 1990), 84.

62. Creed and Ching, "Introduction," 6.

63. George Chauncey, *Gay New York: Gender, Urban Culture, and the Making of the Gay Male World, 1890–1940* (New York: BasicBooks, 1994), 7; Weston, *Long Slow Burn,* 32.

64. For more on the potential of micro-sites, see Elizabeth A. Povinelli and George Chauncey, "Thinking Sexuality Transnationally: An Introduction," *GLQ* 5.4 (1999) regarding "the delicate structures of local corporeal texts" (444).

65. Creed and Ching, "Introduction," 30.

66. For cultural histories of U.S.-based (literary) regionalism, see Richard H. Brodhead, *Cultures of Letters: Scenes of Reading and Writing in Nineteenth-Century America* (Chicago: University of Chicago Press, 1993); T. J. Jackson Lears, *No Place of Grace: Antimodernism and the Transformation of American Culture, 1880–1920* (Chicago: University of Chicago Press, 1994); Susan Hegeman, *Patterns for America: Modernism and the Concept of Culture* (Princeton: Princeton University Press, 1999); Stephanie Foote, *Regional Fictions: Culture and Identity in Nineteenth-Century American Literature* (Madison: University of Wisconsin Press, 2001); Robert L. Dorman, *Revolt of the Provinces: The Regionalist Movement in America, 1920–1945* (Chapel Hill: University of North Carolina Press, 1993); and Judith Fetterly and Marjorie Pryse, *Writing Out of Place: Regionalism, Women, and American Literary Culture* (Champaign: University of Illinois Press, 2005). For a conversational account of regionalism's relation to twenty-first-century globalization, see Butler and Spivak, *Who Sings the Nation-State? Language, Politics, Belonging* (New York: Seagull Books, 2007).

67. Raymond Williams, *Marxism and Literature* (Oxford: Oxford University Press, 1977), 121.

68. Williams, *The Country and the City* (New York: Oxford University Press, 1973), 289.

69. Eve Kosofsky Sedgwick, *Epistemology of the Closet* (Berkeley and Los Angeles: University of California Press, 1990), 36.

70. Alan Sinfield, "The Production of Gay and the Return of Power," in *De-Centring Sexualities*, 21. See also Gayatri Gopinath, "Queer Regions: Locating Lesbians in *Sancharram*," in *Companion to Lesbian, Gay, Bisexual, Transgender, and Queer Studies*, 341–54.

71. Gayatri Gopinath, *Impossible Desires: Queer Diasporas and South Asian Public Cultures* (Durham, NC: Duke University Press, 2005), 11. For complementary studies, see Inderpal Grewal and Caren Kaplan, "Global Identities: Theorizing Transnational Studies of Sexuality," *GLQ* 7.4 (2001): 663–79; Katie King, "Global Gay Formations and Local Homosexualities," in *A Companion to Postcolonial Studies: A Historical Introduction*, ed. Henry Schwarz and Sangeeta Ray (Malden, MA: Blackwell, 2000), 508–19; and Puar, *Terrorist Assemblages*.

72. Halberstam, *Queer Time*, 38.

73. James Baldwin, "Sonny's Blues," in *Going to Meet the Man* (1965; New York: Dell, 1966), 120.

Chapter One

1. Robert M. Dowling, "A Marginal Man in Black Bohemia: James Weldon Johnson in the New York Tenderloin," in *Post-Bellum, Pre-Harlem: African-American Literature and Culture, 1877–1919*, ed. Barbara McCaskill and Caroline Gebhard (New York: New York University Press, 2006), 118. See also Gilbert

Osofsky, *Harlem: The Making of a Ghetto, Negro New York, 1890–1930* (New York: Harper & Row, 1963), 12-15.

2. Lisa Duggan, *The Twilight of Equality? Neoliberalism, Cultural Politics, and the Attack on Democracy* (Boston: Beacon Press, 2003), 50.

3. Ibid., 51.

4. Didier Eribon, "The Flight to the City," in *Insult and the Making of the Gay Self*, trans. Michael Lucey (Durham, NC: Duke University Press, 2004), 20.

5. Judith Halberstam, *In a Queer Time and Place: Transgender Bodies, Subcultural Lives* (New York: New York University Press, 2005), 36–37, 41–42.

6. John D'Emilio, "Capitalism and Gay Identity," in *The Lesbian and Gay Studies Reader*, ed. Henry Abelove, Michèle Aina Barale, and David M. Halperin (New York: Routledge, 1993), 470.

7. Unless otherwise noted, all citations from George Chauncey can be found in Chauncey, *Gay New York: Gender, Urban Culture, and the Making of the Gay Male World, 1890–1940* (New York: Basic Books, 1994).

8. Esther Newton, *Mother Camp: Female Impersonators in America* (Chicago: University of Chicago Press, 1972), 29.

9. Links between modernism and the metropolitan include Joseph Allen Boone, *Libidinal Currents: Sexuality and the Shaping of Modernism* (Chicago: University of Chicago Press, 1998), 205–87; Andreas Huyssen, "Geographies of Modernism in a Globalizing World," in *Geographies of Modernism: Literatures, Cultures, Spaces*, ed. Peter Brooker and Andrew Thacker (New York: Routledge, 2005), 6–18; Nina Miller on "new sophistication" (93) and U.S. urbanity in *Making Love Modern: The Intimate Public Worlds of New York's Literary Women* (New York: Oxford University Press, 1998); Julie Abraham, *Metropolitan Lovers: The Homosexuality of Cities* (Minneapolis: University of Minnesota Press, 2009); and Lewis A. Erenberg on "the split between city sophistication and small-town morality" in *Steppin' Out: New York Nightlife and the Transformation of American Culture, 1890–1930* (1981; Chicago: University of Chicago Press, 1984), 236. For a reconsideration of U.S. modernism and "rural inferiority and backwardness" (906), see Maria Farland, "Modernist Versions of Pastoral: Poetic Inspiration, Scientific Expertise, and the 'Degenerate' Farmer," *American Literary History* 19.4 (2007): 905–36; and Janet Gallingani Casey, *A New Heartland: Women, Modernity, and the Agrarian Ideal in America* (New York: Oxford University Press, 2009).

10. Halberstam, *Queer Time*, 42.

11. For discussions of modernist lesbian urbanity and urbanism, see Terry Castle, *Noël Coward and Radclyffe Hall: Kindred Spirits* (New York: Columbia University Press, 1996), 10–33; Annamarie Jagose, "The Evolution of a Lesbian Icon," *Genders* 34 (2001): 32; Joanne Winning, "The Sapphist in the City: Lesbian Modernist Paris and Sapphic Modernity," in *Sapphic Modernities: Sexuality, Women, and National Culture*, ed. Laura Doan and Jane Garrity (New York:

Palgrave Macmillan, 2006), 17–33; Lisa Duggan, *Sapphic Slashers: Sex, Violence, and American Modernity* (Durham, NC: Duke University Press, 2000); Lillian Faderman, *Odd Girls and Twilight Lovers: A History of Lesbian Life in Twentieth-Century America* (New York: Penguin, 1991), on 1920s "lesbian chic," 62–92; and Patricia White, "Black and White: Mercedes de Acosta's Glorious Enthusiasms," *Camera Obscura* 15.3 (2001): 227–65.

12. Laura Doan, *Fashioning Sapphism: The Origins of a Modern English Lesbian Culture* (New York: Columbia University Press, 2001), 99, 116.

13. Doan, *Sapphism*, 194.

14. Beatriz Sarlo, *Una modernidad periférica: Buenos Aires 1920 y 1930* (Buenos Aires: Nueva Vision, 1988). Quoted in Mary Louise Pratt, "Modernity and Periphery: Toward a Global and Relational Analysis," in *Beyond Dichotomies: Histories, Identities, Cultures, and the Challenge of Globalization*, ed. Elisabeth Mudimbe-Boyi (Albany: State University of New York Press, 2002), 29.

15. Merrill Maguire Skaggs, "Introduction," in *Willa Cather's New York: New Essays on Cather in the City*, ed. Skaggs (Madison, NJ: Fairleigh Dickinson University Press, 2000), 14. I discuss this relationship a bit more in Scott Herring, *Queering the Underworld: Slumming, Literature, and the Undoing of Lesbian and Gay History* (Chicago: University of Chicago Press, 2007), 221.

16. Willa Cather, *Lincoln (NE) Courier*, October 23, 1897, "The Urban Scene: Presbyteria and Bohemia," in *The World and the Parish: Willa Cather's Articles and Reviews, 1893–1902*, vol. 2, ed. William M. Curtin (Lincoln: University of Nebraska Press, 1970), 508.

17. Cather, "The Sculptor's Funeral," *The Troll Garden* (1905; New York: Vintage, 1975), 250.

18. Cather, *Shadows on the Rock* (1931; New York: Vintage, 1971), 31.

19. Unless otherwise noted, all citations from Willa Cather's *The Professor's House* are found in Cather, *The Professor's House* (1925; New York: Vintage, 1973).

20. Elizabeth Shepley Sergeant, quoted in Ann Romines, "Sapphira and the City," *Willa Cather's New York*, 243.

21. Christopher Nealon, *Foundlings: Lesbian and Gay Historical Emotion Before Stonewall* (Durham, NC: Duke University Press, 2001).

22. John P. Anders, *Willa Cather's Sexual Aesthetics and the Male Homosexual Literary Tradition* (Lincoln: University of Nebraska Press, 1999), 105.

23. I have in mind Eve Kosofsky Sedgwick, "Willa Cather and Others," in *Tendencies* (Durham, NC: Duke University Press, 1993), 167–76; and Nealon, *Foundlings*. For a synthesis of these two readings that addresses the importance of both "self-identity" and a "possibility" that can "preclude identification" (88), see Jonathan Goldberg, "Willa Cather and Sexuality," in *The Cambridge Companion to Willa Cather*, ed. Marilee Lindemann (Cambridge: Cambridge University Press, 2005), 86–100.

24. See Solomon Valley/Highway 24 Heritage Alliance, *Weaving the Common Threads of the Solomon Valley Fabric* (Woodston, KS: Western Books, 2002), for a detailed description of this socioeconomically, if not culturally, impoverished geography.

25. "Heartland," *Oxford English Dictionary*, http://www.oed.com/ (accessed February 22, 2008). Cheryl Temple Herr, *Critical Regionalism and Cultural Studies: From Ireland to the American Midwest* (Gainesville: University Press of Florida, 1996); and Victoria Johnson, *Heartland TV: Prime Time Television and the Struggle for U.S. Identity* (New York: New York University Press, 2008), each provide rich overviews of this term's historical evolution.

26. Emily Dickinson, letter to Mrs. J. G. Holland (January 20, 1856). Quoted in *The Letters of Emily Dickinson*, ed. Thomas H. Johnson (Cambridge, MA: Belknap Press of Harvard University, 1958), vol. 2, letter 182, 324.

27. Sedgwick, "Preface," in *Between Men: English Literature and Male Homosocial Desire* (New York: Columbia University Press, 1985, 1992), ix.

28. Ibid.

29. Walt Whitman, *Leaves of Grass*, in *Leaves of Grass, and Other Writings*, ed. Michael Moon, 2d ed. (1855; New York: Norton, 2002), lines 499, 680.

30. See Cather, "Whitman: 'Keen Senses Do Not Make a Poet,'" *Nebraska State Journal*, January 19, 1896. Quoted in *The World and the Parish: Willa Cather's Articles and Reviews, 1893–1902*, ed. William M. Curtin (Lincoln: University of Nebraska Press, 1970), 279–82.

31. Whitman, "Song of Myself," *Leaves of Grass, and Other Writings* (1881), lines 4–5, 26.

32. Quoted in Brian Moylan, "The 'Grass' Is Getting Greener: D.C. to Celebrate 150th Anniversary of Gay Poet Walt Whitman's *Leaves of Grass*," *Washington Blade*, March 25, 2005.

33. George Chauncey, "Manhattan's Roaring Gay Days," *Out Traveler*, Spring 2008, 58.

34. Pratt, "Modernity and Periphery," 40.

35. A sampling of such paintings includes *Box of Tricks* (1933); *Lancaster* (1920); *Modern Conveniences* (1920); *End of the Parade, Coatesville, Pa.* (1920); *Chimney and Water Tower* (1931); *Buildings, Lancaster* (1930); *Buildings Abstraction, Lancaster* (1931); *In the Province (Roofs)* (1920); and *After All* (1933).

36. For general accounts of Egyptomania, see Elliott Colla, *Conflicted Antiquities: Egyptology, Egyptomania, Egyptian Modernity* (Durham, NC: Duke University Press, 2007); and Bridget Elliott, "Art Deco Worlds in a Tomb: Reanimating Egypt in Modern(ist) Visual Culture," *South Central Review* 25.1 (2008): 114–35. For two accounts of *My Egypt* and Egyptomania, see Michael North, *Reading 1922: A Return to the Scene of the Modern* (New York: Oxford University Press, 1999), 23–24; and Robert Hughes, *American Visions: The Epic History of Art in America* (New York: Knopf, 1997), 382.

37. Barbara Haskell, *Charles Demuth* (New York: Whitney Museum of American Art, 1987), 183–84, highlights Demuth's deep connection to Williams; and Karal Ann Marling, "*My Egypt*: The Irony of the American Dream," *Winterthur Portfolio* 15.1 (Spring 1980): 25–39, presents a fine reading of Demuth and irony.

38. Hughes, *Visions*, 382. A sampling of critics that also discusses this painting includes James M. Dennis, *Renegade Regionalists: The Modern Independence of Grant Wood, Thomas Hart Benton, and John Steuart Curry* (Madison: University of Wisconsin Press, 1998), 197–214; Celeste Connor, *Democratic Visions: Art and Theory of the Stieglitz Circle, 1924–1934* (Berkeley and Los Angeles: University of California Press, 2001); and Wanda Corn, *The Great American Thing: Modern Art and National Identity, 1915–1935* (Berkeley and Los Angeles: University of California Press, 1999).

39. Marcel Proust, *Remembrance of Things Past, Volume 2: The Guermantes Way and Cities of the Plain,* trans. C. K. Scott Moncrieff and Terence Kilmartin (New York: Vintage, 1982), vii, 639, 656. See Jonathan Freedman, "Coming Out of the Jewish Closet with Marcel Proust," *GLQ* 7.4 (2001): 521–51, for more on links between urbanized Jews and metropolitan-based queers in Proust.

40. Jonathan Weinberg, *Speaking for Vice: Homosexuality in the Art of Charles Demuth, Marsden Hartley, and the First American Avant-Garde* (New Haven, CT: Yale University Press, 1993), 216.

41. Demuth, letter to Alfred Stieglitz, October 30, 1927. Quoted in *Letters of Charles Demuth, American Artist, 1883–1935*, ed. Bruce Kellner (Philadelphia: Temple University Press, 2000), 104.

42. Robert McRuer, *Crip Theory: Cultural Signs of Queerness and Disability* (New York: New York University Press, 2006), 2. Theorizations of disability studies as they dovetail with queer studies guide much of my efforts here. I have been influenced by McRuer on links between foundational texts of queer theory such as *Epistemology of the Closet* and "the crisis of able-bodied/disabled definition" ("We Were Never Identified: Feminism, Queer Theory, and a Disabled World," *Radical History Review* 94 [2006]: 152); Lennard J. Davis on "ambient society" (41) in *Bending Over Backwards: Disability, Dismodernism, and Other Difficult Positions* (New York: New York University Press, 2002); Sharon L. Snyder and David T. Mitchell on "mobility impairment" (10) in *Cultural Locations of Disability* (Chicago: University of Chicago Press, 2006); and McRuer and Abby L. Wilkerson, "Introduction: Desiring Disability: Queer Theory Meets Disability Studies," *GLQ* 9.1–2 (2003): 1–23.

43. David Serlin, "Disabling the Flâneur," *Journal of Visual Culture* 5.2 (2006): 199.

44. See Kevin Murphy, "Walking the Queer City," *Radical History Review* 62 (1995): 195–201; and Chauncey, *Gay New York*, 180–205.

45. Michael Davidson, "Introduction," *Journal of Literary Disability* 1.2 (2007): i.

46. For further readings of Demuth's oeuvre in relation to modern urbanized queerness, see Juan Antonio Suárez, *Pop Modernism: Noise and the Reinvention of the Everyday* (Champaign: University of Illinois Press, 2007), 185–86; and Weinberg, *Speaking*.

47. Betsy Fahlman, whom I rely heavily on for my biography of Demuth, provides an exemplary description of these locales in *Pennsylvania Modern: Charles Demuth of Lancaster* (Philadelphia: Philadelphia Museum of Art, 1983), 18; and in *Chimneys and Towers: Charles Demuth's Late Paintings of Lancaster* (Philadelphia: University of Pennsylvania Press, 2007), 55.

48. For the queerness of these cabarets, see Shane Vogel, *The Scene of Harlem Cabaret: Race, Sexuality, Performance* (Chicago: University of Chicago Press, 2009).

49. Haskell, *Demuth*, 60; see also pp. 55–59, on Demuth's relationship to queer Greenwich Village subcultures.

50. Social histories of type 2 diabetes and insulin injections appear in Michael Bliss, *The Discovery of Insulin* (Chicago: University of Chicago Press, 1982); and Chris Feudtner, *Bittersweet: Diabetes, Insulin, and the Transformation of Illness* (Chapel Hill: University of North Carolina Press, 2003). Recent conversations between diabetes cultures and disability studies can also be found in McRuer, *Crip Theory*, 38; and Davis, *Bending*, 24.

51. Haskell, *Demuth*, 139–40.

52. Fahlman, *Pennsylvania Modern*, 12.

53. Haskell, *Demuth*, 140.

54. Ibid.

55. See David Walbert, *Garden Spot: Lancaster County, the Old Order Amish, and the Selling of Rural America* (New York: Oxford University Press, 2002), for detailed discussions of Lancaster County's imagined association with rurality at this time.

56. Demuth, letter to George Biddle, August 10, 1927. Quoted in *Letters*, 99.

57. Haskell, *Demuth*, 194.

58. Proust, *Remembrance of Things Past*, 656.

59. Dana Luciano, "Invalid Relations: Queer Kinship in Henry James's *The Portrait of a Lady*," *Henry James Review* 23.2 (2002): 206.

60. The phrase comes from Diana Fuss's description of Proust in *The Sense of an Interior: Four Writers and the Rooms That Shaped Them* (New York: Routledge, 2004), 168. My reading also borrows from Fahlman, in *Chimneys and Towers*, who contends that "[P]recisionism is an intriguing dichotomy, including urban and rural, realist and abstract, descriptively situated in region yet informed by the sophistication of New York and Europe" (98).

61. Demuth, letter to Stieglitz, [July?] 1927. Quoted in *Letters*, 98.

62. Sarlo, *Una modernidad periférica*, 29.

63. Raymond Williams, "Metropolitan Perceptions and the Emergence of Modernism," in *The Politics of Modernism: Against the New Conformists* (London: Verso, 1989), 47.

64. Demuth, letter to Stieglitz, November 28, 1921. Quoted in *Letters*, 38.

65. Siobhan B. Somerville, *Queering the Color Line: Race and the Invention of Homosexuality in American Culture* (Durham, NC: Duke University Press, 2000), 125.

66. Ibid., 119.

67. Ibid., 117.

68. I'm thinking of Cheryl Clarke, "Race, Homosocial Desire, and 'Mammon' in *Autobiography of an Ex-Colored Man*," in *Professions of Desire: Lesbian and Gay Studies in Literature*, ed. George Haggerty and Bonnie Zimmerman (New York: Modern Language Association of America, 1995), 84–97; Phillip Brian Harper, *Are We Not Men?: Masculine Anxiety and the Problem of African-American Identity* (New York: Oxford University Press, 1996), 108–13; and Anne Herrmann, *Queering the Moderns: Poses/Portraits/Performances* (New York: Palgrave, 2000), 115–37.

69. Somerville, *Color Line*, 114.

70. Unless otherwise noted, all citations from James Weldon Johnson's *The Autobiography of an Ex-Colored Man* can be found in Johnson, *The Autobiography of an Ex-Colored Man* (1912, 1927; New York: Vintage Books, 1989).

71. Other considerations of upper-class urbanized queer U.S. white male identity at the turn of the century include Stephanie Foote, "Little Brothers of the Rich: Queer Families in the Gilded Age," *American Literature* 79.4 (2007): 701–24; and Martha Umphrey, "The Trouble with Harry Thaw," *Radical History Review* 62 (1995): 8–23.

72. See Chauncey, *Gay New York*, 233–35, 271–73, on Berlin's gay environs. See also Eribon, *Insult*, 20; Harry Oosterhuis, "Homosexual Emancipation in Germany Before 1933: Two Traditions," in *Homosexuality and Male Bonding in Pre-Nazi Germany: The Youth Movement, the Gay Movement, and Male Bonding Before Hitler's Rise*, ed. Oosterhuis and trans. Hubert Kennedy (New York: Harrington Park Press, 1991), on the "bordellos, private clubs, and friendship circles [that] were apparently already in existence" by "the second half of the nineteenth century" (15); and Dorothy Rowe, *Representing Berlin: Sexuality and the City in Imperial and Weimar Germany* (Burlington, VT: Ashgate Publishing, 2003).

73. Magnus Hirschfeld, *Les homosexuels de Berlin: Le troisième sexe* (Paris: Librairie Médicale et Scientifique, 1908), 55. Translation by Denise Cruz. See also the broad reading offered by Eribon, *Insult*, 21–22, which initially alerted me to the existence of this text.

74. Hirschfeld, *Les homosexuels*, 56. Translation by Cruz.

75. Richard von Krafft-Ebing, *Psychopathia Sexualis with Especial Reference to the Antipathic Sexual Instinct, a Medico-Forensic Study*, trans. Franklin S. Klaf (1886; New York: Arcade Publishing, 1965), 394.

76. Ibid., 396.

77. We might assume that Johnson learned this lesson through his social encounters in Puerto Cabella, Venezuela. It was here that Johnson wrote large chunks of *Autobiography* when he served as the U.S. consulate under president Theodore Roosevelt. See Johnson, *Along This Way: The Autobiography of James Weldon Johnson* (1933; New York: Penguin, 1990); and Jacqueline Goldsby, "Keeping the 'Secret of Authorship': A Critical Look at the 1912 Publication of James Weldon Johnson's *Autobiography of an Ex-Colored Man*," in *Print Culture in a Diverse America*, ed. James P. Danky and Wayne A. Wiegand (Champaign: University of Illinois Press, 1998), 244–71, for more on *Autobiography*'s publication history.

78. The best discussion of how acculturation connects to cultivation remains Raymond Williams's overview of the term "culture" in *Keywords: A Vocabulary of Culture and Society* (New York: Oxford University Press, 1985), 87–93.

79. Kath Weston, *Long Slow Burn: Sexuality and Social Science* (New York, London: Routledge, 1998), 49.

Chapter Two

1. Stuart Scofield, "RFD History," *RFD* 9.3 (1983): 9.

2. For detailed historical, ethnographic, and sociological accounts of the radical faeries, see Harry Hay, *Radically Gay: Gay Liberation in the Words of Its Founder* (Boston: Beacon Press, 1996); Stuart Timmons, *The Trouble With Harry Hay: Founder of the Modern Gay Movement* (Boston: Alyson Publications, 1990); Elizabeth Povinelli, *The Empire of Love: Toward a Theory of Intimacy, Genealogy, and Carnality* (Durham, NC: Duke University Press, 2006); and Peter Hennen, *Faeries, Bears, and Leathermen: Men in Community Queering the Masculine* (Chicago: University of Chicago Press, 2008).

3. Olmo Eric Ganther and Frank S. Grant, "From Hippy to Fairy at Short Mountain Sanctuary," *RFD* 26.3 (Spring 2000): 24.

4. Mitch Walker, *Visionary Love: A Spirit Book of Gay Mythology and Trans-Mutational Faerie* (San Francisco: Treeroots Press, 1980); and the collected essays in *Gay Spirit: Myth and Meaning*, ed. Mark Thompson (New York: St. Martin's Press, 1987), present suspect analogies between gay male faeries and the Native American two-spirit.

5. Scott Morgensen, "Rooting for Queers: A Politics of Primitivity," *Women and Performance: A Journal of Feminist Theory* 15.1 (2005): 257. See also Morgensen, "Arrival at Home: Radical Faerie Configurations of Sexuality and Place," *GLQ* 15.1 (2009): 67–96.

6. B., "Ooo-h-h-h It's One of Those! Reflections and Projections of Faerie Past, Present and Future," *RFD* 30.3 (Spring 2004): 20.

7. Anonymous, "Letter," *RFD* 26.2 (Spring 2000): 4.

8. Gershon Legman, "The Language of Homosexuality," in *Sex Variants: A Study of Homosexual Patterns, with Sections Contributed by Specialists in Particular Fields*, ed. George W. Henry (New York: P. B. Hoeber, 1948). Reprinted in Jonathan Ned Katz, *Gay/Lesbian Almanac: A New Documentary* (New York: Harper and Row, 1983), 582.

9. Ibid.

10. I here invoke and extend Lauren Berlant and Elizabeth Freeman's readings of normative and non-normative queer print cultures in their essay "Queer Nationality" (in Lauren Berlant, *The Queen of America Goes to Washington City: Essays on Sex and Citizenship* [Durham, NC: Duke University Press, 1997], 169).

11. Martin Meeker, *Contacts Desired: Gay and Lesbian Communications and Community, 1940s–1970s* (Chicago: University of Chicago Press, 2006), 223.

12. Donald L. Engstrom, telephone interview by the author, January 12, 2006.

13. James T. Sears, *Rebels, Rubyfruit, and Rhinestones: Queering Space in the Stonewall South* (New Brunswick, NJ: Rutgers University Press, 2001), 306. Framing my argument in this manner, I join Michael Warner, "The Mass Public and the Mass Subject," in *Habermas and the Public Sphere*, ed. Craig Calhoun (Cambridge, MA: MIT Press, 1992), 377–401; Lisa Duggan, *Sapphic Slashers: Sex, Violence, and American Modernity* (Durham, NC: Duke University Press, 2000); Richard Meyer, "*Gay Power* Circa 1970," *GLQ* 12.3 (2006): 441–64; and Margo Hobbs Thompson, "'Dear Sisters': The Visible Lesbian in Community Arts Journals," *GLQ* 12.3 (2006): 405–23. Each has written on the complex interconnections between collective U.S. lesbian and gay identities and modern print cultures.

14. See Halberstam, *In a Queer Time and Place: Transgender Bodies, Subcultural Lives* (New York: New York University Press, 2005), 35; and Kath Weston, *Long Slow Burn: Sexuality and Social Science* (New York: Routledge, 1998), 32, for discussions of these migrations.

15. Rodger Streitmatter, *Unspeakable: The Rise of the Gay and Lesbian Press in America* (Boston: Faber and Faber, 1995), 154–55.

16. Scofield, "*RFD* History," 13.

17. Streitmatter, *Unspeakable*, 50.

18. Scofield, "*RFD* History," 13.

19. Carl Wittman, "A Gay Manifesto," in *Out of the Closets: Voices of Gay Liberation*, ed. Karla Jay and Allen Young (1972; New York: New York University Press, 1992), 340–41.

20. Chicago Gay Liberation, "Working Paper for the Revolutionary People's Constitutional Convention," in *Out of the Closets*, 349.

21. Streitmatter, *Unspeakable*, 150.

22. Ibid., 87. Allan Bérubé (*Coming Out Under Fire: The History of Gay Men and Women in World War Two* [New York: The Free Press, 1990]) and John

D'Emilio (*Sexual Politics, Sexual Communities: The Making of a Homosexual Minority in the United States, 1940–1970* [Chicago: University of Chicago Press, 1983]) provide the most detailed accounts to date on the rise of lesbian and gay "ghettos" in major post–World War II U.S. cities. For a sociological account of 1970s gay male clone cultures, see Martin P. Levine, *Gay Macho: The Life and Death of the Homosexual Clone* (New York: New York University Press, 1998), 31–43. For a contemporary critique of this ideal, see Charles P. Thorp, "I.D., Leadership, and Violence," in *Out of the Closets*, 352–63. For complementary twenty-first-century critiques, see Charles I. Nero, "Why Are the Gay Ghettos White?," in *Black Queer Studies: A Critical Anthology*, ed. E. Patrick Johnson and Mae G. Henderson (Durham, NC: Duke University Press, 2005), 228–45.

23. One exception is Michael Bronski, *Culture Clash: The Making of Gay Sensibility* (Boston: South End Press, 1984), 144–59, who viewed the *Advocate* as a consumable sex object geared toward middle-class gay white men.

24. Pierre Bourdieu, *Distinction: A Social Critique of the Judgement of Taste* (1979, 1984; Cambridge, MA: Harvard University Press, 1996), 218. See also Katherine Sender, "Gay Readers, Consumers, and a Dominant Gay Habitus: 25 Years of the *Advocate* Magazine," *Journal of Communication* 51.1 (March 2001): 73–99; as well as Sender, *Business, Not Politics: The Making of the Gay Market* (New York: Columbia University Press, 2004).

25. José Esteban Muñoz, "The Future in the Present: Sexual Avant-Gardes and the Performance of Utopia," in *The Futures of American Studies*, ed. Donald E. Pease and Robyn Wiegman (Durham, NC: Duke University Press, 2002), 101.

26. Anon., *Advocate*, February 1970, 40.

27. Quoted in Levine, *Macho*, 56.

28. Craig Alfred Hanson, "The Fairy Princess Exposed," *Gay Sunshine*, January 10, 1972, 10. Reprinted in *Out of the Closets*, 266–69.

29. Joseph Litvak, *Strange Gourmets: Sophistication, Theory, and the Novel* (Durham, NC: Duke University Press, 1997), 4.

30. William J. Spurlin, "Remapping Same-Sex Desire: Queer Writing and Cultures in the American Heartland," in *De-Centring Sexualities: Politics and Representations Beyond the Metropolis*, ed. Richard Phillips, Diane Watt, and David Shuttleton (London: Routledge, 2000), 182–98; Michael Moon, "Whose History? The Case of Oklahoma," in *A Queer World: The Center for Lesbian and Gay Studies Reader*, ed. Martin Duberman (New York: New York University Press, 1997), 24–34; and John Howard, *Men Like That: A Southern Queer History* (Chicago: University of Chicago Press, 1999), offer trenchant critiques of what Howard terms the "bicoastal bias" (12).

31. For more on cities such as Chicago as "'extra-regional' exceptions" to geographies such as the U.S. Midwest, see Victoria Johnson, *Heartland TV: Prime Time Television and the Struggle for U.S. Identity* (New York: New York University Press, 2008), 36.

32. See Michael Warner, *The Trouble with Normal: Sex, Politics, and the Ethics of Queer Life* (New York: The Free Press, 1999), 61–66 and 77, for his overview of late twentieth-century mass publications such as *Genre*.

33. Michael Quinion, "Boilerplate," "World Wide Words," http://www.world-widewords.org/qa/qa-boi1.htm (accessed April 24, 2009).

34. Two works that track the political complexities of the U.S. metropolis in the 1960s and 1970s include Cynthia A. Young, *Soul Power: Culture, Radicalism, and the Making of a U.S. Third World Left* (Durham, NC: Duke University Press, 2006); and Laura Pulido, *Black, Brown, Yellow, and Left: Radical Activism in Los Angeles* (Berkeley and Los Angeles: University of California Press, 2006).

35. Del Martin, "If That's All There Is," *Advocate*, October 28–November 10, 1970, 74.

36. Ibid., 75.

37. See Saralyn Chestnut and Amanda C. Gable, "'Women Ran It': Charis Books and More and Atlanta's Lesbian-Feminist Community, 1971–1981," in *Carryin' On in the Lesbian and Gay South*, ed. John Howard (New York: New York University Press, 1997), 241–84; Karla Jay, "No Man's Land," in *Lavender Culture*, ed. Jay and Allen Young (1978; New York: New York University Press, 1994), 63; Stephanie Foote, "Deviant Classics: Pulps and the Making of Lesbian Print Culture," *Signs* 31.1 (2005): 169–90; and Streitmatter, *Unspeakable*, 155–58, for catalogs of lesbian prints published during the 1970s and earlier.

38. Streitmatter, *Unspeakable*, 167.

39. Ibid., 161.

40. Jay, "No Man's Land," 53. See also Jill Johnston, *Lesbian Nation: The Feminist Solution* (New York: Simon and Schuster, 1973); Charlotte Bunch, "Learning from Lesbian Separatism," in *Lavender Culture*, 433–44; Adrienne Rich, "Compulsory Heterosexuality and Lesbian Existence," in *The Lesbian and Gay Studies Reader*, ed. Henry Abelove, Michèle Aina Barale, and David M. Halperin (New York: Routledge, 1993), 227–54; Alice Echols, *Daring to Be Bad: Radical Feminism in America, 1967–1975* (Minneapolis: University of Minnesota Press, 1989); Radicalesbians, "Leaving the Gay Men Behind," in *Out of the Closets*, 290–93; Berlant and Freeman, "Queer Nationality," on the "separatist withdrawal into safe territories" (168); Ann Snitow, "A Gender Diary," in *Conflicts in Feminism*, ed. Marianne Hirsch and Evelyn Fox Keller (London: Routledge, 1990), 9–43; Linda Garber, *Identity Poetics: Race, Class, and the Lesbian-Feminist Roots of Queer Theory* (New York: Columbia University Press, 2001); and Cherríe Moraga, "Preface," in *This Bridge Called My Back: Writings by Radical Women of Color*, ed. Moraga and Gloria Anzaldúa (Watertown, MA: Persephone Press, 1981), xiii–xix, for personal accounts and critical histories of U.S. radical-lesbian feminisms in the 1970s.

41. See http://www.lesbianherstoryarchives.org/exhfashion.htm (accessed February 14, 2006; now defunct). See also Streitmatter, *Unspeakable*, 161–63.

42. Streitmatter, *Unspeakable*, 105, 192.

43. For discussions of this stereotype, see Sender, "Gay Readers," 85.

44. Jay, "No Man's Land," 53.

45. Ibid., 63.

46. Ibid. Besides those listed, scads of national and regional magazines, journals, and newsletters were produced during this pivotal decade, including *Atlanta Lesbian Feminist Alliance Newsletter, Big Apple Dyke News* (New York City), *Lavender Prairie News* (Champaign, IL), *Lesbian Community News* (Lincoln, NE), *Lesbians of Color Newsletter* (San Diego), *Monthly Cycle* (Lawrence, KS), *Sinister Wisdom* (Amherst, MA), *Third World Women's Gay-Zette* (Flushing, NY), *Sisters United: A Lesbian/Feminist Magazine* (Galena, KS), *Womin Energy* (Lexington, KY), and *Lesbian Front* (Jackson, MS). For further listings, see reels 103–4, "Periodicals," in the Lesbian Herstory Archives and Lesbian Herstory Educational Foundation, New York, NY.

47. Ann Cvetkovich, *An Archive of Feelings: Trauma, Sexuality, and Lesbian Public Cultures* (Durham, NC: Duke University Press, 2003), 156–238, overviews the emotional, intellectual, and political convergences of lesbians and gay men at the zenith of AIDS activism in the late 1980s and early 1990s.

48. Meeker, *Contacts Desired*, 232.

49. For analysis of the cultural politics of the radical back-to-the-land movement as well as the countercultural strains that influenced *Country Women*, see Bennett M. Berger, *The Survival of a Counterculture: Ideological Work and Everyday Life Among Rural Communards* (Berkeley and Los Angeles: University of California Press, 1981).

50. David Bell and Gill Valentine, "Queer Country: Rural Lesbian and Gay Lives," *Journal of Rural Studies* 11.2 (1995): 118.

51. See *Lesbian Land*, ed. Joyce Cheney (Minneapolis: Word Weavers, 1985); Angelia R. Wilson, "Getting Your Kicks on Route 66!: Stories of Gay and Lesbian Life in Rural America, c. 1950–1970," in *De-Centring Sexualities*, 199–216; Gill Valentine, "Introduction: From Nowhere to Everywhere: Lesbian Geographies," in *From Nowhere to Everywhere: Lesbian Geographies*, ed. Valentine (Binghamton, NY: Harrington Park, 2000), 1–9; and Valentine, "Making Space: Lesbian Separatist Communities in the United States," in *Contested Countryside Cultures: Otherness, Marginalisation, and Rurality*, ed. Paul Cloke and Jo Little (London: Routledge, 1997), 109–22, for more on the emancipatory politics as well as the ideological difficulties of rural-based feminist/lesbian separatism.

52. Bell and Valentine, "Queer Country," 119.

53. Sherry Thomas and Jeanne Tetrault, "Introduction," in *Country Women: A Handbook for the New Farmer* (Garden City, NY: Anchor Press/Doubleday, 1976), 13. Reels 80–81, "Land," in the Lesbian Herstory Archives and Lesbian Herstory Educational Foundation, also detail rural lesbian-based land cultivations.

54. Thomas and Tetrault, "Introduction," xiii.

55. Sherry Thomas and Jeanne Tetrault, "Statement of Purpose," *Country Women* 1.1 (1973): n.p.

56. Gerald W. Creed and Barbara Ching, "Introduction: Recognizing Rusticity: Identity and the Power of Place," in *Knowing Your Place: Rural Identity and Cultural Hierarchy*, ed. Ching and Creed (New York: Routledge, 1997), 10.

57. Ibid., 4.

58. Barbara, "Retrospective: Feminism and the Unconscious Collective," *Country Women* 2 (1973): 34.

59. Ibid.

60. Scofield, "*RFD* History," 9.

61. *RFD* Collective, "Rustic Fairy Dreams," *RFD* 1 (1974 Autumnal Equinox issue): 3.

62. Anon., "Hop Brook Commune," *RFD* 1 (1974 Autumnal Equinox issue): 11.

63. Lee Mintz, "The Gays—Who Are We? Where Do We Come From? What Are We For?," *RFD* 5 (Autumn 1975): 41.

64. I borrow the phrase "mainstream subculture" from Lauren M. E. Goodlad and Michael Bibby, "Introduction," in *Goth: Undead Subculture* (Durham, NC: Duke University Press, 2007), who use the term to describe contemporary goth group identities.

65. Anon., "As the Butter Churns," *RFD* 7 (1976 Vernal Equinox issue): 4.

66. Scofield, "*RFD* History," 11.

67. Ibid., 13.

68. *RFD* Collective, "Rustic Fairy Dreams," *RFD* 1 (1974 Autumnal Equinox issue): 3.

69. Scofield, "*RFD* History," 9.

70. Lee Mintz, "City/Country," *RFD* 3 (1975 Spring Equinox issue): 9.

71. Anon., "As the Butter Churns," *RFD* 7 (1976 Vernal Equinox issue): 16.

72. Ibid.

73. Critical analyses of "hillbilly" and working-class white representations can be found in Matt Wray, *Not Quite White: White Trash and the Boundaries of Whiteness* (Durham, NC: Duke University Press, 2006); Constance Penley, "Crackers and Whackers: The White Trashing of Porn," in *White Trash: Race and Class in America*, ed. Wray and Annalee Newitz (New York: Routledge, 1997), 89–112; Wendell Ricketts, "Passing Notes in Class: Some Thoughts on Writing and Culture in the Ga(y)ted Community," in *Everything I Have Is Blue: Short Fiction by Working-Class Men about More-or-Less Gay Life*, ed. Ricketts (San Francisco: Suspect Thoughts Press, 2005), 216–42; J. W. Williamson, *Hillbillyland: What the Movies Did to the Mountains and What the Mountains Did to the Movies* (Chapel Hill: University of North Carolina Press, 1995); and John Hartigan Jr., *Odd Tribes: Toward a Cultural Analysis of White People* (Durham, NC: Duke University Press, 2005).

74. Beth Bailey, *Sex in the Heartland* (Cambridge, MA: Harvard University Press, 1999), 4.

75. Meeker, *Contacts Desired*, 223.

76. RFD Collective, "Rustic Fairy Dreams," *RFD* 1 (1974 Autumnal Equinox issue): 1.

77. Sunfrog, "Politics and Poly Tricks: From Confrontation to Community," *RFD* 20 (1994): 17.

78. Meeker, *Contacts Desired*, 214.

79. Mark Monmonier, *How to Lie with Maps* (Chicago: University of Chicago Press, 1991), 43.

80. Lisa Lowe and David Lloyd, "Introduction," *The Politics of Culture in the Shadow of Capital*, ed. Lowe and Lloyd (Durham, NC: Duke University Press, 1997), 25.

81. Anon., *RFD* 2 (1974 Winter Solstice issue): 3.

82. Didier Eribon, "The Flight to the City," in *Insult and the Making of the Gay Self*, trans. Michael Lucey (Durham, NC: Duke University Press, 2004), 19.

Chapter Three

1. I use the term "redneck" here and elsewhere in this chapter knowingly, and not disparagingly. Historically, this slang term has been used against working-class U.S. southern white (and often rural) populations. It has, nevertheless, also become a term of self-identification for this social group.

2. Michael Meads, quoted in Wayne Northcross, "Good Ol' Boys," *Instinct*, March 2003, 95.

3. Anonymous, "SO HOT!!!" November 19, 2003, http://www.datalounge.com/datalounge/forums/index.html (accessed January 23, 2005). Subsequent anonymous quotations about *Eastaboga* and *Alabama Souvenirs* stem from the same DataLounge Web site and the same "SO HOT!!!" posting.

4. For links between "white trash" bodies and pornography, see Constance Penley, "Crackers and Whackers: The White Trashing of Porn," in *White Trash: Race and Class in America*, ed. Matt Wray and Annalee Newitz (New York: Routledge, 1997), 89–112. For the queerness of "white trash," see Joshua Gamson, *Freaks Talk Back: Tabloid Talk Shows and Sexual Nonconformity* (Chicago: University of Chicago Press, 1998), 193–94; and Ann Cvetkovich, *An Archive of Feelings: Trauma, Sexuality, and Lesbian Public Cultures* (Durham, NC: Duke University Press, 2003), 115–17. For "white trash erotics," see David Bell, "Eroticizing the Rural," in *De-Centring Sexualities: Politics and Representations Beyond the Metropolis*, ed. Richard Phillips, Diane Watt, and David Shuttleton (London: Routledge, 2000), 85–90.

5. Thomas Waugh, *Hard to Imagine: Gay Male Eroticism in Photography and Film from Their Beginnings to Stonewall* (New York: Columbia University Press, 1996), xiv.

6. Waugh, *Hard to Imagine*, 54.

7. By "spectatorship" I reference W. J. T. Mitchell in *Picture Theory: Essays on Verbal and Visual Representation* (Chicago: University of Chicago Press, 1994): "The look, the gaze, the glance, the practices of observation, surveillance, and visual pleasure" (16).

8. For more on Eastaboga's racial population breakdown, see "The Skinny On: 36260 (Eastaboga AL)," http://zipskinny.com/index.php?zip=36260. For social histories of working-class and poor rural-identified whites in Alabama and the U.S. South, see Wayne Flint, *Dixie's Forgotten People: The South's Poor Whites* (1979; Bloomington: Indiana University Press, 2004); Flint, *Poor But Proud: Alabama's Poor Whites* (Tuscaloosa: University of Alabama Press, 1989); Julian B. Roebuck and Mark Hickson III, *The Southern Redneck: A Phenomenological Class Study* (New York: Praeger Publishers, 1982); and Rick Bragg, *The Prince of Frogtown* (New York: Knopf, 2008), and *Ava's Man* (New York: Vintage, 2001).

9. Judith Halberstam, *In a Queer Time and Place: Transgender Bodies, Subcultural Lives* (New York: New York University Press, 2005), 37. The archive on queer sexualities and the U.S. South includes John Howard, *Men Like That: A Southern Queer History* (Chicago: University of Chicago Press, 1999); *Carryin' On in the Lesbian and Gay South*, ed. Howard (New York: New York University Press, 1997); James T. Sears, *Rebels, Rubyfruit, and Rhinestones: Queering Space in the Stonewall South* (New Brunswick, NJ: Rutgers University Press, 2001); Lisa Duggan, *Sapphic Slashers: Sex, Violence, and American Modernity* (Durham, NC: Duke University Press, 2000); Angelia R. Wilson, *Below the Belt: Sexuality, Religion, and the American South* (London: Cassell, 2000); *Out in the South*, ed. Carlos L. Dews and Carolyn Leste Law (Philadelphia: Temple University Press, 2001); E. Patrick Johnson, *Sweet Tea: Black Gay Men of the South* (Chapel Hill: University of North Carolina Press, 2008); Charles E. Morris III, "Introduction: 'Travelin' Thru' the Queer South," *Southern Communication Journal* 79.3 (2009): 233–42; and Reta Ugena Whitlock, "'Them Ol' Nasty Lesbians': Queer Memory, Place, and Rural Formations of Lesbians," *Journal of Lesbian Studies* 13.1 (2009): 98–106.

10. With their critical focus on sexual history and identification, Meads's images join debates about queer historiography that have been advanced by Leo Bersani and Ulysse Dutoit, *Caravaggio's Secrets* (Cambridge, MA: MIT Press, 1998); Christopher Nealon, *Foundlings: Lesbian and Gay Historical Emotion before Stonewall* (Durham, NC: Duke University Press, 2001); Elizabeth Freeman on "temporal incongruity" and the anachronisms of the feminist U.S. body in "Packing History, Count(er)ing Generations," *New Literary History* 31.4 (2000): 728; Freeman, "Turn the Beat Around: Sadomasochism, Temporality, History," *differences* 19.1 (2008): 32–70; Halberstam on the "anachronism" of the transgender visual body in *Queer Time*, 15; and Jonathan Goldberg and Madhavi Menon, "Queering History," *PMLA* 120.5 (2005): 1608–17.

11. José Esteban Muñoz, "The Future in the Present: Sexual Avant-Gardes and the Performance of Utopia," in *The Futures of American Studies*, ed. Donald E. Pease and Robyn Wiegman (Durham, NC: Duke University Press, 2002), 98.

12. See Muñoz, "Rough Boy Trade: Queer Desire/Straight Identity in the Photography of Larry Clark," in *The Passionate Camera*, ed. Deborah Bright (New York: Routledge, 1998), 167–77, for a close reading of Clark's queer photographs.

13. Vince Aletti, "Photo: Michael Meads," *Village Voice*, December 11–17, 2002, 79.

14. Meads, "quick update," e-mail message to author, April 13, 2005.

15. Bell, "Anti-Idyll Rural Horror," in *Contested Countryside Cultures: Otherness, Marginalisation, and Rurality*, ed. Paul Cloke and Jo Little (London: Routledge, 1997), 94.

16. Though I am aware that Pater wrote during a moment in Britain's sexual history when a hetero- and homosexual binary was only beginning to cohere, I use the term "proto-gay" because later art historians and lay critics such as Scott McLemee ("Walter Pater [1839–1894]," http://www.glbtq.com/literature/pater_w.html [accessed February 18, 2005]) have reclaimed the critic for an "aesthetic" that supposedly "reflected a homosexual sensibility" (par. 1).

17. Waugh, *Hard to Imagine*, xiv.

18. It is beyond the present scope of this argument to explore Meads's complex conversations with histories of the U.S. South and photographic representation. As my reference to Evans suggests, I believe that a dialogue on these matters does take place, even as Meads prefers to think of himself as rebelling against a specifically gay and a specifically urban-oriented pictorial tradition. For more on southern photography and the politics of visual representation, see Katherine Henninger, "Claiming Access: Controlling Images of Dorothy Allison," *Arizona Quarterly* 60.3 (Autumn 2004): 83–108; and William Stott, *Documentary Expression and Thirties America* (New York: Oxford University Press, 1973).

19. Joan W. Scott, "Fantasy Echo: History and the Construction of Identity," *Critical Inquiry* 27.2 (Winter 2001): 284–304.

20. Meads, "last email with two questions: I promise," e-mail message to author, February 10, 2005. One solid history of "white power" coalitions in the present day is James Ridgeway, *Blood in the Face: The Ku Klux Klan, Aryan Nations, Nazi Skinheads, and the Rise of a New White Culture* (New York: Thunder's Mouth, 1995). For an insightful analysis of "white power" groups, their "cultures of hate," and their terrorism against ruralized queer bodies, see Halberstam, *Queer Time*, 29.

21. Given the current violence waged against Alabama-based queers, such a reading is not unfounded. See Bob Moser, "Unsweet Homo Alabama," *Out.com*, http://www.out.com/ (accessed April 18, 2005).

22. Meads, "forgot to mention," e-mail message to author, April 16, 2005. See also David Shuttleton, "The Queer Politics of Gay Pastoral," in *De-Centring Sexualities*, for his reading of the "elitist and emancipatory, aesthetic and polemical, misogynist and separatist" politics of "the gay pastoral" (129).

23. Jamie Hakim, "Sweet Homo Alabama," *Attitude* (Spring 2004): 31.

24. Howard, *Men Like That*, 306. Johnson, *Sweet Tea* also details homosex practices in the U.S. South—here African American queer and trans-identified men.

25. Ibid., 19.

26. Ibid., 43.

27. Northcross, "Good Ol' Boys," 95.

28. Andrew Robinson, "Men in Their Natural State," *Gay City News*, July 8–14, 2004.

29. This deliberate facade of "everyday life" may also be part of Meads's larger attempt to trouble documentary knowledge concerning rural male intimacy in the U.S. South. See John Ibson, *Picturing Men: A Century of Male Relationships in Everyday American Photography* (Washington, DC: Smithsonian Institution Press, 2002), for its reading of intimate everyday life ideologies in relation to photography and male-male relations.

30. Meads, quoted in Brad Johnston, "The Boys: Growing Up with Michael Meads," *Blue*, November 2003, 42.

31. Waugh, *Hard to Imagine*, 71.

32. Meads, "forgot to mention."

33. For theories of "inaccurate replication," see Bersani and Dutoit, *Caravaggio's Secrets* and *Forms of Being: Cinema, Aesthetics, Subjectivity* (London: British Film Institute, 2004).

34. Though I do not reprint them, most of the "Allen and Justin" series—as well as several of the *Allen: At the Old Confederate Bridge* shots—correspond to images in von Gloeden's *Taormina*. The "Allen" shot of fig. 3.3, in fact, re-stages a von Gloeden image of a young Sicilian male standing on jagged rock looking away from the viewer's gaze.

35. Waugh, *Hard to Imagine*, 85.

36. For critics whose work dialogues directly with the imperial sexual politics of the Mediterranean, the colonialist ideologies of Prussia, and the sexualization of modern Germany, see Robert Aldrich, *Colonialism and Homosexuality* (London: Routledge, 2003); Aldrich, *The Seduction of the Mediterranean: Writing, Art, and Homosexual Fantasy* (London: Routledge, 1993); and Joseph Allen Boone, "Vacation Cruises; or, the Homoerotics of Orientalism," *PMLA* 110.1 (1995): 89–107. For von Gloeden's imperialism in particular, see Waugh, *Hard to Imagine*, 71–86, 97–102; and Allen Ellenzweig, *The Homoerotic Photograph: Male Images from Durieu/Delacroix to Mapplethorpe* (New York: Columbia University Press, 1992), 35–47. For an analysis of how von Gloeden has been fetishized in U.S. gay

male pornography, see Jason Goldman, "'The Golden Age of Gay Porn': Nostalgia and the Photography of Wilhelm von Gloeden," *GLQ* 12.2 (2006): 237–58.

37. Waugh, *Hard to Imagine*, 49–50.

38. Ibid., 71.

39. Ellenzweig, *Homoerotic Photograph*, 4.

40. George Chauncey, "Manhattan's Roaring Gay Days," *Out Traveler*, Spring 2008, 58.

41. This anachronistic time recalls and reformats Anne McClintock's theory of "anachronistic space," or what she defines as a colonial "trope" that situates "colonized people" "in a permanently anterior time within the geographic space of the modern empire as anachronistic humans, atavistic, irrational, bereft of human agency—the living embodiment of the archaic 'primitive'" (*Imperial Leather: Race, Gender, and Sexuality in the Colonial Contest* [New York: Routledge, 1995], 30). Though von Gloeden (and, to some extent, Meads) photographs rural bodies in an "anterior time" that signifies ancient Greece or Rome, he also imports this time into his turn-of-the-century present rather than shunting them permanently to an unspecified past.

42. Roland Barthes, "Is Baron von Gloeden's Work 'Camp'?," trans. Angus Whyte, in *Taormina: Wilhelm von Gloeden* (Santa Fe, New Mexico: Twelvetrees, 1997), n.p.

43. Ibid.

44. Ibid.

45. Waugh, *Hard to Imagine*, 26.

46. Northcross, "Good Ol' Boys," 95.

47. Meads, "Allen," 2005, http://www.michaelmeads.com/allenbio.htm (accessed February 10, 2005).

48. Northcross, "Rural Rhapsody," *Gay City News*, February 21–27, 2003, 34.

49. Muñoz, *Disidentifications: Queers of Color and the Performance of Politics* (Minneapolis: University of Minnesota Press, 1999), 11.

50. For another reading of southern "backwardness" with regards to the state of Mississippi, see Howard, *Men Like That*, 29.

51. Kath Weston, *Long Slow Burn: Sexuality and Social Science* (New York: Routledge, 1998), 54.

52. Meads, "last email with two questions."

53. Meads, quoted in Johnston, "The Boys," 42.

54. "Michael Meads," *New Yorker*, December 16, 2002, 20.

55. Northcross, "Rural Rhapsody," 34.

56. Meads, "forgot to mention."

57. I have in mind Derek Jarman's films and several of Thom Gunn's poems. See Raymond Jean-Frontain, "Caravaggio and Post-Stonewall Gay Culture," in "GLBTQ: An Encyclopedia of Gay, Lesbian, Bisexual, Transgender, & Queer Culture," http://www.glbtq.com/arts/caravaggio,3.html (accessed April 26, 2009), for a brief discussion of these two artists.

58. Meads, "In the Studio," *Alabama Souvenirs*, 2005, http://www.michael-meads.com/studiobio.htm (accessed January 12, 2005).

59. Elliot Lane, "Southern Men: The Work of Michael Meads," *OUTspoken!*, March 2004.

60. Johnston, "The Boys," 42.

61. Howard, *Men Like That*, 304.

62. Meads, "last email with two questions."

63. John M. Coski, *The Confederate Battle Flag: America's Most Embattled Emblem* (Cambridge, MA: Belknap Press of Harvard University, 2005), 97. Complementary readings that scrutinize the Confederate battle flag as it reflects white racial hatred and non-white appropriation include Kim Q. Hall, "My Father's Flag," in *Whiteness: Feminist Philosophical Reflections*, ed. Chris J. Cuomo and Hall (Lanham, MD: Rowman and Littlefield, 1999), 29–35; Bonnie R. Strickland, "Leaving the Confederate Closet," in *Out in the South*, 97–114; James C. Cobb, *Away Down South: A History of Southern Identity* (New York: Oxford University Press, 2005), 290–301; Tara McPherson, *Reconstructing Dixie: Race, Gender, and Nostalgia in the Imagined South* (Durham, NC: Duke University Press, 2003), 33–37; and Houston A. Baker Jr., *Turning South Again: Re-Thinking Modernism/Re-Reading Booker T.* (Durham, NC: Duke University Press, 2001), 21–22.

64. Ibid., 26, 174.

65. Ibid., 305.

66. Meads, telephone interview by author, October 4, 2004.

67. Laura Kipnis, "(Male) Desire and (Female) Disgust: Reading *Hustler*," in *Queer Studies: An Interdisciplinary Reader*, ed. Robert J. Corber and Stephen Valocchi (Oxford: Blackwell, 2003), 116.

68. Released in 1995 by Universal Pictures, the film was directed by Beeban Kidron, produced by Amblin Entertainment, and written by Douglas Carter Beane.

69. My description of Meads's disidentifications also brings to mind Muñoz's description of the performance artist Vaginal Davis's "counterpublic terrorism" (*Disidentifications*, 100).

70. Muñoz, "The Future in the Present," 101.

71. Northcross, "Rural Rhapsody."

72. Bersani and Dutoit, *Caravaggio's Secrets*, 51, 64.

73. Muñoz, *Disidentifications*, x. For discussions of the volatile and violent appropriations of the Union Jack by British queer skinheads, see Kobena Mercer, "Skin Head Sex Thing: Racial Difference and the Homoerotic Imaginary," in *The Masculinity Studies Reader*, ed. Rachel Adams and David Savran (Malden, MA: Blackwell, 2002), 188–200; and Murray Healey, *Gay Skins: Class, Masculinity, and Queer Appropriation* (London: Cassell, 1996), 115–19, 172–97.

74. Bell, "Anti-Idyll Rural Horror," 94.

Chapter Four

1. Unless otherwise noted, all citations from Eli Clare can be found in Clare, *Exile and Pride: Disability, Queerness, and Liberation* (Cambridge, MA: South End Press, 1999). I have also gendered Clare's narrator as female, but I point out that in an essay almost a half decade later Clare writes, "I'm hungry for an image to describe my gendered self, something more than the shadowland of neither man nor woman" ("Gawking, Gaping, Staring," *GLQ* 9.1–2 [2003]: 260). For her achievement of this image, see Clare, *The Marrow's Telling: Words in Motion* (Ypsilanti, MI: Homofactus Press, 2007).

2. Throughout *Exile and Pride*, Clare identifies as "mixed-class," a terms that, for her, signifies a combination of working- and middle-class habitus (42).

3. Unless otherwise noted, all citations from D. A. Miller can be found in Miller, *Bringing Out Roland Barthes* (Berkeley and Los Angeles: University of California Press, 1992).

4. The following lists some of the many works in queer studies that consider dress and fashion: Renu Bora, "Outing Texture," in *Novel Gazing: Queer Readings in Fiction*, ed. Eve Kosofsky Sedgwick (Durham, NC: Duke University Press, 1997), 94–127; Kathryn Bond Stockton, *Beautiful Bottom, Beautiful Shame: Where "Black" Meets "Queer"* (Durham, NC: Duke University Press, 2006), 39–66; Sharon Marcus, "Reflections on Victorian Fashion Plates," *differences* 14.3 (2003): 4–33; Sedgwick, "White Glasses," in *Tendencies* (Durham, NC: Duke University Press, 1993): 252–66; Shaun Cole, *"Don We Now Our Gay Apparel": Gay Men's Dress in the Twentieth Century* (Oxford: Berg, 2000); Danae Clark, "Commodity Lesbianism," in *The Lesbian and Gay Studies Reader*, ed. Henry Abelove, Michèle Aina Barale, and David M. Halperin (New York: Routledge, 1993), 186–201; Diana Fuss, "Fashion and the Homospectatorial Look," *Critical Inquiry* 18.4 (1992): 713–37; and Marjorie Garber, *Vested Interests: Cross-Dressing and Cultural Anxiety* (New York: Routledge, 1997).

5. Diana Crane, *Fashion and Its Social Agendas: Class, Gender, and Identity in Clothing* (Chicago: University of Chicago Press, 2000), 21. General overviews of fashion studies in its urbanist orientations can be found in *Fashion Cultures: Theories, Explorations, and Analysis*, ed. Stella Bruzzi and Pamela Church Gibson (London: Routledge, 2000); Elizabeth Wilson, *Adorned in Dreams: Fashion and Modernity* (New Brunswick, NJ: Rutgers University Press, 2003), 134–54; *Chic Thrills: A Fashion Reader*, ed. Juliet Ash and Elizabeth Wilson (Berkeley and Los Angeles: University of California Press, 1992); Yuniya Kawamura, *Fashion-ology: An Introduction to Fashion Studies* (Oxford: Berg, 2005); and Réka C. V. Buckley and Stephen Gundle, "Fashion and Glamour," in *The Fashion Business: Theory, Practice, Image*, ed. Nicola White and Ian Griffiths (Oxford: Berg, 2000), 37–54.

6. General critiques of urban-based fashion and labor can be found in Robert J. S. Ross, *Slaves to Fashion: Poverty and Abuse in the New Sweatshops* (Ann Arbor:

University of Michigan Press, 2004); Edna Bonacich and Richard Appelbaum, *Behind the Label: Inequality in the Los Angeles Apparel Industry* (Berkeley and Los Angeles: University of California Press, 2000); and Ellen Israel Rosen, *Making Sweatshops: The Globalization of the U.S. Apparel Industry* (Berkeley and Los Angeles: University of California Press, 2002).

7. Wayne Koestenbaum, *Cleavage: Essays on Sex, Stars, and Aesthetics* (New York: Ballantine, 2000), 36.

8. Unless otherwise stated, all citations from Roland Barthes are quoted from Barthes, *Système de la mode* (The fashion system), trans. Matthew Ward and Richard Howard (1983; Berkeley and Los Angeles: University of California Press, 1990).

9. Susan Sontag, "Notes on 'Camp,'" in *Against Interpretation, and Other Essays* (New York: Picador, 2001), 290.

10. For more on the temporal norms of fashion, see Herbert Blumer, "Fashion: From Class Differentiation to Collective Selection," *Sociological Quarterly* 10.3 (1969): 275–91.

11. Edmund White, *States of Desire: Travels in Gay America* (1980; New York: Plume, 1991), 259.

12. Years before the term achieved a wider currency and three years before *Zami*'s publication in 1982, Lorde first used the term "dyke-chic" in an earlier version of her memoir that was published as "'Tar Beach' from Prosepiece, part iii," *conditions five: the black women's issue* (Autumn 1979): 34. Katie King's "Audre Lorde's Lacquered Layerings: The Lesbian Bar as a Site of Literary Production," in *New Lesbian Criticism: Literary and Cultural Readings*, ed. Sally Munt (New York: Columbia University Press, 1992), 51–74, first brought this quote to my attention.

13. Lorde, "'Tar Beach,'" 34.

14. Unless otherwise stated, remaining quotations from Lorde can be found in Audre Lorde, *Zami: A New Spelling of My Name* (Berkeley: Crossing Press, 1982).

15. Lorde, "'Tar Beach,'" 34.

16. I have in mind Lorde's sexual encounters with Ginger once she found "a job running a commercial X-ray machine" in Stamford, Connecticut (129). As Ginger cruises Audre at the Keystone factory, the former exclaims, "That's right. Blue jeans and sneakers on Atlantic Avenue [in Brooklyn] on Thursday night! I said to myself, who's this slick kitty from the city?" (129). Audre then becomes the object of Ginger's idealizations of Greenwich Village lesbianism, an idealization that she fails to live up to. Lorde writes: "A piece of me was invested in her image of me as the gay young blade, the seasoned and accomplished lover from the big city" (141).

17. Cathy J. Cohen, *The Boundaries of Blackness: AIDS and the Breakdown of Black Politics* (Chicago: University of Chicago Press, 1999), 71.

18. Lorde, "'Tar Beach,'" in *The Persistent Desire: A Femme-Butch Reader*, ed. Joan Nestle (Boston: Alyson Publications, 1992), 129.

19. Quoted in Madeline Davis, Amber Hollibaugh, and Joan Nestle, "The Femme Tapes," in *The Persistent Desire*, 254. Further reparative readings of butch-femme relations include Nestle, *A Restricted Country* (Ithaca, NY: Firebrand, 1987); Amber Hollibaugh and Cherríe Moraga, "What We're Rollin' Around in Bed With: Sexual Silences in Feminism," in *Powers of Desire: The Politics of Sexuality*, ed. Ann Snitow, Christine Stansell, and Sharon Thompson (New York: Monthly Review Press, 1983), 394–405; and Leslie Feinberg, *Stone Butch Blues* (Ithaca, NY: Firebrand, 1993).

20. Gayle Rubin, "Of Catamites and Kings: Reflections on Butch, Gender, and Boundaries," in *The Persistent Desire*, 474.

21. The archive recording this debt is vast. See King, "Audre Lorde's Lacquered Layerings"; Sarah E. Chinn, "Feeling Her Way: Audre Lorde and the Power of Touch," *GLQ* 9.1–2 (2003): 181–204; Linda Garber, *Identity Poetics: Race, Class, and the Lesbian-Feminist Roots of Queer Theory* (New York: Columbia University Press, 2001), on Lorde's "poetics of location" (97); Lynda Hall, "Passion(ate) Plays 'Wherever We Found Space': Lorde and Gomez Queer(y)ing Boundaries and Acting In," *Callaloo* 23.1 (2000): 394–421; Robert McRuer, "Boys' Own Stories and New Spellings of My Name: Coming Out and Other Myths of Queer Positionality," in *Eroticism and Containment: Notes from the Flood Plain*, ed. Carol Siegel and Ann Kibbey (New York: New York University Press, 1994), 260–84; Sharon P. Holland, "To Touch the Mother's C(o)untry: Siting Audre Lorde's Erotics," in *Lesbian Erotics*, ed. Karla Jay (New York: New York University Press, 1995), 212–26; and Cheryl A. Wall, *Worrying the Line: Black Women Writers, Lineage, and Literary Tradition* (Chapel Hill: University of North Carolina Press, 2005), 41–58.

22. I don't want these dates to neglect the fact that lesbian-identified chic was also central to the historical emergence of an Anglo-identified middle-class lesbian identity in the United States and Britain in the 1920s. As we saw in chapter 1, sapphic modernity was viewed by some as a constrictive form of metronormativity rather than a celebratory subculture.

23. Pierre Bourdieu, *Distinction: A Social Critique of the Judgement of Taste*, trans. Richard Nice (1979, 1984; Cambridge, MA: Harvard University Press, 1996), 56.

24. Sharon Bridgforth, "Preface," *The Bull-Jean Stories* (Austin, TX: RedBone Press, 1998), n.p.

25. Ibid.

26. Bridgforth, "Personal Statement," http://www.wymnwriting.blogspot.com/2005/10/personal-statement-sharon-bridgforth-i.html (accessed October 23, 2006; now defunct).

27. Bridgforth, "Preface," n.p.

28. Ibid.

29. Bridgforth, telephone interview by author, April 2, 2007.

30. Detailed accounts of Western lesbian aesthetics and lesbian chic can be found in Lisa Walker, *Looking Like What You Are: Sexual Style, Race, and Lesbian Identity* (New York: New York University Press, 2001); Karen Tongson, "Introduction: Lesbian Aesthetics, Aestheticizing Lesbianism," *Nineteenth-Century Literature* 60.3 (2005): 281–90; Marguerite Moritz, "Lesbian Chic: Our Fifteen Minutes of Celebrity?," in *Feminism, Multiculturalism, and the Media: Global Diversities*, ed. Angharad N. Valdivia (Thousand Oaks, CA: Sage Publications, 1995), 127–44; Clark, "Commodity Lesbianism"; Karman Kregloe and Jane Caputi, "Supermodels of Lesbian Chic: Camille Paglia Revamps Lesbian/Feminism (while Susie Bright Retools)," in *Cross-Purposes: Lesbians, Feminists, and the Limits of Alliance*, ed. Dana A. Heller (Bloomington: Indiana University Press, 1997): 136–54; and Inge Blackman and Kathryn Perry on the "high fashion urban look" in "Skirting the Issue: Lesbian Fashion for the 1990s," *Feminist Review* 34 (1990): 69.

31. Unless otherwise noted, all quotations from Jodi R. Schorb and Tania N. Hammidi are found in Schorb and Hammidi, "Sho-Lo Showdown: The *Do's* and Don'ts of Lesbian Chic," *Tulsa Studies in Women's Literature* 19.2 (Autumn 2000): 255–68.

32. Susan McCully, "Out on the Edge: 1996 Festival of Lesbian and Gay Theater," *Theatre Journal* 49.3 (1997): 368. Further Bridgforth notices can be found in Jewelle Gomez, "But Some of Us Are Brave Lesbians: The Absence of Black Lesbian Fiction," in *Black Queer Studies: A Critical Anthology*, ed. E. Patrick Johnson and Mae G. Henderson (Durham, NC: Duke University Press, 2005), 295; and Joni L. Jones and Iya Omi Osun Olomo, "Cast a Wide Net," *Theatre Journal* 57.4 (2005): 598–600.

33. Bridgforth, interview, April 2, 2007.

34. "Michigan Womyn's Music Festival," "Absolute Michigan: All Michigan, All the Time," http://www.absolutemichigan.com/dig/media/michigan-august-event-calendar/ (accessed March 6, 2009).

35. Bonnie J. Morris, "At the Michigan Womyn's Music Fest," *Gay and Lesbian Review Worldwide* 10.5 (2003): 16. For more on the Michigan Womyn's Music Festival, see Ann Cvetkovich, *An Archive of Feelings: Trauma, Sexuality, and Lesbian Public Cultures* (Durham, NC: Duke University Press, 2003), 83–87, 111; and Cvetkovich and Selena Wahng, "Don't Stop the Music: Roundtable Discussion with Workers from the Michigan Womyn's Music Festival," *GLQ* 7.1 (2001): 131–51.

36. Michigan Womyn's Music Festival, August 5–10, 2008, brochure, n.p.

37. "General Festival Information," http://www.michfest.com/festival/index.htm (accessed July 28, 2007).

38. For explorations of queer solo performance in the 1990s, see *O Solo Homo: The New Queer Performance*, ed. Holly Hughes and David Román (New York: Grove Press, 1998), 1–15; José Esteban Muñoz, *Disidentifications: Queers of Color and the Performance of Politics* (Minneapolis: University of Minnesota Press, 1999); Jill Dolan, *Utopia in Performance: Finding Hope at the Theater* (Ann Arbor: University of Michigan Press, 2005), 35–88; Ann Pellegrini, *Performance Anxieties: Staging Psychoanalysis, Staging Race* (New York: Routledge, 1996), 49–64; and Román, *Acts of Intervention: Performance, Gay Culture, and AIDS* (Bloomington: Indiana University Press, 1998), 116–53.

39. Bridgforth, interview, April 2, 2007.

40. Elin Diamond, *Unmaking Mimesis: Essays on Feminism and Theater* (London, New York: Routledge, 1997), 52.

41. Ibid., 53.

42. Dolan, *Utopia*, 88.

43. For a complementary account of such queer temporality, see Michael Hanchard, "Afro-Modernity: Temporality, Politics, and the African Diaspora," in *Alternative Modernities*, ed. Dilip Parameshwar Gaonkar (Durham, NC: Duke University Press, 2001), 272–98.

44. Bridgforth, "quick question about no mo blues," e-mail message to author, October 25, 2006.

45. Ibid.

46. Bridgforth, "Preface," n.p.

47. Bridgforth, *no mo blues* (unpublished manuscript), 5.

48. Ibid., 17.

49. Bridgforth, interview, April 2, 2007.

50. Critical accounts of the word "dyke" or "dike" in African American cultures can be found in Richard A. Spears, "On the Etymology of Dike," *American Speech* 60.4 (1985): 318–27; Clarence Major, *Juba to Jive: The Dictionary of African-American Slang* (New York: Penguin, 1994), 71; Anne Stavney, "Cross-Dressing Harlem, Re-Dressing Race," *Women's Studies* 28.2 (1999): 127–56; Eric Garber, "Gladys Bentley: The Bulldagger Who Sang the Blues," *OUTLook: National Lesbian & Gay Quarterly* 1 (1998): 52–61; and Garber, "A Spectacle in Color: The Lesbian and Gay Subculture of Jazz Age Harlem," in *Hidden from History: Reclaiming the Gay and Lesbian Past*, ed. Martin Duberman, Martha Vicinus, and George Chauncey Jr. (New York: Meridian, 1989): 318–31. For accounts of the term "bulldagger" in queer of color studies, see Ekua Omosupe, "Black/Lesbian/Bulldagger," *differences* 3.2 (1991): 101–11; Cathy J. Cohen, "Punks, Bulldaggers, and Welfare Queens: The Radical Potential of Queer Politics?," in *Black Queer Studies*, 21–51; and Kara Keeling, *The Witch's Flight: The Cinematic, the Black Femme, and the Image of Common Sense* (Durham, NC: Duke University Press, 2007).

51. Bridgforth, interview, April 2, 2007.

52. For more on this dilemma, see Elizabeth Lapovsky Kennedy, "Telling Tales: Oral History and the Construction of Pre-Stonewall Lesbian History," *Radical History Review* 62 (1995): 58–79.

53. Toni Morrison, *Beloved* (New York: Knopf, 1987), 191.

54. Bridgforth, "a note from the author," *no mo blues*, 2.

55. Hazel Carby, "The Politics of Fiction, Anthropology and the Folk: Zora Neale Hurston," in *Cultures of Babylon: Black Britain and African America* (London: Verso, 1999), 168–85, provides an extended discussion of this problematic. See also Madhu Dubey, *Signs and Cities: Black Literary Postmodernism* (Chicago: University of Chicago Press, 2003), 144–185, for her reparative critique of postmodern black literature's representation of the folk, which presents "the rural South of a bygone era as an imaginary elsewhere to postmodern urban existence" (144). On the concept of performative utopias, see Muñoz, "Cruising the Toilet: LeRoi Jones/Amiri Baraka, Radical Black Traditions, and Queer Futurity," *GLQ* 13.2–3 (2007): 353–67; and Dolan, *Utopia*, on the "small but profound moments in which performance calls the attention of the audience in a way that lifts everybody slightly above the present" (5).

56. Sharon P. Holland, "Foreword: 'Home' Is a Four-Letter Word," in *Black Queer Studies*, xii.

57. Dilip Parameshwar Gaonkar, "On Alternative Modernities," in *Alternative Modernities*, ed. Parameshwar Gaonkar (Durham, NC: Duke University Press, 2001), 23.

58. Bridgforth, *no mo blues*, 10.

59. Anon., "Urban Chic," *Curve* 17.3 (2007): 35.

60. Bridgforth, "A wo'mn called sir," *Curve* 12.4 (2002): 46.

61. E. Patrick Johnson, "'Quare' Studies, or (Almost) Everything I Know About Queer Studies I Learned From My Grandmother," in *Black Queer Studies*, 140.

62. Bridgforth, "wo'mn," 47. See Carol B. Stack, *Call to Home: African Americans Reclaim the Rural South* (New York: Basic Books, 1996), for the definitive history of post–World War II narratives of African American return migration; and Farah Jasmine Griffin, *"Who Set You Flowin'?": The African-American Migration Narrative* (Oxford: Oxford University Press, 1995), on musical representations of black counter-migration.

63. Bridgforth, "Preface," n.p.

Chapter Five

1. Brian Lauskies, "Pennsyltucky," Urban Dictionary, http://www.urbandictionary.com/ (accessed June 6, 2008).

2. Fred Norris, "Pennsyltucky," Urban Dictionary, http://www.urbandictionary.com/ (accessed June 8, 2008).

3. Unless otherwise noted, all citations from Alison Bechdel's *Fun Home* can be found in Bechdel, *Fun Home: A Family Tragicomic* (New York: Houghton Mifflin, 2006).

4. Scholars often approach "Appalachia" as a social and geographic space that primarily encompasses regions in Tennessee, Kentucky, North Carolina, and West Virginia. I also envision Appalachian geographies that stretch from the state of Maine to the valleys of north-central Alabama, and that include regions such as central Pennsylvania, Maryland, and New York. On the difficulties of historically defining this region, see Dwight Billings and Ann Tickamyer, "Uneven Development in Appalachia," in *Forgotten Places: Uneven Development and the Loss of Opportunity in Rural America*, ed. Thomas A. Lyson and William W. Falk (Lawrence: University Press of Kansas, 1993), 7–29. For general histories of Appalachia and its diverse cultures, see Richard B. Drake, *A History of Appalachia* (Lexington: University Press of Kentucky, 2001); David E. Whisnant, *All That Is Native and Fine: The Politics of Culture in an American Region* (Chapel Hill: University of North Carolina Press, 1983); Allen Batteau, *The Invention of Appalachia* (Tucson: University of Arizona Press, 1990); and Kathleen Stewart, *A Space on the Side of the Road: Cultural Poetics in an "Other" America* (Princeton: Princeton University Press, 1996).

5. Analyses that follow the trauma of these losses include Ann Cvetkovich, "Drawing the Archive in Alison Bechdel's *Fun Home*," *WSQ* 36.1–2 (2008): 111–28; and Jennifer Lemberg, "Closing the Gap in Alison Bechdel's *Fun Home*," *WSQ* 36.1–2 (2008): 129–40. For links between visualization and verbalization in comics, comix, graphic novels, and graphic memoirs, see Mario Saraceni, *The Language of Comics* (New York: Routledge, 2003); Scott McCloud, *Understanding Comics: The Invisible Art* (New York: HarperCollins, 1993); Hillary Chute, "Comics as Literature? Reading Graphic Narrative," *PMLA* 123.2 (2008): 452–65; and Chute and Marianne DeKoven, "Introduction: Graphic Narrative," *Modern Fiction Studies* 52.4 (2006): 767–82.

6. Kate Burns, "Cartoons and Comic Books," in *Lesbian Histories and Cultures: An Encyclopedia*, ed. Bonnie Zimmerman (New York: Garland Publishing, 2000), 149–50, offers a brief history of queer comics and comix for and about women. Also, for Cruse's influence in Bechdel's art, see "Alison Bechdel," in *Dyke Strippers: Lesbian Cartoonists A to Z*, ed. Roz Warren (Pittsburgh: Clies Press, 1999), 9.

7. Bechdel, "Introduction: On the Occasion of the Twentieth Anniversary of 'Dykes to Watch Out For,'" *Dykes and Sundry Other Carbon-Based Life-Forms to Watch Out For* (Lost Angeles: Alyson Books, 2003), n.p.

8. See Bechdel, *The Indelible Alison Bechdel: Confessions, Comix, and Miscellaneous Dykes to Watch Out For* (Ithaca, NY: Firebrand Books, 1998); and Bechdel, *The Essential Dykes to Watch Out For* (New York: Houghton Mifflin Harcourt, 2008), on the historical and personal background of *Dykes*'s origins.

9. "Interstate 92—New England (Unbuilt)," http://www.bostonroads.com/roads/I-92/ (accessed June 14, 2008).

10. Bechdel, "Dykes to Watch Out For: Life in a Box: Frivolous, Aimless Queries," http://dykestowatchoutfor.com/frivolous-aimless-queries/ (accessed November 17, 2007).

11. Bechdel, interview with Hilary Chute, *Modern Fiction Studies* 52.4 (2006): 1005.

12. Craig Alfred Hanson, "The Fairy Princess Exposed," *Gay Sunshine*, January 10, 1972, 10. Reprinted in *Out of the Closets: Voices of Gay Liberation*, ed. Karla Jay and Allen Young (1972; New York: New York University Press, 1992), 266–69.

13. Michael Moon, review of Bechdel, *Fun Home: A Family Tragicomic*, "Gutter Geek," http://www.guttergeek.com/2006/September2006/funhome/funhome.html (accessed October 28, 2007).

14. See Hans Kurath, *A Word Geography of the Eastern United States* (Ann Arbor: University of Michigan Press, 1949), 32–36, for more on Pennsylvania argot; and Craig M. Carver, *American Regional Dialects: A Word Geography* (Ann Arbor: University of Michigan Press, 1987), 187–89, for more on central Pennsylvania dialects. On queer dialectology, see *Beyond the Lavender Lexicon: Authenticity, Imagination, and Appropriation in Lesbian and Gay Languages*, ed. William L. Leap (Amsterdam: Gordon and Breach Science Publishers, 1995); *Queerly Phrased: Language, Gender, and Sexuality*, ed. Anna Livia and Kira Hall (New York: Oxford University Press, 1997); Deborah Cameron and Don Kulick, *Language and Sexuality* (Cambridge: Cambridge University Press, 2003), 74–105; and *Speaking in Queer Tongues: Globalization and Gay Language*, ed. Leap and Tom Boellstorff (Champaign: University of Illinois Press, 2004).

15. "Bumpkin," *Webster's New World College Dictionary*, ed. Michael Agnes, 4th ed. (Foster City, CA: IDG Books Worldwide, 2001), 194.

16. I poached these definitions, respectively, from the following sources: Online Etymology Dictionary, http://www.etymonline.com/index.php?term=bumpkin; Merriam-Webster's Online Dictionary, http://www.merriam-webster.com/dictionary/bumpkin; and The Free Dictionary, http://www.thefreedictionary.com/bumpkin. All were accessed on June 15, 2008.

17. Batteau, *The Invention of Appalachia*, analyzes this hillbilly stereotype as it evolved across the nineteenth and twentieth century.

18. Walt Wolfram and Natalie Schilling-Estes, *American English: Dialects and Variation*, 2nd ed (Malden, MA: Blackwell Publishing, 2006), 41.

19. Ibid., 128.

20. Ibid., 404.

21. A brief sampling of analyses that focus on queer migrations without, within, and across the urbanized United States could cite Eithne Luibhéid, *Entry Denied: Controlling Sexuality at the Border* (Minneapolis: University of Minnesota

Press, 2002); *Queer Migrations: Sexuality, U.S. Citizenship, and Border Crossings*, ed. Luibhéid and Lionel Cantú Jr. (Minneapolis: University of Minnesota Press, 2005); Erica Rand, *The Ellis Island Snow Globe* (Durham, NC: Duke University Press, 2005); and *Passing Lines: Sexuality and Immigration*, ed. Brad Epps, Keja Valens, and Bill Johnson González (Cambridge, MA: David Rockefeller Center for Latin American Studies, 2005).

22. Outside of "hillbilly horror" (David Bell, "Eroticizing the Rural," *De-Centring Sexualities: Politics and Representations Beyond the Metropolis*, ed. Richard Phillips, Diane Watt, and David Shuttleton [London: Routledge, 2000], 87–89), there remains a paucity of writing on Appalachian-identified queers. Exceptions also include Kate Black and Marc A. Rhorer, "Out in the Mountains: Exploring Lesbian and Gay Lives," in *Out in the South*, ed. Carlos L. Dews and Carolyn Leste Law (Philadelphia: Temple University Press, 2001), 16–25; Jeff Mann, "Appalachian Subculture," *Gay and Lesbian Review Worldwide* 10.5 (2003), 19–21; Mann, *Loving Mountains, Loving Men* (Athens: Ohio University Press, 2005); and Mary Gray, *Out in the Country: Youth, Media, and Queer Visibility in Rural America* (New York: New York University Press, 2009).

23. I borrow my history here from Mark H. Rose, *Interstate: Express Highway Politics, 1941–1956* (Lawrence: Regents Press of Kansas, 1979). For complementary accounts of U.S. roadways, see Owen D. Gutfreund, *Twentieth-Century Sprawl: Highways and the Reshaping of the American Landscape* (Oxford: Oxford University Press, 2004); Clay McShane, *Down the Asphalt Path: The Automobile and the American City* (New York: Columbia University Press, 1994); and Pierce Lewis, "The Urban Invasion of Rural America," in *The Changing American Countryside: Rural People and Places*, ed. Emery N. Castle (Lawrence: University Press of Kansas, 1995), 39–62.

24. "Interstate: History," http://www.interstate-guide.com/i-080.html (accessed April 7, 2009).

25. For a history of the interstate in Pennsylvania, see *The Story of the Keystone Shortway* (Williamsport, PA: Keystone Shortway Association, 1970); and "Keystone Shortway Z. H. Confair Memorial Highway," http://www.pahighways.com/interstates/I80.html.

26. Author unknown, "Interstate: Pennsylvania 80," *Keystone Shortway*, 7.

27. Paul W. Horn, "The Keystone Shortway Story," *Keystone Shortway*, 11.

28. Charles N. Johnson, "Political Aspects of the Shortway," *Keystone Shortway*, 19.

29. "September 17, 1970," "FHWA By Day: A Look at the History of the Federal Highway Administration," http://www.fhwa.dot.gov/byday/fhbd0917.htm (accessed June 21, 2008).

30. Raymond P. Shafer, "Letter," *Keystone Shortway*, 4.

31. Histories that focus on the importance of roadways for male-identified queer sex cultures include John Howard, *Men Like That: A Southern Queer History*

(Chicago: University of Chicago Press, 1999), 99–115; and Tim Retzloff, "Cars and Bars: Assembling Gay Men in Postwar Flint, Michigan," in *Creating a Place for Ourselves: Lesbian, Gay, and Bisexual Community Histories*, ed. Brett Beemyn (New York: Routledge, 1997), 227–52. For histories that focus on the importance of roadways for women, see Lillian Faderman, *Odd Girls and Twilight Lovers: A History of Lesbian Life in Twentieth-Century America* (New York: Penguin, 1991) on working-class female hoboes during the thirties, or "'sisters of the road,' as they were called by male hoboes" (94); and Elizabeth Lapovsky Kennedy and Madeline D. Davis, *Boots of Leather, Slippers of Gold: The History of a Lesbian Community* (New York: Penguin, 1993), on the importance of automobile culture to pre-Stonewall working- and middle-class lesbians in Buffalo, New York, and its surrounding vicinities.

32. For more on Stonewall mythology and its material relations to Christopher Street public spheres, see Lauren Berlant and Michael Warner on "the thousands who migrate or make pilgrimages to Christopher Street" ("Sex in Public," in *Queer Studies: An Interdisciplinary Reader*, ed. Robert J. Corber and Stephen Valocchi [Oxford: Blackwell, 2003], 177); Richard Meyer, "*Gay Power* Circa 1970," *GLQ* 12.3 (2006): 441–64; Martin F. Manalansan IV, "In the Shadows of Stonewall: Examining Gay Transnational Politics and the Diasporic Dilemma," *GLQ* 2.4 (1995): 425–38; Manalansan, "Race, Violence, and Neoliberal Spatial Politics in the Global City," *Social Text* 84–85 (2005): 141–55; and Warner, *The Trouble with Normal: Sex, Politics, and the Ethics of Queer Life* (New York: The Free Press, 1999), 129.

33. Hank O'Neal, "Introduction," in *Gay Day: The Golden Age of the Christopher Street Parade, 1974–1983* (New York: Abrams Image, 2006), 6–11, presents a succinct history of the parade that also includes documentary photographs of its festivities.

34. Michèle Aina Barale, "Queer Urbanities: A Walk on the Wild Side," in *Queer Diasporas*, ed. Cindy Patton and Benigno Sánchez-Eppler (Durham, NC: Duke University Press, 2000), discusses how metropolitan street signs can influence "the not at all uncommon tale of a country youth's discovery of the urban erotic" (210).

35. Anna Lowenhaupt Tsing, *Friction: An Ethnography of Global Connection* (Princeton: Princeton University Press, 2005), 6.

36. Judith Halberstam, *In a Queer Time and Place: Transgender Bodies, Subcultural Lives* (New York: New York University Press, 2005), 37.

37. Pierre Bourdieu, *Language and Symbolic Power*, trans. Gino Raymond and Matthew Adamson (Cambridge, MA: Harvard University Press, 1995), 46.

38. Ibid., 53–54.

39. Ibid., 54.

40. Though I concentrate on post-1969 flights in this chapter, pre-Stonewall flights are just as feasible and just as mythic.

41. Kath Weston, *Long Slow Burn: Sexuality and Social Science* (New York: Routledge, 1998), 40.

42. Warner, *The Trouble with Normal*, 190.

43. Jean Laplanche and Jean-Bertrand Pontalis, *The Language of Psycho-Analysis* (New York: Norton, 1973), 211. This definition hints at the differences and the definitional overlaps between incorporation and introjection in psychoanalytic thought. Incorporation can sometimes take on a pejorative sense of failed mourning while introjection appears as the supposedly successful internalization of the lost object—though not always. For more discussions of these matters, see W. R. D. Fairbairn, *Psychoanalytic Studies of the Personality* (London: Routledge, 1992); Christopher Bollas, *The Shadow of the Object: Psychoanalysis of the Unthought Unknown* (New York: Columbia University Press, 1987), 153–54; and Nicolas Abraham and Maria Torok, *The Shell and the Kernel: Renewals of Psychoanalysis*, vol. 1, ed. and trans. Nicholas T. Rand (Chicago: University of Chicago Press, 1994).

44. Unless otherwise noted, all citations from *The Psychic Life of Power* can be found in Judith Butler, *The Psychic Life of Power: Theories in Subjection* (Stanford, CA: Stanford University Press, 1997).

45. Sigmund Freud, "Mourning and Melancholia," in *The Freud Reader*, ed. Peter Gay (New York: Norton, 1989), 586, 589.

46. Ibid., 586.

47. Ibid., 587.

48. I cross-reference John Bowlby, *Attachment and Loss*, vol. 3, *Loss: Sadness and Depression* (New York: Basic Books, 1980), on this claim: "Ever since Freud's early contributions to the clinical problems of mourning, *the process of identification with the lost object* has been a cornerstone of every psychoanalytic theory. Although at first Freud believed the process to occur only in pathological mourning, subsequently he came to regard it as a principal feature of all mourning" (29).

49. One of the sharpest readings of gay melancholia and queer activism remains Douglas Crimp, "Mourning and Militancy," *October* 51 (1989): 3–18. Other queer theorizations of loss and melancholia that have influenced my thinking include Eve Kosofsky Sedgwick, "White Glasses," in *Tendencies* (Durham, NC: Duke University Press, 1993), 252–66; Leo Bersani and Ulysse Dutoit, *Forms of Being: Cinema, Aesthetics, Subjectivity* (London: British Film Institute, 2004), on "new relational modes" inspired by mourning (103); and Elizabeth Freeman, "Time Binds, or, Erotohistoriography," *Social Text* 84–85 (2005): 57–68.

50. Weston, *Long Slow Burn*, 41.

51. Halberstam, *Queer Time*, 37.

52. All subsequent quotations from Eli Clare, *Exile and Pride*, can be found in Clare, *Exile and Pride: Disability, Queerness and Liberation* (Cambridge, MA: South End Press, 1999).

53. Michael Balint, *The Basic Fault: Therapeutic Aspects of Regression* (1968; Evanston, IL: Northwestern University Press, 1992), 4.

Coda

1. See Eithne Luibhéid, *Entry Denied: Controlling Sexuality at the Border* (Minneapolis: University of Minnesota Press, 2002); *Queer Migrations: Sexuality, U.S. Citizenship, and Border Crossings*, ed. Luibhéid and Lionel Cantú Jr. (Minneapolis: University of Minnesota Press, 2005); Cantú, *The Sexuality of Migration: Border Crossings and Mexican Immigrant Men*, ed. Nancy A. Naples and Salvador Vidal-Ortiz (New York: New York University Press, 2009); and Cantú, "*De Ambiente*: Queer Tourism and the Shifting Boundaries of Mexican Male Sexualities," *GLQ* 8.1–2 (2002): 139–166.

2. Laurence Tate, "How They Do It in West Texas," *Gay and Lesbian Review Worldwide* 13.4 (2006): 26.

3. Edmund White, *States of Desire: Travels in Gay America* (1980; New York: Plume, 1991), 259.

Index

Note: Page numbers in *italics* indicate illustrations.

Krafft-Ebing, Richard von: *Psychopathia Sexualis*, 56–57
Kramer, Larry: *The Normal Heart*, 153
Ku Klux Klan, 11, 119
"Ky-Ky," 132–33, 134, 146

Ladder: A Lesbian Review, 69, 79
Lancaster, Pennsylvania, 14, 36, 44, 46, 47–50, 52, 60
lang, k. d., 139
language games, concept of, 8, 12, 14, 26
Laplanche, Jean, 171
Larry Clark: 1992 (Clark photos), 104
Lavender (film), 9
Leaves of Grass (Whitman), 41–42
Lesbian Connection, 81
lesbians: anti-fashion stereotype and, 80–81; commune-based separatists, 22, 69, 79–87, 89, 96; fashionability and, 34–35, 125–28, 132–37; Greenwich Village, pre-Stonewall, 5, 14, 17, 36–38, 132–37, 212n16; metronormativity and, 28, 168–69; mid-nineties chic, 139–40; race and, 131–37, 140–47; *RFD* printed by, 86–87; urbanized white middle-class, 34–35, 37–38, 139–40, 174; working-class rural, 9–10, 81–87, 89–90, 125, 126, 138–39, 140–47
Lesbian Tide, 81
Let Us Now Praise Famous Men (Agee and Evans), 107
Lewis, Edith, 36, 38
Liberty, Tennessee, 64
Life Outside (Signorile), 11, 12
literature: anti-urban stylistics and, 35–43; metronormativity and, 32, 54–59
Litvak, Joseph, 74
Lloyd, David, 95
Locke, Alain, 42

Lock Haven, Pennsylvania, 155, 178
London, England, 33, 34; as fashion center, 127
Longjohns series (Meads), 116–17, 127
Long Road to Mazatlán, The (film), 9
"Look Out! It's Luppies" (Bechdel), 152
Lorde, Audre, 17, 27, 127, 128, 131–37, 141, 147, 212n12, 212n16
Los Angeles, California: African American district, 139; image as glamour center, 19, 74–75, 163–64; lifestyle publications, 68–78
Lowe, Lisa, 95
Luciano, Dana, 49

Macon, Georgia, 14
Madonna, 139
Mann, Thomas, 33; *Death in Venice*, 34
Martin, Del, 79, 80
Marx, Leo, 12
Mattachine Review, 69, 70, 71
Mattachine Society, 32, 64
Maurice (Forster), 153
McClintock, Anne, 209n41
McRuer, Robert, 9, 46, 197n50, 213n21
Meads, Michael, 52, 209n41; African American male depicted by, 116, 122; *Alabama Souvenirs*, 100–109, 113–14, 122–23; *Allen*, 106–9; Caravaggio and, 115–16; "closet anarchy" approach, 103, 114–15, 116, 119, 120; *Eastaboga* exhibition, 99–103, 120–21, 144; interviews with, 117–18; *Longjohns* series, 127; staging of photographs, 109–15; *In the Studio* series, 115–19, 121; von Gloeden photographs and, 110–13; woman depicted by, 116, 122
Mediapolis, 100
Meeker, Martin, 67, 81, 92

Nealon, Christopher, 38, 194n23, 206n10

Nestle, Joan: *The Persistent Desire: A Femme-Butch Reader,* 135

new media, metronormativity and, 99–101. *See also* Internet

Newton, Esther, 21–22, 34

New York, New York: Chelsea, 1, 2, 3, 99–102, 121; Demuth's depictions of, 50, *51,* 52; as fashion center, 127; Greenwich Village, 11, 14, 31–32, 36–38, 47–48, 75, 132–37, 169, 175, *176,* 177, 212n16; guidebooks for, 33, 42, 47; Harlem, 145; image as promised land for queers, 1, 3–4, 10, 68–78, 112, 165, 167, 178; Interstate 80 and, 154, 158, 160–65; Johnson's disenchantment with, 55–56; as lesbian iconic space, 34–35; "outer boroughs," 3; as taste-maker, 18–19, 20, 53–54; Tenderloin, 32, 55–56; walking and, 47–48. *See also* Christopher Street, New York

New Yorker, 99

Nicodemus, Kansas, 40

Nikolai Fine Art Gallery, 99–103

no mo blues (Bridgforth), 26–27, 128, 140–48

non-metropolitan spaces. *See* rural

Normal Heart, The (Kramer), 153

North Carolina, 3, 94

nostalgia, 170

Novi, Michigan, 96

Nugent, Richard Bruce, 33

NuSouth Apparel, 119

Oakland, California, 14, 49, 125, 174

O'Hara, Frank, 33

O'Keeffe, Georgia, 44

ONE: The Homosexual Magazine, 69, 71

ONE Inc., 32

One of Ours (Cather), 37

Out, 75

OUTspoken!, 117

Out Traveler, 42, 58, 61

painting: anti-urban stylistics and, 35–36, 43–52

paper-cut politics, theory of, 23, 95

Paris, France, 112, 182; as fashion center, 14, 127, 128–31; guidebooks, 33, 34; reputation of, 32

Parks, Sonja, 144, 145

Pater, Walter, 101, 105–6, 110, 115, 121, 207n16

Pavement Web site, 104

Pennsyltucky, 149–50, 154, 156, 165, 167–68

Persistent Desire, The: A Femme-Butch Reader (Nestle), 135

Philadelphia, Pennsylvania, 48

Pig Belly, 2003 (Meads photo), 104–5

Playboy, 83

Pleasant Grove, Alabama, 142

Politics of Modernism, The (Williams), 52

Pontalis, Jean-Bertrand, 171

poodle, *Advocate* image of, 72–73, *73*

Port Orford, Oregon, 14, 125, 174

Portrait of a Lady, The (James), 49, 153

Povinelli, Elizabeth, 9, 10, 191n64, 199n2

Pratt, Mary Louise, 43

Precisionism, 44, 48, 49–50, 52

Presber, Rodolphe: *Les types de la capital,* 56

Professor's House, The (Cather), 36, 37, 38–43, 46, 52, 58

Proust, Marcel, 58, 61; *À la recherche du temps perdu,* 33, 34, 44, 46, 153; *Sodome et Gomorrhe,* 44, 46, 48–49

Provincetown, Massachusetts, 48

64–65; working-class gays, 99–101, 116–19; working-class lesbians, 9–10, 81–87, 89–90, 140–47
rurality, queer, 50, 66, 92–93, 167–74; gay male, 86–97, 99–101, 107, 150, 155–56; lesbian, 79–86, 89–90, 140–47; "white trash" stylistics and, 10, 12–13, 26, 99–101
Rush, Benjamin, 11

St. Vincent Millay, Edna, 38; *A Few Figs from Thistles*, 36; *Renascence, and Other Poems*, 36
Saint John the Baptist in the Wilderness (Caravaggio), 115–16
San Francisco, California: image as promised land for queers, 5, 19, 68–78, 74–75; Interstate 80 and, 154, 165
Sapphism, 17, 34–35, 36, 38, 213n22
Saussure, Ferdinand de, 128
Schorb, Jodi R., 139–40
Scofield, Stuart, 69, 86, 90
Scott, James, 34
"Sculptor's Funeral, The" (Cather), 37
Sears, James T., 67
Sedgwick, Eve Kosofsky, 28, 40–41, 194n23, 211n4, 221n49
semiology, 128, 137
Sergeant, Elizabeth Shepley, 31, 37
Serlin, David, 47
sexology, 55, 56, 66
"sexual assimilation," 19, 58, 103, 127, 136
Shadows on the Rock (Cather), 37
Shafer, Raymond, 160
Sharon, Pennsylvania, 164
"sho-lo" haircut, 140, 182
Sicily, von Gloeden's photographs, 110–13
Signorile, Michelangelo: *Life Outside*, 11, 12, 13

Skaggs, Merrill Maguire, 37
slumming, 100
Small Town Gay Bar (film), 9
social death, 1, 131, 167
Social Text, 174
Sodome et Gomorrhe (Proust), 44, 46, 48–49
Solomon Valley, Kansas, 14, 36, 39–43, 46, 54, 60
Somerville, Siobhan, 53, 54–55
Sontag, Susan, 17–18, 21
sophistication: *Advocate* depiction of, 72–73; counteracting, 94; definition of, 16; early 20th-century, 53–54, 57–58, 59; as metronormative idealization, 22, 34; in rural settings, 39, 60; stereotypes of, 85
Southern Comfort (film), 9
Southern Voice, 19
Spivak, Gayatri Chakravorty, 189n43, 192n66
Spurlin, William J., 201n30
State College, Pennsylvania, 155
States of Desire: Travels in Gay America (White), 18–19
Stein, Gertrude, 34, 46, 49
Stieglitz, Alfred, 46, 52
Stieglitz Circle, 44
Stone, Sharon, 139
Stonewall Inn, 162, 169
Stonewall riots, 17, 160, 162–63, 174; queer mythology of, 162
Streitmatter, Robert, 80
structuralism, 128–31
stylistics: anarchic, 85; anti-urbane, 36; centrality of, 190n48; class hegemony and, 20, 34, 39, 53–59, 69–78; counter-, 6, 22–26, 29, 61, 96–97, 182–83; definition of, 23; gay male, 33–34, 70–78, 126–27, 155; habitus and, 20–21, 33; lesbian, 131–41; lesbian critiques of, 79–81;

stylistics (*continued*): metronormativity and, 16, 17–21, 33–34, 53–54, 70–78, 84, 90, 120–21, 125–31, 182; pre-Stonewall, 72–74, 100–101, 132–37, 155; rural, 6, 22–23, 41–43, 48, 50, 68, 83–97, 103, 107, 114–15, 143–48, 167, 182; rural-identified bodies and, 12; as tactics of the weak, 34; use as weapon, 23; "white trash," 10, 12–13; working-class, 21–22, 34, 38–43, 81–87, 89–90, 100, 116–19, 138–39
subcultural style, 5
suburbia, 187n21
"Sun-Bath, A" (Whitman), 42
Sunfrog, 93
Système de la mode (Barthes), 128–31, 132, 134, 137

Taormina, Italy, 110–13, 123
Taormina (von Gloeden photos), 110–13, 116, 208n34
taste: Bourdieu on, 19–21; metronormativity and, 16, 17–19
Teenage Lust (Clark photos), 104
Tennessee, 10. *See also* Memphis
Tetrault, Jeanne, 83–84, 203n53
Their Eyes Were Watching God (Hurston), 143–44
Thomas, Sherry, 83–84, 203n53
Tongson, Karen, 187n21, 190n48
To Wong Foo, Thanks for Everything! Julie Newmar (film), 118, 120, *120*
"trailer trash," 100
Trouble with Normal, The (Warner), 3–4, 11, 170
Troubridge, Una, 35
Tsing, Anna Lowenhaupt, 164
Tulsa (Clark photos), 104, 108
Tyler, Parker, 33
types de la capital, Les (Presber), 56

unfashionability, 125–48, 182; as critique, 22, 25; Barthes on, 128–31; lesbian separatism and, 80–81; meaning of, 128–31; rural black southern dykes and, 140–47; rural stylistics and, 89; stigma of, 129–37, 147–48
urban: cowboy craze, 173; definition of, 7–9, 13; sprawl, 7–8, 13; white gay male ghettos, 69–70, 71, 75, 84, 92, 96
urbanity, queer: coinage of, 186n13; compulsory, 25, 33–34, 53–55, 58, 68–78, 114, 126, 154; disability and, 44, 46–50, 61; historicization of, 42; lesbian Luppies, 150, 152; metronormativity and, 3–7, 14, 16–19, 22, 32, 33–34, 85, 127, 139–40, 168, 172–73; post-Stonewall gay male, 1, 3–5, 17, 72–73, 126, 160, 162–65, 174; pre-Stonewall gay male, 17, 32, 53–59, 155, 169–70; pre-Stonewall lesbian, 14, 17, 34–35, 132–37; queers of color and, 17; rejection of, 40; in rural settings, 38–43, 48, 154, 155–56; transnationalism and, 28, 42, 52–59, 61, 182–83

Vanity Fair, 139
Van Vechten, Carl, 33
Venice, Italy, 33
Vidal, Gore, 33
Village Voice, 99, 104
Vogel, Lisa, 142
Vogue, 129

Warner, Michael, 5, 200n13, 220n32; *The Trouble with Normal*, 3–4, 11, 170
Washington, D.C.: image as sophisticated, 19

About the Author

SCOTT HERRING teaches in the Department of English at Indiana University. He is author of *Queering the Underworld: Slumming, Literature, and the Undoing of Lesbian and Gay History.*